People's Art

Working-Class Art
from 1750 to the Present Day

Emmanuel Cooper

MAINSTREAM
PUBLISHING

EDINBURGH AND LONDON

This book is for Nigel Young

First published in Great Britain in 1994 by
MAINSTREAM PUBLISHING COMPANY (EDINBURGH) LTD
7 Albany Street
Edinburgh EH1 3UG

ISBN 1 85158 108 1

A catalogue record for this book is available from the British Library

Typeset in Monophoto Stempel Garamond by Lasertext Ltd., Stretford, Manchester
Printed in Hong Kong by H. Y. Printing Co

CONTENTS

ACKNOWLEDGMENTS

Many people have helped in the preparation of *People's Art*. I would particularly like to acknowledge the contribution from the original discussion group 'Visual Art and the Working Class' 1982–86 who were Barry Prothero, Michael Regan, David Ketteridge, Judy Collins and Hugh Adams. Others who have made invaluable suggestions include David Cheshire, David Horbury, Jeffrey Weeks, Peta Levi, Arnold Rattenbury, Andras Kalman, John Titchell, Paul Wombell, Bernie O'Donnell, Johnny Marr, Brian Blench, Hilda Ellis, William Wilson, Simon Watney, Celia Southers, Tim Binding, Katie Hazell, Helen Clark, Eileen Lewenstein, June Freeman, Martina Margets, Abigail Frost, John Gorman and Nigel Young. Many thanks to them and to the museums and collectors who have patiently answered questions and provided photographs. I also gratefully acknowledge project funding from the Gulbenkian Foundation, London, and from the Crafts Council, London.

INTRODUCTION

People's Art looks at visual art made by the great mass of working people on the mainland of Britain within the historical period which roughly coincides with the Industrial Revolution, beginning at its earliest date of 1750, but concentrating on the period from 1780 to the present day. In identifying and describing visual art by men and women, who include skilled workers, artisans, housewives, semi-skilled operatives, unskilled workers and labourers, the book illuminates a currently unstudied and little acknowledged element of our cultural heritage. It discusses the importance of visual art as a communicative process of working-class life; it also questions the accepted definition of 'art' and puts forward arguments for extending it.

There has been a long tradition of art made within rural pastoral societies, of objects and decorations produced in traditional fashion by people with little or no formal training. Such work, usually known as folk art, was intended for everyday use and ornament or for such rites of passage as births, weddings or funerals. Folk art is seen as a largely autonomous tradition with its own characteristics, with techniques passed on from generation to generation, and with patterns and designs changing little. Though influenced from time to time by professional art, folk art retained its basic characteristics. The Industrial Revolution radically transformed this; much folk art was lost or incorporated in different ways of working but the need to create continued. Increases in population saw a movement of people to towns and cities with a corresponding growth in urban living. Factory-based work replaced home industry, with most workers earning a wage; new technology replaced traditional skills which were abandoned or adapted to new conditions using different materials. The introduction of compulsory education helped further sharpen the distinction between work and leisure as well as making people more conscious of the critical values of high art.

Within industrial society the urge to make and decorate took new forms as creative minds responded to different techniques and materials. This is what I call people's art; it reflects the working and living conditions of an industrial, often urban, society, it was made in or around the home or the workplace and is discussed within the context in which it was made. Strategies are put forward for its assessment.

Appreciating the expressive qualities of people's art involves discussion of its relationship with the cultural traditions of high art, for it is these which form the basis for aesthetic judgments. Though some people's art is influenced by and is partly a response to high art, the majority is separate and represents different creative expressions. For many years there has been a generally accepted theory that the working class has produced little or no art, for it has not been made in the refined mode of classical art; nor does it appear to measure up to formal comparisons with the fine arts of painting, drawing, sculpture or fine craft. Such a view, however, ignores the diversity of creative energy which can take many forms.

Even such a distinguished commentator as Professor J. K. Galbraith doubted the creative talents of 'the poor'. Speaking on *Economics and the Arts* (1983) he said:

Deep in the inner soul and psyche of the poor there is – or must be – an instinctive artistic expression. It has only to be discovered. There is folk art, proletarian art, the art by implication of the masses. Surely these are superior to bourgeois art, art that has been blighted by exposure to money . . .

It is only when other wants are satisfied that people and communities turn generally to the arts; we must reconcile ourselves to this unfortunate fact. In consequence, the arts become a part of the affluent standard of living. When life is meagre so are they.

Professor Galbraith's argument that the poor produce little or no art ignores the immense body of creative, expressive work made by the vast majority of people who form the working class.

Galbraith implies that the arts include only those of the fine arts of painting and sculpture, classical music, the ballet, opera, and the theatre, usually known as our cultural heritage. But there are other rich and diverse artistic traditions; these have rarely been written about, are poorly represented in museums and art galleries and have not been widely collected. The relatively low status of the work is reflected in the absence of agreed terms to describe it. These may include popular art, low art, working-class art, alternative art, outsider art, naïve art and peasant art. Low art conveys an impression of inadequacy, alternative art suggests oppositional non-skilled work, while outsider art has come to be identified with the fascinating but obsessional work of individuals motivated by an inner determination to create art for themselves. Naïve art is now used to describe a particular style, while peasant (and folk) art refers to pre-industrial rural society. A useful alternative is the term people's art; it lies outside other definitions, has no already proscribed meaning and is an accurate description of art produced by working-class people in industrial society.

Despite the differences between folk art and people's art, there are significant overlaps and similarities. While the long history of folk art is based in pastoral communities and

people's art came out of industrial society, for many years factories were set up in rural settings enabling many traditional forms to be absorbed by factory workers. Carving wood – one of the longest and most popular types of folk art, used for busk stays, knitting sheaths, love spoons and the like – traditionally carried out by minders of flocks, all but died out during the nineteenth century as agricultural methods changed; but the traditional forms, motifs and symbols were adopted for use on such objects as patchwork quilts, while workers in industry used new techniques such as marquetry to decorate such objects. Shoes cut from flat pieces of brass for use as mantelpiece ornaments combined skill with the conventional use of footware as a symbol of good luck, as did similar small objects carved from coal by miners. While it is a contradiction in terms to describe people's art as industrial folk art, it does convey much of its spirit, its sense of continuity and communal belonging which is so vital a part of this creative work.

This book sets out with the basic proposition that many 'ordinary' people, who have not had highly specialised contact with art schools and colleges, can create works of art and craft which have a genuinely expressive value. To describe these as works of art immediately raises the problem of defining what is art. When placed in the context of 'high art', many (though by no means all) of the objects written about in this book seem out of place; a few may seem to be 'crude' and insignificant. Their qualities can only be fully appreciated when separated from the dominant tradition of classical academic art, and seen as serving a completely different purpose.

The fundamental question of whose interest people's art serves and whose it represents can only be answered by looking at the context within which it was made and at its likely audience. Art as it is generally thought of in our society has long been seen as the sole preserve of the academies, a part of the tradition moulded literally in the courts of popes and kings, and in the great houses of the aristocracy. Even in today's relatively egalitarian society, art is firmly placed within the tradition of high art, accessible in the main only to an educated élite. The work described and illustrated in this book is not a part of that tradition, although some of it has been influenced by it. People's art is an integral part of working-class culture and needs to be appreciated within that context.

Though the term 'art' presents problems, it is not necessary to abandon it for the sole use of the high tradition. The body of work described here imaginatively conveys the aspirations, the self-identity and the pride of its makers. It has an expressive significance which extends beyond the usual sense of 'crafts' and, often, beyond the common distinction between 'art' and 'craft'. Indeed, much of the work illustrated in this book is highly relevant to the current debate about the boundaries between fine art and craft.

People's art has its own cultural values and traditions. It is not bound up with the prevalent artistic, social and aesthetic values of a culturally dominant class to which it does not belong; it does not have a complex system of a learned visual code, nor is there a preoccupation with depicting the world through the use of the renaissance invention of perspective, the visual representation of the three-dimensional world on a flat surface; nor is there a self-conscious attempt to be 'detached' or 'objective', to stand back from the world and give an overview of it. In people's art artists may use skills acquired as a part of their trade and their artistic sensibility to produce visual work calling on tradition and innovation to represent their own feelings and responses, which will in itself embody a recognisable and understood language.

Like any art, people's art is produced within an economic, social and cultural context which helps shape its meaning. The 'aesthetics' of people's art is largely determined by the people who make it rather than outside bodies. A useful example of changed emphasis is in photographs taken by working-class photographers. Many did not have access to expensive lenses or sophisticated equipment and, as a result, they are unlikely to be as technically accomplished as those by professional photographers. Their interest is more likely to lie in the subjects which were often events and people of daily life rather than in the handling of light and shade or the compositional qualities of the image. These 'family albums' of working-class life can be seen objectively as pictorial 'history' by social scientists, or personal (if partial) accounts by those who took the photographs, appeared in them or knew the subjects or places with every detail of background accepted and understood. Their enjoyment (or criticism) would be more likely to be based on their view of the accuracy of the image or the mood conveyed in terms of their own experience or memory, rather than formal discussion of photographic aesthetics or social record.

Little has been done to construct a useful theoretical framework for the study of people's art. The extant literature is of only limited use and some of the most basic questions remain contentious. In comparison with the Continent, Britain would appear to have produced little or no actual folk art. This is partly the result of the system of medieval land ownership, partly to do with the development of a puritan aesthetic of plainness and partly because of the disruption of long-established customs by the early start of the Industrial Revolution. Ethnographers have been more concerned with indigenous culture of other countries rather than in investigating the richness of their own. This is in marked contrast to countries where folk art has been greatly admired as a valid and rich part of cultural heritage. In the United States of America, for example, it is studiously collected and displayed. In 1924 the Whitney Studio Club (now the Whitney Museum of American Art) organised an exhibition of American naïve art. At much the same time museums of folk art were set up on the Continent, while central European folk art has been carefully collected and studied.

One of the aims of this book is at least

to fill partially the absence of any coherent social, artistic and aesthetic study of the huge body of people's art, to indicate its size and range and to give it an historical perspective. There are practical as well as theoretical difficulties in writing about people's art: often there is little accurate information about who made the objects, when or where they were produced and so on; people's art is rarely discussed in histories of the arts nor is it generally considered to be a significant area of human communications. There is, however, a growing awareness of its importance. Newly set-up museums of labour history are now conscious of it and keen to adequately represent it; one or two serious collectors have turned their attention to it and it is now sold at auctions at major London houses. While there are examples of such work in large national collections such as the British Museum, the Victoria and Albert Museum, the National Museums of Wales and the major Scottish museums, it is displayed in a dispersed and incoherent form. Some museums have started to give the work serious study, most notably the People's Palace in Glasgow, the Highland Folk Museum in Kingussie, the Welsh Folk Museum, Beamish Open Air Museum in County Durham and the Castle Museum in York, but there is still no institution devoted solely to the study and preservation of people's art.

Many museums with holdings of people's art often know little, or sometimes nothing at all, about the origins of the objects they have or who made them. While this would present few problems when discussing 'high' art, where status and conventions are well established, it presents serious difficulties for the proper and full assessment of people's art which all too often is seen as 'quaint' or 'eccentric'. The lack of information reflects the generally pervasive attitude which regards these artefacts as mere curiosities. Associated with this low grading is the fact that until recently working-class art and artefacts have had very little monetary value.

For the purpose of this book it is useful to know the identity or social status of the maker. In some cases objects may be virtually indistinguishable in terms of materials, style or technique from work made professionally. Ships' models, for example, were often made by captains and by deckhands. Textiles is another area which presents similar problems. Patchwork was carried out by middle-class people as a leisure-time hobby, often purchasing new fabric, while working-class people used available materials and the patchwork cover was as much for warmth as decoration. Many of the objects here have not been approached in this particular way before and wherever possible the name of the makers and their status is acknowledged.

Of the studies already carried out, none has identified people's art. Enid Marx and Margaret Lambert in *English Popular Art* looked enthusiastically at the whole field, concentrating on folk art, though in no systematic way, while in *Unsophisticated Arts*, Barbara Jones paid particular attention to the art of everyday objects. John Gorman's *Banner Bright* examined in detail the history of trade union banners, while Robert Leeson's *United We Stand* dealt with trade union emblems. Most other studies have either told the story of the Labour Movement in pictures – *The Pictorial History of the Labour Party* (Labour Party) or Patrick Rooke's *The Trade Union Movement* – or were concerned with showing how conventional artists have depicted the Labour Movement, for example, *Work and Struggle* by Edward Lucie-Smith and Celestine Dars. Peter Brears's *North Country Folk Art* is the most relevant and useful book so far published. Outside of the visual arts, *Useful Toil* (edited by John Burnett), a collection of autobiographical writings by working people from the 1820s to the 1920s, provided much contextual information as well as furnishing evidence of literary creative work.

People's Art makes use of these important works but is more directed in its scope and inevitably questions current definitions of art as being too limited. The need to 'make a mark' has never been stronger. Just as some fifty years ago homes

Plate 1 Joseph and Margaret Cordiner with the ship garden they have been building in their home at Peterhead, Scotland, for more than 30 years. Their most recent addition is a sailing ship, the *Hope*, in the background. A model of the *Cutty Sark* is planned. 1991 (Photograph Murdo MacLeod)

were ornamented, so they are today. On the Isle of Wight one householder cemented stones and shells in decorative patterns, turning an ordinary house into something special and individual, another in Scotland covered an old bus with shells and stones. In Bath a dweller in a basement flat has created a grotto of fantastical delights in the area between the street and house. Made up of plastic figures, small tables, moss, stones, gnomes and such like, the work is an unfettered creation of whimsical delight. In another town a householder added a pair of giant human ears to the outside of his house, a startling and surreal way of making a mark. In Derbyshire one proud household painted 'Swiss chalet' decorations on their home. The cultivation of gardens (see Plate 1), the decoration of mass-produced cars, the making of 'private worlds' continues. People's art has a rightful place in society, a part of our cultural heritage to be enjoyed and appreciated. This book, I hope, has a creative part to play in this process.

Solidarity by Geoff Gibbons (see p209)

Chapter One

WORKING-CLASS ART: WORKING-CLASS ARTIST

In 1986 Chris Bowers appeared on the popular Sunday evening television programme *That's Life* to draw attention to the difficulties of obtaining insurance for his car. He had painted the outside of a basic Ford model to his own design and refitted the interior with exotic upholstery (see Plate 2). The production-line model was transformed into a work of art in which the impersonal but stylish Ford took on some of the personality of its owner. Unemployed and living in Birkenhead, Chris Bowers' insurance problem caught the attention of television, our most influential medium. For a brief few minutes living-rooms across the country saw imaginative and inventive examples of people's art, not displayed in art galleries, museums or even labelled art, but as part of contemporary life – albeit one on which no monetary value could be placed.

Other television programmes have featured a woman in north London who turned the entire interior of her house into a magic grotto, and a Welsh plasterer who carved

Plate 3 *Country Scene* by Jessie Radford oil on canvas, 11 × 8 inches, 1950s

huge visionary sculptures in wood. Each is remarkable for wanting to convey their ideas in visual form, to be an artist, though it is unlikely that any would apply such a label to themselves.

As a lad in a small Derbyshire coal-mining village I saw small intensely painted oils, rarely measuring more than 10 × 6 inches, produced by Jessie Radford, a woman who had had little or no training. Idyllic pastoral landscapes, thatched country cottages and overgrown forests were depicted with vivid realism (see Plate 3). Fairy-tale qualities conveyed an impression of peaceful countryside far removed from the coal-mining area where we lived. One day I discovered a carved bone apple-corer made probably some hundred years ago. About five inches long and cut from a sheep's shin bone, its handle had an incised pattern of crossed and hatched lines conveying good luck. The inventiveness and care which went into making it impresses me still (see Plate 4).

In the village a woman, the wife of a

Plate 2 Customised Ford car with painted bodywork and upholstered interior by Chris Bowers, 1986

coal-miner with a large family, sat for many hours by her open door making pegged rugs from scrap fabrics. Helped at various times by her family, Cis Taylor patiently cut old clothes into narrow strips before prodding them systematically through a piece of washed sacking bearing a simple geometrical chalked design she had made. Thick and bulky, the completed rugs felt generous and comforting,

Plate 4 Apple-corer, carved mutton bone with incised decoration, about 6 inches long, nineteenth century

the muted colours and restrained patterning surprisingly conservative in taste. Colours were dependent on available fabrics and flashes of red or yellow were viewed with suspicion. Miners made inventive use of waste pieces of metal. My uncle, a coal-miner, fashioned an ornate toasting fork with an inlaid design in copper from scrap metal, while on the mantelpieces of miners' homes stood flat brass wall or shelf ornaments, often cut in the shape of shoes or boots, made

from waste pieces of brass and incised with minimal patterns (see Plate 5).

What these diverse objects share is a form of creative expression into which the makers wanted to put some part of themselves. The carved bone and pegged rugs are traditional, passed on from one generation to the next, which makers interpreted according to their own ideas; but the painted car, brass ornaments and toasting fork belong entirely to contemporary society though the intention of their creators to make individual objects is similar. This chapter discusses the extent of people's art, looks at its relationship with high or academic art, and suggests various strategies for appreciating its qualities.

Discussion of people's art needs to say what it is, what its boundaries are, what qualities distinguish it from high art and folk art, the contexts or 'institutions' within which it is produced, and whether any definition needs to concentrate on the work of individuals or eccentrics who make their presence known, or attempt to give shape to wider areas of work. Recognition must also be given to the extent to which people's art crosses over the boundaries of art and craft, often reducing or eliminating such differences. I argue in this book that art need not be the

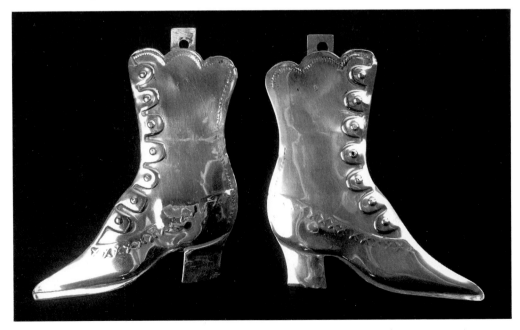

Plate 5 Flat brass ornaments with incised and raised decoration made from waste metal, anon, nineteenth century

sole preserve of fine art but can embrace many sorts of styles of art including people's art; it can be a collective as well as an individual expression, a means of communicating and sharing ideas and ideals, effectively altering and influencing the space in which the work is placed. Like any art, people's art can be appreciated more fully with some knowledge of the society and conditions within which it was produced.

For the purpose of this book the boundaries of people's art can broadly be defined as far as geographical area and time span are concerned as that produced by working-class men and women on the mainland of Britain in the period which approximately starts with the Industrial Revolution (c.1750) coming up to the present day. The majority of it was and is produced for the home with much of it made in or around the home. Even items made in workshops and factories often ended up in the home. In some areas close links between home and workplace continued during many years of the industrial period, but for some the separation was much more dramatic so objects made in the factory and taken home were a way of bringing the two areas of life together. Before discussing the objects themselves, the emotive terms 'working class' and 'art' require consideration.

Many social scientists today dispute the existence of a working class in its historical sense, but others recognise its presence albeit in a changed form. While few would deny that an identifiable working class existed in the nineteenth century, some argue that modern society has altered so radically that the term is now redundant and cannot be usefully applied to the men and women who occupy this economic and social position. Definitions of what constitutes class have concerned leading socialists and political philosophers for many years. Deep and far-ranging changes in society such as the demise of a manufacturing base, the growth of service industries and large numbers of unemployed people have further complicated this task. But many traditional economic differences remain.

Workers continue to sell their labour and they have no control or access to the means of production. Despite the increase in home ownership and the acquisition of consumer items, these are dependent on substantial mortgages and loans and, rather than bring freedom, prove to be further liabilities. Economic indices suggest that the gap between the better-off and the poor grows, while some jobs pay such minimal wages that many hours overtime need to be worked to achieve a reasonable wage. Despite all the complexity of the contemporary situation and all the changes which have taken place, many of which are touched on in this book, I would argue that class divisions remain and a distinct working-class culture continues to exist. What is still to be discovered is the extent and richness of visual art within working-class culture and the importance of its role within social and economic structures.

Technical evidence that the working class continues came in a document from HM Government's Office of Population Census and Survey advocating abandoning the established practice of grading people by social class. '1990 – AND WHITEHALL ABOLISHES THE WORKING CLASSES' proclaimed the *Daily Mail* headline of 31 October 1987. The new scheme proposed using 'more suitable' definitions taking account of job, income, education and lifestyle. People are listed under six different job categories. The first includes judges, the second teachers, the third shopkeepers, while artisans come in class four, the semi-skilled in class five and class six is made up of unskilled workers like porters and domestics. In such groupings cultural background of each class or division, of which typical jobs are given here, is not taken into consideration as the emphasis is on status and income. However, the groupings confirm class divisions, albeit in complex form.

If the term 'working class' appears problematic because of the changes in society, this is relatively insignificant when compared to the contentious use of the word 'art'. Art is accepted as signifying aspects of societies' most civilised behaviour, a part of creative expression with a cultural history dating back to ancient Greece and Rome; it has a visually sophisticated language, a critical literature to accompany it and rich codes of reference to define its role. To apply the definition 'art' to work by men and women with no training in the concepts or skills of the visual arts may appear a contradiction in terms. But until relatively recent times any medium of artistic expression was regarded as an expression of skill, whether made by a weaver, a medieval stone-carver, or a limner's painted wall decoration; creativity was judged not by the discipline but by the individual piece of work.

During the industrial period the value of the creative work of the artisan, whether man or woman, changed within industrial processes as old skills died and new ones took their place. The appreciation of traditional craft skills was especially highlighted by the Romantic Movement which industrialisation produced. 'Art' was idealised to distinguish it from mechanical work and craft, and elevated as the work of gifted individuals who produced items for the middle and upper classes. Artisan art and academic or high art became separated, giving rise in part to the formation of the Arts and Crafts Movement in the nineteenth century which sought to reunite them. People's art, closely aligned with artisan art, found new and different forms of expression.

The relationship between high art and people's art can be compared to that between the canals and rivers: one is skilfully engineered and carefully maintained to create a measured, fully controlled system of movement; a constant battle is waged to ensure good working order against the intrusion of nature. In contrast the river flows free; it finds its own route and moves effortlessly along, fed by innumerable springs and streams, varying in speed, rising and falling, its width and depth depending on the land over which it flows.

It is a picturesque description successfully evoking two separate and unconnected systems. Each is a part of the complex spectrum of art with a place within society taking forms which range from the most sophisticated abstract and minimal expressions of high art to the carved knife of the sailor or furniture built from scrap wood by an unemployed Londoner. Like high art, people's art must be seen within the contexts and institutions within which it is produced, the materials used acknowledged, the forms examined, and the iconography identified and some assessment made of its visual success. The artistic intention of the maker must also be recognised as a vital part of the production process.

Comparisons have also been made between the 'natural flow' of people's art and that produced by children or found in exotic ('primitive') work. The absence of any deep understanding of, or concern with, the laws of perspective or the representation in two-dimensional form of space or volume is often as evident in people's art as it is in the work of children; 'primitive' art may also appear to share common characteristics but people's art differs in virtually every other respect. In people's art the handling of technique is highly competent – the skill of execution of objects produced by professional artisans, for instance, is of the finest level; subtlety of expression varies from individual to individual. Equally, within people's art different and identifiable styles or genres can be traced. Nor is people's art totally free from a learnt visual language whether derived from traditional or contemporary sources. Equally (unlike children's art), such work can be discussed, critical judgments can be made – and are made – by the audience for whom such work is produced.

The range and diversity of visual art within working-class culture has yet to be fully acknowledged. While the culture of the middle and upper classes is dominant, clearly defined and representative of a well-organised and articulate group, working-class culture, however widespread and extensive, is disparate and fragmented. The proponents and exponents of each appear to talk the same dialect of knowledge but, whilst sharing a common language, fail to understand each other. A government advertising campaign which appeared in the national press early in 1986 for the Youth Training Scheme (YTS) graphically illustrated popular perceptions of the two cultures. Advertisements contrasted two 16-year-old youths; one, dressed in bleached jeans worn skinhead-style at half-mast, was spraying 'Spurs' on a grimy brick wall in large but loosely drawn lettering, by implication committing an act of vandalism. The other youth, neatly dressed in a pair of white dungarees was painting 'Tottenham Hotspur Football Club' on a notice-board in crisp Roman-style lettering; even the brick wall on which the board was fixed had been whitewashed (see Plate 6).

The contrast between the two youths could hardly be greater. One is rough, direct, impulsive, unfettered and wild, apparently acting on instinct; the other ordered, trained, respectable, tasteful and acceptable. Though deliberately set up to conflict, the images encapsulate some of the perceived differences (or prejudices) between the two cultures. With education and training the advertisement suggests, one could replace the other. The two contrasting lettering forms amplify difference; the roman style connotes literacy, culture and history, while the spray-canned slogan appears sloppy, careless, insensitive and crude. Yet both accurately convey some of the ideas and aspirations of their class. Working-class culture often displays strength in its visual imagery and in the way materials

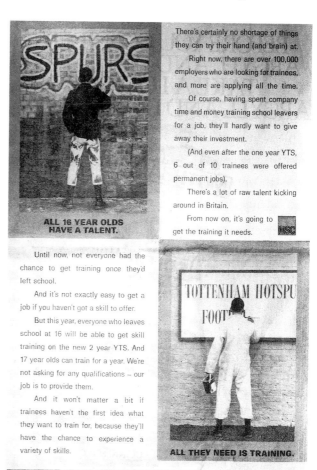

Plate 6 Advertisement for the Youth Training Scheme, the *Guardian*, 1986

are used which has little to do with conventional education or artistic training but is a response to a wider range of conditions – an intimate part of the lives of the men and women who made it.

WHY DECORATE?

Why so much time and energy went into the decoration as well as in the making of objects, particularly those intended for a specific use, is a central issue in people's art. Despite the fact that materials and leisure time were limited, people still found the resources, energy and drive to enhance the appearance of objects made for their own pleasure and use. Some decoration clearly cost little more in terms of effort than a plain finish and may even have been called for by the technique being used or the resources available. Work with textiles, for example, or woven baskets both require planning. The design of a pegged rug can be worked so it incorporates the limited range of different coloured fabrics available, while much the same situation occurs with patchwork. But for most objects additional decoration means more time and effort. Many of the objects illustrated in this book demonstrate the desire to make something special out of something ordinary.

The central question 'why decorate?' when no material advantage is apparent, can be partly answered by reference to the desire to make objects which carry identity, to make a personal mark whether on the actual piece or as part of a wider scheme; such work proclaims the owner's skill and imagination and adds visual diversity, whether to items of clothing or to home objects. No complete answer is forthcoming just as there is no total explanation of the question why anyone makes any sort of art. Nevertheless, when appraising people's art the presence of inventive and sensitive decoration requires recognition, indicating as it does some basic human need which cannot be fully explained.

EDUCATION AND LEISURE

People's art arose and developed within the industrial period against a rapidly changing social and economic background. Major influences included the growth of leisure time and leisure pursuits and the introduction of free state education.

Self Help

At the beginning of the nineteenth century a commonly held view was that leisure was a snare and a danger, a time when employers had little control over the workers and therefore when 'trouble' could arise. When Robert Owen told a parliamentary commission that he thought it unnecessary for children under ten years of age to work in mills, he was asked whether or not there would 'be a danger of their acquiring vicious habits for want of regular occupation?'.[1] Fortunately Owen's more enlightened view prevailed. Until the 1870s, though there was little provision for the education of the working class, there were many self-help groups teaching reading and writing. Local 'dame schools' taught some younger children, there were church schools, Mechanics' Institutes opened, and there was a steady demand for instructional literature. The Penny Encyclopaedia was a great success in giving workers a general idea of the principles underlying the tools and machinery in common use. In 1833 it was estimated that one-third of all working-class children in England had no schooling at all. Literacy remained a problem until well after the 1870 Education Act which brought in elementary education for all children under 13.

Within the often grim picture of working-class life in Britain it would be all too easy to assume that there was little time or energy after a long working day for pursuing personal and individual interests, whether this was learning to write or any other activity. Yet this was far from the case. As well as acquiring literary skills, many found time to make decorative pieces, judging by the number of objects that exist. Published diaries and autobiographical accounts by working-class people clearly demonstrate the breadth of their concern and interest in recording details of their own lives and experiences.

Though there were few opportunities for adult education, whenever they did arise, despite the long hours of labour, full use was often made of them, particularly by skilled workers. Mechanics' Institutes were founded to teach young mechanics or the 'children of the labouring poor'. Employers objected to the Institute because they thought it would make workpeople restless if their education was improved. The Secretary of the Institute, Isaac Ironside, was dismissed for allowing 'subversive or chartist books in the library'.[2] The Institute continued to ban books on politics. The first Institute opened in London in 1832, rapidly followed in the same year by another in Glasgow. Manchester Mechanics' Institute was founded in 1834 and other industrial cities quickly followed suit. Usually rooms were rented and a library of books, prints, models and so on, was kept. Lectures were organised on literary and scientific subjects as well as the fine arts, though it was the introductory classes on elementary education which were most popular.

Gradually Mechanics' Institutes were set up in most major towns. By 1850 there were 622 Institutes in England and Wales with over 600,000 members. Many attracted workers from the lower middle as well as the working class, though Newcastle and the Scottish towns were an exception. In Manchester in 1842 the mix was typical, including 'merchants, manufacturers, clerks, shop-keepers, tradesmen, artists'.[3] More working class in character probably because they were cheaper, were the three Lyceums of Manchester and Salford. The subscription was only two shillings a quarter, and, as well as libraries and evening schools, included news-rooms and provision for music, gymnastics and dancing. Separate classes were set up for teaching women reading, writing, grammar, sewing and knitting, with the greatest care being taken to 'guard against any species of impropriety'.[4] In the classes for women at the Ancoats Lyceum the average attendance in 1841 was from 32 to 44 and this included 'some from the factories'.[5] The Newcastle Mechanics' Institute was thought one of the best. At the Saturday popular lectures and concerts held in connection with it, there were likely to be audiences of some

700 'chiefly workmen and some young men from shops and warehouses'.[6]

In Scotland a well-organised education system ensured a good level of literacy. Most people could read and write, except for immigrant English and Irish. In the English midlands and the north, in spite of National Schools, Sunday Schools, night schools and the determination of a few self-educated workers, a high percentage of illiteracy remained. In 1840 the Registrar-General of births, deaths and marriages of Manchester-Salford reported that 60 per cent of the population could not sign their own names.

Yet despite the absence of proper and formal education for all, the first Public Library Act in 1850 decreed that towns could levy a rate to open public libraries; in 1854 the act was extended to Ireland and Scotland. By 1860 some 25 towns had opened libraries. At much the same time art galleries were being set up in many towns and cities, with free entry. Towards the end of the nineteenth century in London the National Portrait Gallery, the National Gallery of British Art (now the Tate Gallery) and the Wallace Collection were opened. The National Gallery had an important extension added and Queen Victoria laid the foundation stone for the Victoria and Albert Museum which incorporated the South Kensington Museum. Outside the capital, the Whitworth Institute opened in Manchester. A network of museums and public art galleries was opened across the land displaying the art of the middle and upper classes. Admission was usually free, a practice which continues still and should remain.

Education

In 1870 the Education Act ordained that, for the first time, schools should be provided for every child up to the age of 13. Education was made compulsory in 1880 when sufficient school buildings had been provided. Higher education was still left to private, community and work-centred institutions with little if

any state help. Yet still elementary schooling was not free for everyone: those who could pay had to do so. Abolition of school fees in elementary schools did not take place until 1891 and even then there were only provisions for children to attend schools for half a day and work for the other half. After 1918 all children received full-time education up to the age of 14, though classes continued to remain large in size. The school leaving age was not increased to 15 until the 1945 Education Act, and to 16 years of age in 1972.

The effects of education – whether from school, institutes or museums and art galleries – were far-reaching, particularly on the perceptions of 'ordinary people' who produced visual art. Imagery, which had hitherto come from local or work-centred sources, now came from many directions. High art, abstract sculpture and painting, mass-produced cultural images, whether in newspapers, the cinema or on television, were seen as examples to emulate. Furthermore, teachers often encouraged the imitation of this work. The artist Julian Trevelyan, who was closely involved with Mass Observation – set up in the 1930s to study everyday life in Britain, relying on 2,000 voluntary observers to produce a popular sociology – met and encouraged many 'Sunday painters'. He found in their art a powerful and personal quality; untutored and produced from a strong sense of conviction, it had a vital communicative strength. In his view, the majority of the post-war years' huge increase in the number of Sunday painters had not retained this quality but had often become slick and imitative.

This aspect of education relates importantly to the whole range of visual arts as well as to painting and sculpture. Model-making, for example, increased but was seen as a craft rather than an art. Many model-makers were engineers who made miniatures of large machines, or enthusiasts who produced models based on familiar machines or even events. Within high art such work was seen as craft, skilled making rather than 'expressive' work. The aesthetics of high art formed the basis of the evaluation of the

work. Amateur and Sunday artists were encouraged to make things which related more closely to the concepts of aesthetics as defined by the middle and upper classes.

More recently, model-making has become a popular and absorbing hobby, a means of being creative in its own right. The 1986–87 56th Model Engineer Exhibition contained over a thousand models. Some makers were professional, others modelled because they wanted to create their own work. A typical maker was described in the *Daily Telegraph* as

middle-aged, a trifle introspective, intelligent, probably a family man, often as not a skilled artisan or white-collar worker. David Rowe, 50, from Newton Poppleford, Devon, is typical; a school technician who constructs working dioramas, set-piece landscapes in which trains, trucks and cranes move, canal locks fill and empty and thumbnail children swing and skip outside chocolate-box cottages. He spends all evening, every evening, making them, 14 hours a day in the school holidays, using 'old rubbish' to make scenery and disused washing motors to bring it all to life.[7]

The effects of education, whether from school, or later from films or television, were far-reaching. Whereas in the past knowledge had been limited by experience with critical judgments derived from within the community, the advent of new and different ideas both stimulated and inhibited creative output. A wider range of references often resulted in indigenous work receiving little or no praise, while examples of high art were held up to demonstrate what was thought to be superior and 'truly creative'. Art, it was thought, was put into working-class life, an element of culture which was identified as having a civilising influence, uplifting and educational.

Leisure

In the second half of the nineteenth century conditions of labour slowly improved. In 1851 there was no legal restriction on the hours of employment of adult men and no legislation affecting the hours of any workers outside the textile and coal-mining industries. In 1867 an Act was passed bringing all premises within the purlieu of the law by defining a workshop as 'any room or place whatsoever, whether in the open air or under cover, in which any handicraft is carried on by any child, young person or woman and to which and over which the person by whom such child, young person or woman is employed has the right of access or control'. The term 'employed' meant 'occupied in any handicraft, whether for wages or not, under a master or under a parent', and therefore included home industry. At this time the total male population of England and Wales was 7.7 million. Out of this, 1.1 million were defined as the skilled labour class, 3.8 million as the less skilled labour class and 2.8 million as agricultural workers and unskilled labourers. By 1870 the working hours of textile workers were reduced from 13 to 10 a day, and Saturday was made a half holiday.

Leisure, though limited, for the first time for many became meaningful. In the larger cities and towns public parks were opened. Preston, in Lancashire, was the first in 1844. Though Sheffield was considered to be 'singularly destitute'[8] of open spaces, Manchester opened three parks, the first in 1846. A journalist coming to sample these 'now somewhat famous parks of Manchester'[9] a few months later, 'learned from eyesight that even during the rain these parks are resorted to by workmen . . . It is certainly something to know that mechanics, glad of recreation, will play of ninepins, under an ungenial sky, in preference to indulging in the more seasonal attraction of the tap'.[10] Besides the ninepins there were bowls and gymnastics appliances, with swings and seesaws for the children. Twelve years later another observer noted that a secluded portion of Peel Park was 'set apart for girls to allow them also some small chance of proper muscular development'.[11] Swimming baths were also opened by local authorities, often in conjunction with public baths and wash houses.

Many of the sporting activities and interests of the time did not, however, take place in urban parks. Bull-baiting was known to have continued until as late at 1840 (at Wells) though an Act of 1833 had forbidden this and similar cruel sports. Cock-fights, dog-fights, cock-shies and the like continued well into the century. There was much prize fighting and a ready supply of would-be boxers. Regular sport, whether brutal such as the Lancashire 'purring' matches or kicking fights in clogs, or the non-brutal such as whippet-training and pigeon-flying, were most often found in mining villages, among navvies working on the railways, or the semi-rural industrial population, than in the towns themselves.

While the industrial age introduced leisure time, post-Second World War society brought a leisure industry, a whole system for the provision of entertainment and activities for the non-working hours. Travel, do-it-yourself, books and magazines all dealt with leisure, marketing and defining a new aspect of consumer spending. While the traditional concept of leisure has changed, there is no evidence of any diminution of creative energy or the need to express ideas in visual form. This energy has found new directions such as in the decoration of mass-produced objects like cars, motor-cycles, 'ghetto-blasters' and even Doc Marten boots. Much time is spent decorating and creating the home; as well as carrying out basic maintenance, the making of attractive interiors is seen as an important part of individual identity. Gardens, too, have become for many works of art, as have window displays at Christmas. Significantly, these are often arranged so that passers-by in the street can enjoy them, rather than being done solely for the enjoyment of the makers.

STRUCTURES AND INSTITUTIONS

Patronage for academic art has been a vital force in nurturing its shape; such powerful institutions as Church, State, court, civic authorities and private patrons commissioned and displayed work giving it and the artist official recognition. Active interchange between such institutions and artists established subjects and themes. Work produced was intended to become part of private or public collections and have a recognised market value; it was likely to be carefully maintained and bequeathed from one generation to the next. Painters, sculptors and (more recently) photographers studied in recognised studios or schools using particular materials considered suitable for artistic expression with some, such as precious metal, having intrinsic value. Institutions and bodies such as academics, public collections and educational bodies approved work either overtly or covertly, imposing standards of taste which stressed the creative and individual role of the artist adapted to the needs of the institution. Within the fine arts innovation occurred partly in response to the needs of such institutions with a system of interaction reflecting the interests and tastes of the ruling élite. Despite controversy and resistance the basic system continues largely unchanged.

People's art is produced very differently. Major 'institutions' are the workplace, the home and leisure time; though operating more informally, they impose their own requirements whether associated with size, quality or suitability for purpose. Little or none of the work is commissioned though much is seen as fulfilling a particular purpose (such as apprentice pieces) or having a specific use within the home. Objects made at work may relate to the establishment of status or artistic expression beyond that directly required to meet the needs of function. In the home this is more likely to be concerned with items which may have a decorative as well as a practical use. Within this area fall the high art categories of painting, drawing and sculpture.

Within people's art few of the materials used have intrinsic value – wood, common clay, textile, bone and base metal as opposed to bronze, porcelain, ivory, gold and silver. Objects are likely to be intended for a known and specific audience and until recently such items had little or no sale value, nor was their 'life' likely to go much beyond the generation within which they were produced. In many cases this may have been a considerably shorter period. People's art is rarely passed on from one age to another for it relates directly to and is a part of the community within which it is produced with much of its significance dependent on that context. It was kept alive within the community because of its relevance to it. Away from this society people's art was unlikely to survive and if it did it was unlikely to retain its 'meaning'. An immediate and direct contact was often established between maker and user (the consumer), setting up a direct line of communication, giving the object a particular and precise meaning and value.

THE PRIMITIVE IN ART

The basis for the appreciation of any visual art is an agreed language which accurately describes the qualities of the work. Such terms as 'primitive', for example, need explanation if they are to be usefully applied to people's art, whether for two-dimensional painting or drawing, three-dimensional pieces made as sculpture or as objects associated with particular craft skills. Clear and important distinctions exist between 'primitive work' which is produced by self-taught and unsophisticated artists, and 'primitivism', a sophisticated style of art which consciously adopts and promotes primitive characteristics. Even

Plate 7 *Pit Lad* by G. Fowler, hammered and raised in lead, about 12 inches tall, 1906

the description 'primitive' contrasts with 'sophisticated' and by implication suggests more limited work. Nevertheless, despite the problems of language, some creative work can legitimately be called primitive, meaning that it is artistically untaught and directly expressed. An object to usefully discuss in this context is the sculptural head, 'Pit Lad', in York Castle Museum, hammered and raised in lead in 1906 by Mr G. Fowler, a plumber in Northallerton (see Plate 7).

The piece itself takes the conventional form of a portrait head but it is not of a particular character or individual person but rather of a recognisable 'type'. The head is strongly modelled and is in black; the smiling mouth is open, revealing gleaming white teeth. The eyes, equally bright, stare out of the head to give a peaceful if surreal interpretation. The head is both an expression of technical skill and artistic interest. Inside the base is written 'Raised without seam', a reference to the ability of the plumber to beat out a globe from a single sheet of lead. Sphere-like, the head has added facial details; the stand to which the head is attached is in the basic form of the hopper, an item placed at the top of a drainpipe to collect water. Inverted, the hopper serves as a stepped stand to complete the effect.

The fact that the plumber linked together two of the basic processes of the craft, fashioned them into the head 'Pit Lad' and wrote his achievement inside, suggests a degree of pride and a desire to use skill in an artistic form. The knowledge that lead will blacken easily probably prompted the subject. 'Pit Lad' is not a sophisticated piece of work in the conventional artistic sense even though the making is skilled; but its directly expressive quality and creative aspects can usefully be described as primitive in that they achieve a powerful effect rather than an accurate physical representation of a portrait head.

A different group of lead objects, made or collected at the turn of the century by Mr Manning, a plumber, and in the collection of Ipswich Museum, also indicates the deep involvement of skilled workers with their craft (see Plate 8). Mr Manning made tobacco jars and other pieces which included a seamless hollow lead globe to demonstrate technical skills. The collection reflects his fascination with his chosen material and the various skills required to fashion it.

Metal, an ideal material for fashioning heavy, durable objects, could be successfully worked to give a range of effects; it is adaptable to many kinds of artistic inventions,

Plate 8 Lead tobacco jars from the collection of Mr Manning, *c.*1920

but it also poses limits on how it can be handled, as 'Pit Lad' illustrates. Particularly effective examples of objects made from metal which have a 'primitive' strength are the metal trade signs made in the form of chimney-sweeps produced in the second half of the nineteenth century, and intended to stand outside a house or shop. The 'Chelten-

Plate 9 RIGHT Chimney-sweep, carved wood painted black, about 46 inches tall, anon, c.1890, LEFT Chimney-sweep, metal, about 48 inches tall, anon, c.1900

ham Sweep' at Cheltenham Art Gallery and Museum is a powerful, almost alarming, graphic image: the face is black and the eyes stare out, white and clear, while the rigid stance is as much an effect imposed by the restraint of the metal sheet bent and hammered to form the overcoat as of artistic intention (see Plate 9).

The stiff and lurching static pose con-

trasts with the more assured and conventional London chimney-sweep carved in wood some years earlier and now in the Horniman Museum. The stiff metal coat and the top hat confirm the skilled status of the sweep. Until displayed in Cheltenham Art Gallery and Museum the trade sign stood outside 43 Sherbourne Street in the town. The working of the metal is ideally suited to the image required and vividly conveys the impression as well as the appearance of a chimney-sweep. Whether the metal figure was made by the sweep or blacksmith is not known, but like 'Pit Lad', the metal sweep has a 'primitive' simplicity and strength. The Kalman Collection in London has a variety of metal trade signs, including one for a blacksmith of a silhouette showing the smith at work and a near life-size cow for a butcher's shop. Other impressive metal objects include weather vanes cut in the form of a cockerel and one showing a hound walking elegantly along (see Plate 10).

Both 'Pit Lad' and the Cheltenham and London chimney-sweeps make full use of the three-dimensional qualities of the object, but surface decoration can in its simplicity and directness achieve a dynamic sense of involvement. A particularly delicate example of work

Plate 10 Weather vane in the form of a hunting dog, copper and iron, 32 inches long, late nineteenth century

Plate 11 Warming pan, brass lid with incised design of leaves and bird, about 12 inches across, c.1800

on metal, in Reading Rural Life Museum, is on the brass lid of an early nineteenth-century warming pan (see Plate 11). The flowing design of a bird in full song surrounded by stylised branches of foliage, emblematic of peace and hope, is sensitively fitted to the round shape; the overall pattern suggests the design may have been adapted from an engraving, but it also relates to other traditions such as those found on slip-decorated earthenware dishes.

Comparing the incised cover with the decorated brass twist boxes made by miners in South Wales (now in Swansea Maritime and Industrial Museum, see Plate 12), reveals very different skills and intentions. The boxes carry relatively crude designs which incorporate the makers' names. The technique of engraving into the surface or using metal stamps of various kinds suggests an industrial rather than a rural background and one in which skilled working with metal was less important than making an object personal to them. In this case the boxes had particular significance to coal-miners. Colliers can physically carry few of their own objects below ground and are forbidden to take matches or lighters which could cause fires or explosions. Twist boxes, often made in the machine workshops by the miners, could be taken down the mines to hold twists of chewing tobacco as a substitute for smoking, a habit common in the late nineteenth and early twentieth century. Such items could also have served as a talisman, a personal object thought to bring good luck and protect the owner from accident. The name on the box and the individual decoration could also help identify a miner in the case of an accident. Some boxes received much detailed attention and

Plate 12 Brass twist boxes, stamped and engraved with name and address of owner, about 3 inches across, c.1900

care, with carefully considered arrangements of patterns and names.

The primitive in people's art was more likely to be a spontaneous response to depict the material world rather than as a consciously thought-out style. While most makers had a great knowledge of their materials and how they could be worked, few were familiar with the language of high art and its conventions, whether with perspectival representation, anatomically correct figures or classical and romantic styles. A few workers did look to the conventions of high art but the majority were more involved in achieving strong expressive qualities rather than sophisticated interpretation.

The difficulties of finding suitable language are further illustrated in the use of such misleading terms as 'charming' or 'naïve'. These definitions marginalise the expressive qualities of people's art and are better avoided. Even the description 'amateur' may imply that these artists model their work on the conventions and styles of high art but do not achieve the necessary standard. This is quite separate from the use of the word to denote 'non-professional'. Amateur art is, however, usually placed within the spectrum of high art. Hobbyist or enthusiast, relatively recent terms, are equally problematic in suggesting an interest with little relationship to either history or the community.

An equally difficult concept is that of 'self-expression'. While much people's art is undoubtedly an expression of individual response and understanding, it is often in too direct and personal a form to be given such an all-embracing description. In schools the term 'self-expression' has become a vital and important part of education, enabling individuals to reveal ideas and desires which cannot be spoken or written about but can be put into plastic or visual form. While children can do this without self-consciousness, adults may need to overcome many inhibitions to achieve such spontaneity. Objects produced by working-class artists are different to those which result from the therapeutic teaching of skilled instructors. Within people's art the concept of 'self-expression' is of limited use, carrying connotations of work which is of interest and value only as a part of a process of self-discovery rather than of creative expression.

Work that is 'old' presents other problems. It is often associated with nostalgia, an uncritical evocation of a time gone by when conditions, despite hardships, were thought to be better. In the past, family life and community support may often appear to have had a deeper, more significant importance. While it may be tempting to evoke a past which appears to cast a sentimental and non-critical light on working-class lives, this would be false and does not reflect recorded experiences. Discussion of working-class society cannot be based on the simplistic and inaccurate assumption that society was better in the 'good old days'. People were and are good and bad, hardworking and industrious or not. Equally, within working-class society there is a deeply conservative element, resistant to change, even when this may lead to improvements in living conditions.

NEW DEVELOPMENTS

Dramatic changes within society such as the widespread influence of television and the growth of multi-racial society further complicate – and enrich – working-class culture. Unemployment too, is a crucial factor within culture.

Of all the cultural changes since the Second World War, one of the most far-reaching is the advent of television, making knowledge of world events available in their own home to everyone, no matter what their social and economic class, in a way unimaginable before. It also shapes the way we perceive it. The coronation of Queen Elizabeth II in 1953, broadcast in black and white, was a terrific spur for the new medium and many acquired their own receiving sets. Commercial television, started in 1955 and funded by advertising, brought a choice of programmes and many working-class people identified with its more popular image.

The introduction of colour television in the 1970s, the extension of broadcasting hours, additional channels and video cassette players have further extended the influence of this mass form of entertainment. The number of hours of television watched, one of the chief indicators of the importance of the medium, is remarkably high. Today, all except some 2 per cent of homes in the UK have a television, and they are a common sight in bars, fish and chip shops and cafés. The cultural impact of television is vast and far reaching though there is still a temptation to write or speak of it as a temporary phenomenon which may at any time disappear, rather than to acknowledge its integration into late twentieth-century life.

Relevant to the cultural influence of television is the contrast between the ideology which informs it and that of working-class culture. Many people who produce and direct television programmes belong to influential and well-organised groups; the values and ideas they express reflect this. Television has great power to influence taste whether in providing characters for working-class artists to paint, such as those in *Coronation Street* depicted by George Davies at the bottom of a Staffordshire pit, or in presenting new how-to-do-it techniques. While working-class sports such as darts or snooker have been given new life through being featured on television, at the same time these have been appropriated by the middle class. Occasionally programmes look seriously at working-class visual arts. Ken Sprague's *Everyone a Special Kind of Artist* (Channel 4, 1983), presented different artists and their work with understanding and insight.

While a large percentage of the population can appreciate the value of having a job which provides income, defines status and much of their identity, this does not exist for the unemployed. Indeed, they are often portrayed as 'worthless scroungers' who do not want to work. Within the last 14 years the rise in unemployment, often highest in traditional industrial areas, has had a profound effect on working-class leisure time and cultural expression. Many cultural establishments have recognised the impact of unemployment: art galleries and museums, for example, offer concessionary admission rates to the unemployed, though these are often still pitched too high. Community and art centres set up courses for people out of work while part-time courses, in some areas, are open to the unemployed at nominal charges. The Inner London Education Authority (ILEA), abolished in 1990, was particularly sensitive to this need. Exhibitions of work by the unemployed have been featured across the country. In Edinburgh the Gateway Exchange, for anyone over 14, is run on co-operative lines. Exhibitions of paintings, drawings, sculptures and photographs by the young unemployed made clear their feelings of frustration and anger.

Imaginative projects have been conceived to provide professional teaching for the unemployed whilst allowing opportunities for individual expression. At Lyth Arts Centre in the north of Scotland, a woven tapestry was produced by a group of local unemployed people working with a professional weaver. Each weaver was encouraged to design and make their own panel taking local life such as sheep-shearing, farming and fishing as the theme. When completed the panels were stitched together to form a whole (see Plate 13). A later scheme for local people to make a large tapestry depicting the saint associated with the area attracted several hundred people, though only a dozen or so could finally be involved in its making.

A very different project repeated for several years was the opening of Camberwell School of Arts and Crafts in London for several weeks during the summer holiday. Funding came from the ILEA and a variety of courses were on offer. The only criterion was that students had to be unemployed. Registration was taken on a first come, first accepted basis, and courses were full within an hour. At the end of the period an exhibition of work was mounted. There was evident pride and much satisfaction in being able to 'make art' in well-equipped premises with staff on hand to advise and instruct.

'Multi-culturalism' has become a major concern in the wider consideration of culture. By and large the term 'working class' relates to the long tradition of mainly white people in Britain. This tradition is unlikely to be accepted by black people who often have their own rich and vibrant art forms. The writer and playwright Farrukh Dhondy, writing in 1978, commented with insight on the problems of multi-culturalism and the dangers of making broad assumptions about working-class culture:

> This is, of course, an absurd view of culture, a nationalist one. It lumps the 'values' and the 'assumptions' of working-class culture, the ideas and interests that come out of the working-class British, together with those that emerge from Britain's Imperial history and high-cultural artefacts.[12]

He highlighted the difficulties of tokenistic gestures and false assumptions about what may appear to be common ideas – recognition of cultural difference within the spectrum of class remains fundamental.

Evidence of the strength and creativity of people's art is abundant. It is not only associated with forms traditionally identified as people's art such as apprentice pieces, patchwork quilts, and heart-shaped pincushions, but is also an active response to changes in society, finding different and often challenging forms. Mass production may offer a relatively low-price range of goods but many rebel against its impersonal bland image. Leather jackets are painted with cult images while ghetto-blasters are decorated with complex and brightly coloured patterns. All offer a unique glimpse into a world in which art has an easy and unself-conscious role – a true and unfettered mode of creativity.

Plate 13 *The Farmer and his Wife* by Tom Baikie, about 12 × 7 inches, detail from *The Caithness Croft* tapestry (entire piece 66 × 49 inches), 1979. The tapestry illustrates aspects of traditional farming and suggests the hard toil involved, with the farmer and his wife having faces lined by long hours of hard outdoor work (Photograph William Wilson)

Chapter Two

'PURE GENIUS'

'Pure genius', the phrase often used to acknowledge the skill and ingenuity of ordinary workers in producing individual and inventive objects, can well be applied to the making and decoration of tools and machines and the fabrication of a wide range of artefacts in the workplace. Despite all the odds – of a long working-day, of limited resources in time and materials, of often appalling working conditions – workers still found time and energy to produce objects for their friends and families or for their own use, as well as to make their own mark on tools and machines.

PEOPLE'S ART IN INDUSTRY

As a leading manufacturing and trading nation and a major producer of basic raw materials such as iron and coal, great importance in Britain was placed on a skilled and hard-working labour force. Economic prosperity depended as much on the continued efforts of workers who would toil virtually without ceasing as on the ability of owners and managers to respond to new markets. Poems, mottos and texts extolling the value of work ('If any man would not work, neither should he eat' – Saint Paul) gave labour moral as well as social and economic importance.

Though a hard-working labour force ensured national prosperity, particularly for the owners, it also provided a huge measure of satisfaction and pride for the workers themselves. Many trades and professions had conventions whereby skill could be demon-strated and recognised, while workers them-selves utilised spare minutes and 'waste' materials to make objects to take home, carry in processions or display. Workers were defined largely by the work they did, the materials they used and the skills they acquired. Early glaziers, for example, were known as plumbers because of their use of lead cames. Later, when putty was used to hold the glass in place, glaziers handled linseed oil, a material used by painters. All were united within a craft tradition in which each material had its own trade or trades. Some workers wore special clothes which indicated their profession. When posing for photographs workers not only wore their particular clothes but often held the tools of their trade or carried fine examples of their work, emblems of status, pride and achieve-ment (see Plates 20 and 86).

Few if any of the special pieces made by workers had much in common with the new aestheticism which arose in the late eighteenth century. Aestheticism saw the process of 'art' as something special and separate, a gift to be nurtured and fostered. The word aesthetics, used to describe the philosophy or theory of taste, or of the perceptions of the beautiful in nature and art, was not coined until the mid-eighteenth century. Within new theories on 'the artistic', it was argued that art should be autonomous, self-sufficient, refer principally to itself and that it need serve no ulterior purpose. A clear separation developed between 'art', which was seen as refined, special and unique, and 'craft' which was thought to apply to skilled but mechanical work carried out by artisans. Art was associated with ideas, craft with production. Some believed that too close a connection between art and work would mar or stifle the creative imagination.

Such separations fell clearly along class lines with the 'real' or academic artist regarded as creative and intelligent, while craft was left to workers who had served full apprenticeships and knew how to handle and work material. In addition, working-class people had little access to see or appreciate 'fine art' until museums and art galleries were established in the second half of the nineteenth century. Most objects made in factories or workshops involved workers as machine operatives or artisans carrying out designs prepared by others; few had the opportunity to create in their own right. In contrast, sculptors who wanted their ideas carried out often had to employ carvers and cutters, few being sufficiently skilled in basic techniques to realise their own designs.

Guilds which originated in the thirteenth and fourteenth centuries to supervise the training of new entrants to a craft through apprenticeships, and to give recognition to skilled and able work, retained only vestiges of their power in the industrial age. Each guild, company or 'fellowship of crafts and mysteries' had its oaths and charges of acceptance, entrance fees and so on, and these continued within the new trade associations. Strictly bound apprenticeships, a central part of the guild system, survived in many industries, although new machinery and making methods had reduced their length from seven years to a much shorter period.

Professional Pride

In the manufacturing trades many workers found time to produce special objects similar to but separate from those made in the daily course of work. Some, closely related to work practice, were intended to demonstrate levels of achievement and illustrate technical virtuosity. But others were made simply for the workers' own enjoyment and use. Such items do not fall into clear-cut categories, whether in terms of purpose, technique or style. Some closely followed traditional themes though these were often elaborated and adapted, a few borrowed from the styles and subject matter of high art, while others were inventive in their own terms, expressive of a creativity which owed little to the concepts of aestheticism or the unique and privileged position of artist.

The objects share a common theme – a knowledge of and respect for the material from which they are made. Whether of wood, metal, slate, clay, leather, stone, straw or fabric, workers knew their chosen material, how to handle, fashion and reveal its unique qualities. A simple classification based on the material used is useful but has to accommodate awkward comparisons. Within the category 'ceramics' fall fine porcelains as well as everyday products of 'country' potteries such as spirit and pilgrim flasks, water bottles, stewpots, watchstands and candelabra. All are made from clay but their iconographic themes, their purpose and location within the domestic environment, give them very different status. Many pieces are intended principally to be used, while others are for occasional use or only display. Some are made in quantity and are relatively low-priced while others are one-offs and have no readily identifiable commercial market. Despite its limitations, a classification based on material offers a way of appreciating the makers' achievement within its own context.

Professional pride – a desire to celebrate skill as well as produce useful objects – was an important element in the work. For special objects, pieces to be displayed and appreciated on their own terms, makers took much more trouble. Evidence of skill was one of the bases for appreciation, taking into account how well the material was handled, how neat the joints, how good the finish and how suitable the object was to the intended function.

MAKING A MARK

Skilled workers often used their knowledge of materials and techniques to make objects in their free time for their own pleasure and satisfaction. Glass-blowers, for example, used their professional skills, while coal and slate-carving was carried out by miners who had a fascination with the material with which they worked. So-called apprentice pieces, made in a wide range of trades, constitute one group of objects. Some have a specific use, such as butter-coolers, fireplace surrounds, clock-cases and the like, while others are more decorative, almost ritualistic objects, often made as charms to ward off bad luck. Most are superbly crafted with an innovative and creative use of material, and expressive of an absorbing fascination with form and function.

Apprenticeship

The role and importance of tradition, is a major aspect of people's art. Skills, forms, customs and rituals transferred from one generation to the next in a continuous chain were accompanied by a vital quality of innovation and change. Tradition and innovation, two crucial but often conflicting forces in people's art, are essential for its survival. Knowledge, passed on in a multitude of ways, continued to evolve and adapt to new circumstances. People's art belongs to a period of great and profound change when established modes of learning and communication were disrupted, different techniques and processes introduced, and new ways of living separated work, home and leisure. While much traditional-based production continued within extended family units in small workshops attached to the home, work in factories took different forms. Apprentice schemes were established in potters' workshops, the blacksmiths' forges, glass-blowers' work-shops, woodworkers' shops and so on, with accepted and recognised training and learning opportunities. Within them modes were devised by which trainees could demonstrate skill, attainment and status either through 'apprentice-pieces', objects made for trade processions or making special virtuoso pieces such as the large goblet in Plate 14 for display.

Plate 14 Goblet in saltglaze inscribed 'J BRIGHT, J MILSOM, E MELSOM, IN COMMEMORATION OF THE POTTERS WHO RESISTED THE TYRANICAL CONDUCT OF W & T POW**LL, DECEMBER 4 1818 GOD SAVE THE KING', commemorating a group of young potters employed by T. & H. Powell, Bristol, put on trial for striking in support of a dismissed workmate, so breaking the 1799 Combination Act

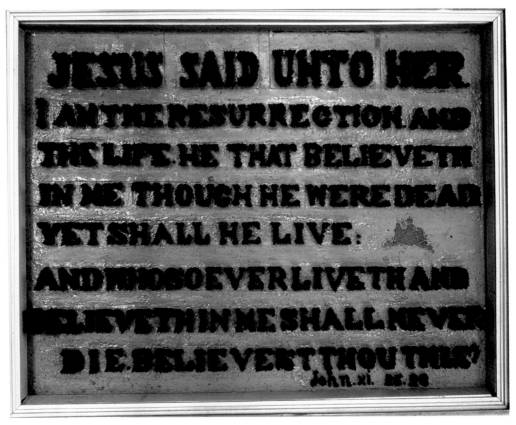

Plate 15 Biblical text: 'I AM THE RESURRECTION AND THE LIFE...' with each letter made of black bristle mounted on a wooden board which also bears the transfer printed emblem of the Brushmaker's Company – a shield bearing the Craft Tool of the Brushmaker supported by a Russian peasant and Bear and surmounted by a tun (barrel); made either as a sampler or more probably by an apprentice in the brush trade; 24½ × 30 inches, c.1850

Some pieces took a traditional theme, either as miniature versions of larger items, particularly popular in the furniture trade, or as more decorative objects which could be for amusement. In the glass industry for instance, these took such forms as a Jacob's ladder or the bell-like shape of a 'flip-flop', an object which could be made to emit a sharp cracking sound. The Biblical Text (see Plate 15) in Leicester Museum made by a brush apprentice using bristle to trace out the lettering is an intricate piece of work with moral and approving overtones. Shoemakers often made presentation pieces such as the pair of boots shown in Plate 16 which were made in 1888, the soles of which were stamped with the mark of the Kettering Joint Statement recording the marks awarded for making and finishing, samples of workmanship which often formed the basis for agreements on wages and quality. Some apprentice

pieces were scaled-down models of production items, miniature but properly made pieces of work which made evident the abilities of the maker, demonstrating skill and ingenuity – of creativity within a particular craft. This tradition, particular in the woodworking trades, continued a practice well established by such great furniture makers as Chippendale in the eighteenth century, of making miniature-sized pieces to show to prospective clients. Easily portable they could be used as samples by the sales force to attract orders or be shown in shop windows or display cases. Other important miniatures include working models of machines made by engineering workers.

The Great Exhibition of 1851 included numerous miniature pieces, partly because this enabled a larger number of objects to be shown, and partly as additional evidence of skilled making. Such official recognition

stimulated the making of miniature pieces
whether as examples of attainment by apprentices or as samples of production. Many
items can be dated to the second half of
the nineteenth century though the practice
continued well into the second half of the
twentieth century. Technical engineering
apprentices still make intriguing objects
which require machine-turning to a high level
of precision if the different pieces are to fit
neatly and smoothly together (see Plate 17).

Because apprentice work is not a precise, well-defined category it is often used as
a general term to embrace a wide and diverse
range of objects with little attempt to differ-
entiate why pieces were made. A beautifully
made model of a dresser dating to around
1860, about 12 inches tall, in the People's
Palace, is both a skilled apprentice piece and
one which is sufficiently portable for a sales
person to display to attract orders. The scale
model of an ornate curved staircase made
around the turn of the century is as much an
object of pride as a working model (see Plate
18). It is also likely to be very different to
the sort of stair its maker would have had in
his own home. Foundry workers also made
miniatures such as detailed fireplaces and
figures, some only a few inches high. At the
other end of the scale were giant, oversized
objects such as the enormous shoe in Plate
19 made by workers at the Scottish Co-
operative Wholesale factory. In Sheffield,
giant saws and scissors were unlikely to
be for personal use, but were instead to
demonstrate the skills of the makers.

Workers' pride in their trades is further
illustrated in photographs taken in the workplace. Invariably they are shown with a piece
of their work or holding the tools of their
trade, identifying them with a particular craft.
Photographs in Whitby Museum record the
skills of local joiners Harry Russell and W.
Clark Brown. The two men, wearing white
shirts and waistcoats, were pictured around
1890 in the formal setting of a photographer's
studio. In their hands they hold familiar tools
of their trade — a saw and a plane marker.
Another photograph shows Mr E. Varley

Plate 16 Boots with soles decorated with brass studs
and coloured leather, made for trade test by W. W.
Grange, shoemaker of Great Harwood, near
Blackburn, c.1888

standing with a bureau he had made in the
style of the eighteenth century. A newspaper
report testified to his and his brothers' devo-
tion to workmanship, and their lifelong
admiration for classic English designs, particularly the Sheraton, Hepplewhite and
Chippendale styles. Many of Mr Varley's
pieces were based on masterpieces of antique
furniture by these famous English makers.

Plate 17 Apprentice pieces by technical engineering
apprentices from the Ipswich-based firm of Ransome
and Rapier's waterside works, 1960s and 1970s

Plate 18 Staircase model by Thomas Fish while studying joinery at Ipswich School of Art (1877–80), about 20 inches tall

both in skills and in the tendency to show less interest in more 'home-spun' furniture.

Many skilled trades required workers to find their own tools and they were only accepted as fully qualified when they had a complete set. Tools also had to be replaced as needed. Cabinet-makers had an elaborate toolbox, costing up to £30 in the mid-nineteenth century. This held all necessary tools which fitted into their appointed place; many tools were home-made and carried individual decoration on handles and on the box, stamping it with the maker's identity. Some tools were decorated with the maker's particular skills such as veneer inlays and beautifully made joints and served as an excellent 'sampler' of skills.

The woodworker's box of tools was less ornate, usually left plain on the outside, but sturdily built. In contrast to the outside, the interior was carefully constructed to accommodate the range of tools and items required, sometimes with neatly fitting drawers and racks. This chest stayed in the workshop or went on journeys but was not taken on 'day' jobs. As a valuable and necessary item the chest would be handed down from generation to generation or sold on the death of the owner. As more industrial methods of making were used, over the years

Classic and well-known styles were often more highly thought of than vernacular work, and were a challenge to the skills of the maker. But in adapting and learning how to produce them, changes took place and individuals made their own versions. The change from local vernacular styles and methods of working to more established mainstream work marked a significant shift

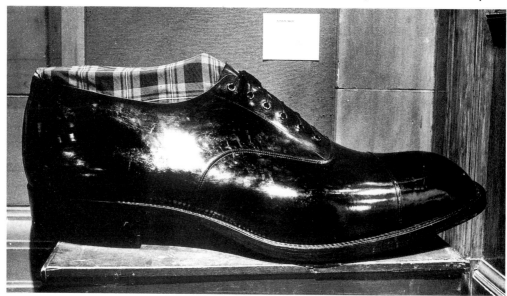

Plate 19 Scottish Co-operative Wholesale Society shoe, size 36, one of a pair made at the SCWS Boot and Shoe factory in Shieldhall for the Empire Exhibition held at Bellahouston, Glasgow, about 30 inches long, 1938

the toolbox became simpler. Paul Martinson (b.1914), who was trained as a cabinet-maker, worked at a factory in the East End of London making sideboards. He had to have his own tools which then cost five pounds, which included different sized chisels, a grooving plane, a tenon-saw and a handsaw: 'My boss taught me every aspect of the trade and at an early age I could do almost anything in the trade. I could veneer, make joints, dovetail and almost make a job right out myself.' Ironically, whether the tools were hand-made or manufactured, they were often disposed of when they were no longer of use.

John Gorman's father, a skilled carpenter, threw away most of his old woodworking tools (many of them hand-made by his father) when he retired, arguing that they were a part of a different age, that new technology had made them obsolete and that as they had lost their use they had no value. They may also have been associated with a hard-working past and hence had no sentimental romantic attachments. But other workers may have felt their skills had been devalued by new technology and threw away their tools in anger and disgust.

WOOD

The long history of working with wood, whether for building homes or ships, furniture or carvings, was regarded as part of the artisan tradition rather than artistic practice. Woodworkers carried on many older traditions, adapting and elaborating conventions which embraced sawn and cut decoration, caricature and exaggeration, as well as an uninhibited use of colour and gilding. Readily available and responsive, most wood can be worked with the knife, saw and chisel. It can be carved, whittled, sawn or even chopped into useful and decorative items. Small items fashioned in wood, described as treen, are numerous, reflecting the widespread interest in making individual objects and the attractive qualities of the material itself for small-scale work. These are discussed in Chapter Four.

Academic sculptors worked almost exclusively in bronze and marble in the second half of the eighteenth century, ignoring the importance of wood within British tradition. In contrast vernacular carvers, unencumbered by such concerns, continued the long-established traditions of wood-carving, including the use of colour and gilding. Not regarded as academic sculptors, their work was based on a solid system of apprenticeship with the finest work able to stand as works of art in their own right. Much of the difference between academic, classically inspired work

and that made by decorative carvers was not so much in quality as in status, with one claiming intellectual superiority and the other offering technical ability. Decorative carving is included in this book because, although it was produced to order, it often embodied a level of individual creativity in which carvers were able to express their own ideas and qualities. These include trade signs, ships' figureheads and fairground animals and decorations, items which were likely to be brightly painted. This latter group were often made by professional carvers (though not always) and are included because often the work

Plate 20 Marshal George Strapps (centre), woodcarver, holding a carved fish, photographed outside his shop in the late nineteenth century. The other workers hold the tools of their trade

transcends mere skilled handling to become expressive and inventive in its own terms.

Carpenters and carvers, familiar with the materials and the tools, produced creative work of high quality. Invariably it is the 'show pieces' which have survived, work which demonstrates in detailed form the skill and inventiveness of the artist. Marshal George Strapps, who had been employed as a postman, then as custodian at the Wisbech Working Men's Institute, was entirely self-taught in the art of wood-carving. Photographed outside his 'shop' in the late nineteenth century with other carpenters, he holds a carved fish, while the others carry such tools of their trade as a plane, saw, trowel, scribe and drill (see Plate 20). George Strapps's work, ornate and heavily carved in low relief, can be seen on a magnificent 'gothic' chair, while a carved wooden dresser bears designs based on traditional English work. One carved panel – 'Blind Man's Buff' (based on a work by Wilkie) – in the Wisbech and Fenland Museum is full of movement, as the blindfolded figures feel their way round the room in search of partners.

Carved and painted wood trade signs, ships' figureheads, fairground animals, roundabout figures and carved decoration on canal boats were a means of providing colour and animation to attract trade as well as enhance carnival and create pageantry. They were bold in size and in the treatment of the subject.

Plate 22 Trade signs in the form of giant tools, late nineteenth century. LEFT: Locksmith's trade sign in the form of a lock, wood, about 40 inches tall. CENTRE: Hardware trade sign in the form of a pair of pliers, wood, about 40 inches long. RIGHT: Locksmith's trade sign in the form of a key, soft wood, 44 inches long

Many forms were part of a well-established tradition but carvers, whether local carpenters or anyone able to wield a chisel, were free to interpret and improvise, often with powerful and expressive results. Trade signs belonged to urban rather than rural communities, and were carved locally; they stood outside shops indicating by a striking visual image the nature of the trade conducted within. The more exotic and colourful they were, the more eye-catching, the most usual and effective being giant-sized objects typical of the particular trade. When shopkeepers took over premises with a well-known sign and retained it even though the trade was different, a certain amount of ambiguity occurred. Unusual figures include a naked boy for undertakers, an artichoke or pineapple for nurserymen and the civet cat for perfumers or chemists. A large collection displayed in Huntly House Museum in Edinburgh includes unique as well as more usual items.

More familiar trade signs are the three gold balls for the pawnbroker, an outsize pestle and mortar, and a unicorn or a carved bust for the apothecary and chemist. Booksellers used busts of literary figures, while stationers used bibles, books, a large bottle of ink or, impressively, giant-sized stamps which stood nearly five feet tall. Hosiers often put up a carved wooden leg, glovers hung out a wooden hand or glove, while shoemakers displayed a carved wooden calf-

Plate 21 Fishmonger's trade sign in the form of a carved and painted fish, wood, about 30 inches long, c.1900

length boot. Barbers advertised with a red and white striped pole and chimney-sweeps used a golden pole or the figure of a chimney-sweep. The tradition continues: a pine furniture shop in south London has built a huge pine bed breaking through the wall.

Outsize objects were popular and made a striking visual impact. These would include giant fish, cricket bat and stumps, a pair of pliers, a lock, and a key, as well as a kettle and large pair of spectacles all made out of wood and placed outside appropriate shops (see Plates 21, 22 and 23). Pigs, cows and other farm animals often stood outside butchers' shops, while large and impressively carved reliefs would signify the name of an inn.

Tobacconists attracted some of the most arresting figure signs which included sailors or 'Jack Tars'. Some signs, larger than life, may have been placed outside the shop; others, half life-size, stood in windows or inside doorways. The 'black boy' or 'Black-amoor' was one of the most popular figures. In Scotland the kilted Highland man often stood outside tobacconist and snuff shops, some even offering a free pinch of snuff to passers-by (see Plate 24). Highlanders may have been used to identify shops selling Scots snuff as opposed to that which came from Bristol. Though most trade signs were carved in wood, others were fashioned from other materials – such as the metal chimney-sweep discussed in Chapter One and the fat gilded stone pig that stood outside a butcher's shop in Goole (see Plate 25).

Plate 24 Tobacconist's trade sign in the form of a Highland soldier sitting on a whisky cask, about 46 inches tall, mid-nineteenth century

Plate 23 Ironmonger's trade sign in the form of a giant kettle, metal, about 36 inches tall, late nineteenth century

Figureheads, often elaborately carved and painted, remained a prominent feature on the bows of ships and boats until wooden sailing ships were superseded by those made from metal. From the early nineteenth century ships of the line had at the prow figureheads emblematic of their names, usually ornately carved and painted by carvers in shipyards. By the mid-eighteenth century the human figure was replacing the lion as the most popular emblem for smaller naval vessels. In 1796, however, the Royal Navy ordered that figureheads could not be fitted to new ships and that old ones should be replaced with an abstract scroll or billet-head.

Nevertheless, figureheads continued to appear, usually of a single human figure, sometimes full length but more commonly

Plate 25 *Fletcher's Pig* – butcher's trade sign in the form of a gilded pig, limestone with gilt and paint, about 40 inches tall, mid-nineteenth century

but variations were introduced. Figures in Highland dress were sometimes used on Scottish vessels, and a figurehead of a woman with a targe and claymore belonged to the ship *Caledonia* of Arbroath, wrecked at Morwenstow in Cornwall in 1842, when travelling from Odessa to Gloucester with a cargo of wheat. Carvers at small remote shipyards sometimes produced particularly lively and striking figureheads. In Southwold Museum there is a Victorian figure with a bunch of grapes in her hand which may have been borne on a fruit schooner (see Plate 26). A particularly sensual figurehead, carved in the mid-nineteenth century and now in Mer-

just a bust of head and shoulders. The theme usually related to the name of the ship. Many vessels bore the names of heroes and heroines from Greek mythology, of which there is an extensive collection in the National Maritime Museum, London. Though carving on ships of the Royal Navy declined and figureheads disappeared, they continued to flourish on merchant vessels. Throughout much of the nineteenth century British ships dominated world trade, and businesses including ship-building expanded. The greatest merchant ships – such as those used by the East India Company for trade with the Far East – closely followed naval tradition.

In larger ports there were specialised workshops which carved figureheads and ship decoration. The two brothers J. and R. R. Laurie of Glasgow were one such firm. Later they carved fairground horses and religious figures for churches. Individual carvers are, however, rarely mentioned in reports of new ships. Most figureheads were carved in the shipyard, probably by one of the builders who had a particular skill. Design and format of the single figure tended to be traditional

Plate 26 Ship's figurehead, woman with a bunch of grapes, possibly from ship engaged in the wine trade, about 30 inches tall, early nineteenth century

seyside County Museum, is of a Welshwoman with one breast revealed, while a caricature of a 'gentleman' is featured on a figurehead in the Maritime Museum on the Isle of Wight. The broadness and vigour of the carving more than makes up for the less skilful hand (see Plate 27).

A few carvers are known by name and their work identified. William Dodd, one of the Liverpool ship carvers, was at work from the 1850s until about 1900. Unusually, he also carved a striking self-portrait bust and one of his sketchbooks has survived. Another famous carver, A. E. Anderson of Bristol, much of whose work is in Bristol Maritime Museum, carved trade signs which incorporate scrollwork of the kind often used for trailboards. As the need for ship carving declined, Anderson, along with many others, turned to the production of spirited and imaginative fairground horses.

Subjects for figureheads were wide ranging and, as well as mythological figures, included warriors, statesmen and characters from popular literature. Portraits of wives were common, though for smaller vessels where personal names or the identity of the

ship were unknown, portraits of sweethearts and daughters were often carved. One example in the North Devon Maritime Museum is of a directly carved and incised seagull from the wooden ketch *Bessie Clark*, built at Bideford in 1881. More than likely it was the work of one of the crew, carved some time after the launch of the vessel.

Plate 27 Ship's figurehead, portrait of man in early nineteenth-century dress, about 36 inches tall, late nineteenth century

CLAY

Alongside the large and efficient ceramic industry which developed and flourished in Stoke-on-Trent from the late eighteenth century, many smaller workshops continued, reflecting and serving the needs of local communities. Small pottery workshops had existed for hundreds of years, usually in rural areas or on the edge of towns where there was plenty of space and where kilns could be fired without problems. The type and range of pots produced were determined by the requirements of the local community, whether pastoral or industrial, providing items for use on farms alongside those required for workers in industry. Hundreds of pottery bottles used by colliers and steelworkers for carrying beverages to work were made by, among others, the Jenkins family

at Ewenny. These items were later replaced by less costly and more durable metal and enamel alternatives. In Oldham Museum a miner's bottle, made locally, bears a chipped design showing an anchor surrounded by the name of the miner, John Stafford Head (see Plate 28). Head worked in several pits in Oldham from the age of 12 until his retirement, and decorated this bottle in 1864 whilst a miner at Rhodes Bank Pit, a small colliery close to Boustree, which operated from c1770 until 1874. The desire of the owner to identify his own bottle is reminiscent of the decorated tobacco tins made by miners in South Wales.

Items made in small potteries can be divided roughly into two sorts. The larger group consists of the functional wares produced for use in the home, on the farm or

Plate 28 Chipped miner's drinking bottle from Rhodes Bank pit, Oldham, by John Stafford Head, 1864

later in industry. At Fremington Pottery, North Devon, these items included seven sizes of pans, some 15 inches diameter, cooking-pots including pipkins, owlsheads, gallipots, butterpots, and oval and round baking dishes. The pottery also made 'steins' for pickling pilchards in Cornwall, colanders, large oval dishes for hams, drainpipes, tiles and chimney-pots. Other potteries made

Plate 29 Water-jar dated 1828 with slip decoration of bird, Ewenny Pottery, Glamorgan, about 24 inches tall

miners' water-bottles and candlestick holders, stew-pots and mugs. The main production method was throwing pots on the potter's wheel, a specialised and skilled process. Some potters still decorated these everyday pieces. A store jar with its bird design and the date is both effective and charming (see Plate 29).

Less skilled methods include assembling objects from flat slabs of clay, made either by hand or formed inside or over clay moulds. Knife boxes, Dutch ovens, baking dishes and salt jars all had functional use, while such items as miniature top hats, elaborate chests of drawers, rocking chairs and toy cradles were more decorative and playful (see Plates 30 and 31). These items are of particular interest because the making methods allowed considerable flexibility and, therefore, scope for improvisation; their flat surfaces were also ideal for inventive decoration.

Many decorated pots which fall into the 'produced for sale' category carried individual designs, often creative interpretations of established motifs. At their strongest they were minimal and assured, with natural forms such as birds and foliage. The press-moulded dish with a slip-trailed bird motif successfully integrates personal creativity with established design (see Plate 32). Commercial concern seems less important than the desire to produce pieces which carried the mark of the maker – many of which, while not adding greatly to the price, offer scope for invention and ingenuity. That such everyday items were decorated affirms the desire to show visual invention as well as mechanical skill.

The other group of wares consists of more decorative and special items which enabled potters to exercise their imagination and use their skills to creative and expressive effect. Some of these pieces were made to order, such as those for the celebration of weddings and marriages; others were made 'on spec' in the hope of finding new markets. Many items were based on traditional forms which were often freely interpreted by the potter. In this section fall loving-cups, tygs, wassail-bowls and, from the North Devon potteries, harvest jugs, the surfaces of which were covered with abundant decoration (see Plate 33). Traditionally, these were used to serve refreshment to the harvesters and had a ritualistic as well as a practical purpose.

Wassail-bowls such as that shown in Plate 34 were much more elaborate and included a lid and a bowl. The ancient New Year custom of wassailing was practised in Glamorgan, as in other parts of Wales, in the nineteenth century. Parties of wassailers, progressing from house to house with traditional greetings for the health and prosperity of the inhabitants, were acknowledged with spiced ale, sometimes with a concoction of apples and cakes, dispensed in a wassail-bowl carried round by the party. The wassail ceremony itself brought together several originally distinct rural traditions, notably that of the Mari Lwyd (Grey Mary) in which a horse's skull, dressed and decorated, was paraded by the party to the exchange of traditional or impromptu verses and to the custom of carrying round a perllan, a symbolic orchard consisting of an apple and a model tree on which perched a bird. The revival of interest in the ceremony was part of romantic nationalism and an attempt to re-establish links with the past and restore a sense of community. The elaborate decoration of Ewenny bowls reflects a convergence of various designs. Traditional motifs include modelled animals associated with rural life such as foxes, hens and dogs, as well as sheaves of corn and trees, while scratched designs include various plants such as hop flowers; others were often very up-to-date: one bowl carries the names 'Langan' and 'Spring' and refers to the protagonists in a celebrated prize fight at Chichester in 1824. Wassailing virtually died out in Glamorgan towards the end of the nineteenth century, though wassailing-bowls were produced as nostalgic reminders of the 'good old days'.

Decorative designs similar to those on wassail-bowls appeared on puzzle jugs, also made at Ewenny Potteries. A complex system of hollow handles and tubes, with a pattern of holes in the neck, posed the problem of how to drink from the jug without spilling

Plate 30 Chest of drawers in red clay with slip-trailed decoration, about 6 inches tall, nineteenth century

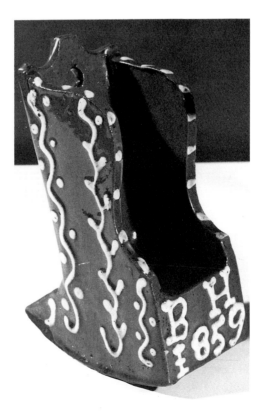

Plate 31 Rocking chair, slab-built red earthenware with slip-trailed decoration, initialled BH and dated 1859, Cliviger Pottery, 8 inches tall

Plate 32 Dish, moulded with slip-trailed decoration of bird, initialled EW and dated 1796, 15¼ inches diameter

the contents. The trick was to suck the spout at the top of the handle. Decoration, carved through a covering of white slip (a thin, creamy white layer of clay for coating and decorating pottery), included birds pecking at foliage, as well as stem and leaf patterns and hop flowers. Some included the name of the owner, the maker and the date.

Money-boxes, decorative and relatively quick to make, were produced at many potteries. At Ewenny they were made in the form of birds and were similar to the hen and chicken money-boxes made in Staffordshire. Another type of money-box had birds modelled on the top of a thrown bottle. Incised decoration through white slip often bore the name of the recipient, for example:

William Jones / Aged three years /
16 Jany 1859

Plate 33 Devon harvest jug, Barnstaple ware with incised decoration of mariner's compass, cock with floral motifs and the verse: 'Harvest is come all/Busy now in making. Of the Barley mow if/You the Barley Mow/Neglect A good ale you/Cannot then Expect/August 1838/John Prouse/Harland', 9½ inches tall, 1838

At Halifax money-boxes were made in the shape of a miniature chest of drawers. Containers for holding ale took the form of jugs in the shape of an animal, the head of which came away to serve as a mug. 'Sussex Pigs' were thrown on the wheel before modelled legs were added. More elaborate are the lidded jugs made in the mid-eighteenth century in the Midlands, particularly at Nottingham and Staffordshire, in the form of bears (see Plate 35). The bear sits upright holding a dog between its front legs which it is presumably crushing to death; the head of the bear served both as a lid and a mug. Bits of clay stuck on the body of the bear suggest the animal's fur, and the freely modelled head and legs are amusing but macabre. The salt kit in Plate 36, made for a blacksmith in the north-east, is a particularly fine example of 'personalised' ware, bearing not only the owner's initials but also the emblems and tools of the blacksmith's trade.

Many smaller pottery factories combined industrial production with hand making to give a 'handmade' look. The effect, consciously or not, was unsophisticated, making full use of modelling and freely drawn lettering. This method of production did have advantages: potteries could produce smaller quantities and be flexible in the range of work they made – a particular advantage when a large proportion of the market was relatively local, and allowed orders for individually marked wares to be accepted. In this way they operated more like country or small potteries, taking orders for individual requirements bearing names and dates for special commemorative pieces.

Even such everyday items as teapots could be made personal by the application of names or special modelled designs. Teapots, salt jars and cheese dishes were some of the range of domestic items made at potteries in Scotland. At the Cumnock Pottery in Ayrshire, inscribed handwritten lettering commemorated particular events:

Mr and Mrs McGregor / married at
Kintore / 7th November 1879

Plate 34 Wassail-bowl and cover, red earthenwear with white slip, incised decoration, lettering and glaze, from the Ewenny Pottery, Glamorgan, about 20 inches tall

The Seaton Pottery in Aberdeen produced a range of individual items. Some, in marbled red and white clay, were impressed with the name of the owner. Cheese bells bear such names as:

Mrs Scott and Mary Ann / 1895

In factories in Stoke-on-Trent there is a tradition of making 'joke' pots for workers getting married. Thus a teapot may be given three spouts, or a jug several handles. Miniature lavatory basins were often converted into smoking pipes while chamber-pots had witty mottos added. The imaginative use of available components by workers in factories has received scant attention.

Relatively slow to make compared with pots thrown on the potter's wheel, as well as time-consuming to decorate and embellish, the hand-built and/or decorated items could satisfy both maker and user. They lie between

Plate 35 Beer jug and cover in the form of a seated bear clasping a dog to its chest, covered with clay chippings to simulate fur, white saltglaze; the removable head has a chain through its snout, Staffordshire, about 6 inches tall, c.1760

at the start of the nineteenth century and this was continued by his family until the early years of the twentieth century, making practical items for use in rural homes and industries. While most of the functional wares have long since disappeared, some of the more unusual items remain, in particular pieces made by Fishley when he was in his 70s and 80s and partly retired.

Typical items are mantelpiece ornaments and watch-stands, some four to five inches tall and decorated with applied red, white and dark brown clays in a crowded assemblage of modelled fruit, animals, human figures, masks and moulded rosettes. These pieces, stamped with his name and the date, suggest they were special to him. Many individual components were moulded from other forms and assembled with only small areas individually modelled. These pieces, many of which are in the collection of the Royal Albert Memorial Museum in Exeter, were quite separate from the regular range of production items made by the pottery.

the basic production ware and the individual pieces. While all the products of Ewenny or Seaton and other similar sized workshops were made for sale, some pieces would be given special attention, providing scope for individual invention and creative expression. Personalised and decorated plates, dishes, cups and so on, would be treasured and displayed on the top shelves of dressers, stored out of reach, safe from the risk of breakage. Adept at handling their skills, potters improvised special pieces particularly to mark public occasions, or for celebrations of birth and marriage or to commemorate death. In Stoke-on-Trent terracotta gravestones decorated with slip-trailed lettering and designs were made by potters for friends and family.

Individual expression by potters is well demonstrated by pieces such as the watch-stand in the shape of a grandfather clock in Manchester City Art Gallery (Plate 37), and by the decorative wares made by George Fishley (1770–1865) at the Fremington Pottery near Barnstaple. Fishley set up the pottery

Plate 36 Salt jar, red earthenware with white slip, incised and painted decoration of initials and masonic signs and anvil. Probably made for a blacksmith, about 10 inches tall, 1857

Plate 37 Watch-stand in form of a grandfather clock, red
earthenware with applied clay decoration and modelled
figures, about 6 inches tall, early nineteenth century

to exercise their imagination. Pots were usually moulded and, short of making many-
spouted or multi-handled teapots and the
like, their own ideas could only be expressed
in the decoration. In factories whose wares
had hand-painted decoration, painters and
paintresses were taught particular skills.
Wares produced at such factories as Royal
Worcester Porcelain and Derby Porcelain
were aimed at the well-to-do middle and
upper classes who were able to afford such
luxury items. 'Taste' was conservative and
traditional, aiming for neat patterns or skilfully rendered representational scenes. Nevertheless, painters carried out their own designs.
At Pountney's Pottery in Bristol, Charlie
Smith painted a plate depicting three hum-
orous fire-watchmen in the war which hung
in the headquarters; earlier Reg Williams
painted idyllic landscapes on commercially
made plates at home which were fired in the
factory (see Plate 39). These were known as
'foreigners'. In South Wales plates were
painted with freely drawn designs with details
of deaths and tragic accidents in coal-mines,
the event more important than slick presentation.

One of the few factories to break away
from 'tasteful' design was that of Clarisse
Cliff. She ran her own studio in Stoke-on-
Trent between the wars after being trained

Towards the end of the nineteenth century
special items made at the pottery included
large lidded bowls on stems and candelabra.
Made in red clay with the applied decoration
in white clay of fruits, flowers and seeds, this
gives the impression of an abundant harvest
cornucopia (see Plate 38).

Clearly George Fishley knew his chosen
material well and enjoyed working with clay,
and in his old age felt able to spend time
making what may have seemed to his family
a whimsical indulgence. His inspiration came
partly from his traditional work as a potter
and partly from Victorian contemporary taste
for crowded and rich imagery, but its
interpretation in clay is his alone. Equally, the
ornamental forms and the resulting decorative
treatment – which also combined an element
of function in that they could display the face
of a pocket-watch – were entirely the result
of his imgination.

Few workers in the ceramic factories
of Stoke-on-Trent had similar opportunities

Plate 38 LEFT: Mantel ornament by George Fishley with
moulded decoration in brown and white clays, 6¾
inches tall, 1855; CENTRE: Bowl and cover by Robert
Fishley in red clay with applied modelled white clay
motifs, 14 inches tall, 1844; RIGHT: Candelabrum by
William Fishley Holland, 10½ inches tall, c.1950

Plate 39 Plate with pastoral scene painted at home by
Reg Williams and subsequently fired in Pountney's
factory, Bristol, about 9 inches across, c.1930

as a paintress. Unusually, Cliff worked her way up the factory and, though she spent a brief period at art school, her colourful and bold designs were outside the boundaries of what was considered good taste. Though beyond the concerns of this book, her work is relevant in shedding light on 'working-class taste'. Just as canal people and fairground workers liked decorations to be new and brightly coloured in preference to the darker, more subtle tones achieved with the patina of age, so Clarisse Cliff's brightly decorated pots were popular with working-class as well as middle-class people. She felt able to explore without inhibition her own delight in colour and stylised pattern.

METAL

The working of iron formed the backbone of the Industrial Revolution with metal used widely for machines, tools, railways and structures for buildings and bridges, as well as a huge range of practical and decorative objects. From around 1780 the iron industry was centred in the West Midlands, the 'Black Country', though iron was also worked in other areas. By 1823 there were 237 blast furnaces spread across Britain, and in 1856

industrial steel production began.

Rolled wrought-iron, and later steel, was used by blacksmiths, as well as specialist smiths such as chainmakers and farriers, and by the engineering industry. Shipbuilders and boilermakers were the main users of plates and sheets, but these were also used by engineers. Blacksmiths, who worked usually with wrought-iron, had a central position in any pre-industrial community, making tools

Plate 40 Model of inside of blacksmith's shop by George Bissell, metal, about 18 inches square, 1870–86

Plate 41 Firegrates made by blacksmiths, about 20 inches long, nineteenth century

for the farm or builder, and, when industry required tools and shovels, it was blacksmiths who provided them. Later the job of smith and farrier was often combined.

By 1831 there were some 58,000 blacksmiths in the country, probably half of whom were engaged in rural occupations. This figure also includes workers in the Sheffield trades. From among blacksmiths and wheelwrights developed most of the large-scale makers of agricultural implements and machinery, though the ordinary day's work and the usual scale of business among blacksmiths and wheelwrights was little changed throughout much of the nineteenth century. The occupational census of 1851 revealed that not one blacksmith in seven employed three or more men, while most had only a labourer and a lad. Wheelwrights likewise only employed one or two assistants.

A fascinating insight into the blacksmiths' skills can be seen in the model of the inside of a blacksmith's shop which existed in London a hundred years ago (see Plate 40). Highly detailed, the model was made by George Bissell between 1870 and 1886 and is now at the Science Museum in London. Bissell, a blacksmith in Stepney, east London, turned and fashioned with beautiful precision all the tools, the various machines, the bellows and hearth and so on. So accurate is the scaling down of the pieces that it is hard to accept their miniature size. The model served both as a demonstration piece and as an expression of professional pride; as a useful piece to show to prospective customers, it

illustrated the skilled work of the smith, but the degree of thought and effort evident in the model suggests that this was far more than a simple exercise in dexterity. It bears the hallmarks of skilled workers concerned with their profession, bringing to it a creative imagination which was both enterprising and clever. Blacksmiths also made imaginative items such as weather vanes (see Chapter

Plate 42 Brassware made from waste brass, which includes spill holders, a 'tidy' in the form of a crown, a 'good luck' horseshoe, a lucky locket, a show on a stand and a boot on a stand, nineteenth century

Plate 43 Miniature cradle and (behind) money-box in form of stool made by John Cairns from scrap steel used in the construction of the Forth Railway Bridge, about 5 inches long, c.1885

One), decoy ducks and animated models of animals with legs that can be made to walk.

The creative work of operators in machine-shops and of blacksmiths in providing objects for local and personal needs is well illustrated by the range of objects produced for the home. These include a number of bannock spades and trivets, all fashioned with slightly different designs. Many incorporated a design of hearts, the symbol of love, and were often presented as love tokens. The range of variations suggests great care and ingenuity was required to ensure each one was different. In Scotland typical items include candlesticks made by twisting a strip of metal into a spiral, griddles with various forms of patterning as well as fire grates with simple but effective decorative treatment (see Plate 41). Equally fascinating are the brass ornaments, trivets and brush and comb containers made in the industrial

areas of the north-east of England and the Midlands from waste pieces of brass (see Plate 42). The metal was cut and fashioned into silhouettes of deer, boots and shoes and bent to make tidies for brushes and combs, spill holders, matchbox-stands and the like to sit brightly polished on the mantelpiece. Workers on the Forth Railway Bridge fashioned such miniature items as cradles and fenders from pieces of scrap metal from the enterprise (see Plate 43).

Metal, whether formed into rivets and nails, huge ships and machines or trivets for the hearth, involves a detailed understanding of the material, a skill which encourages the making of decorative objects. In 1815, to demonstrate the possibilities of iron (more efficient production had lowered the price from £20 to £12 a ton), John Wilkinson made himself a one-person exhibition, building iron chairs, and pipes and vats for breweries. He spoke of houses made out of iron and was even buried alive in an iron coffin.

In Sheffield, the centre of the metal trade, great steelworks at Brightside existed alongside flourishing businesses in knives, cutlery, scissors, files, razors and edge tools. Much of the trade was in the hands of small traders known as 'little mesters', where only one or two workers were employed. A 'mester' needed little capital to set up business: all that was required was an anvil, a few tools, raw materials and a smith's forge, a fireplace and a grinding wheel. Most of the workshops were small and were often attached to the house. To become a cutler a lad was bound apprentice by an indenture until he was 21. At this age he had to take out his mark and freedom by presenting a

Plate 44 Detail of decorative file by Hiram Younge showing a view of Wentworth Woodhose, seat of the Earl of Fitzwilliam, file 30 inches long, 1811

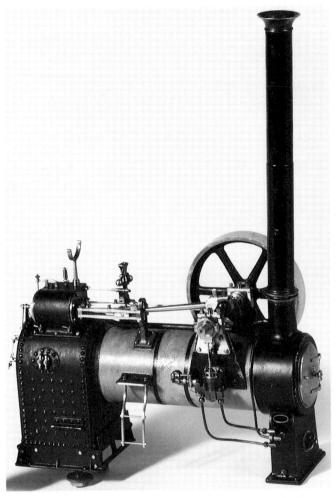

Plate 45 Model overtype semi-portable steam engine made by J. Robson, Gateshead, scale 1:32, about 6 inches tall. This is an accurate working reproduction of an engine made by Marshall Sons & Co, Gainsborough, about 1905. Built over several years using a kitchen table as a working bench and only hand-tools, the model was awarded First Prize in its class in the North-East Coast Exhibition of 1929

piece of work before starting as a journeyman cutler. Working conditions were often appalling. Describing the file-cutting shop, Ebenezer Elliot said:

There are about twelve to twenty men crowded in a small room about four yards wide and three yards high. They are seated five feet apart and there is no ventilation. This causes tiredness and there are frequent journeys to the beershops for stimulant. Dry grinding is most unhealthy for the men breathe particles of dust, which eventually clog the air passages to the lungs and cause the fatal disease known as grinders' asthma.

Making files and rasps was highly specialised work. Great skill was required to accurately forge and grind a file which was oval in section and tapered towards one end; the teeth were cut with a single triangular chisel and hammer suited to the size and grade of the file being cut. The hammer weighed four pounds, and as often as not 100 teeth per minute were cut on a large file. On smaller files, often cut by women working at home, a rate of 250 teeth per minute could be achieved. On these smaller files there could be as many as 100 teeth per inch, each perfectly spaced. Hand-cutting the teeth provided the opportunity to produce highly skilled and decorative scenes. Fine examples are in Kelham Island Industrial Museum.

Plate 46 Miniature firegrate with mantel ornaments, about 9 inches tall, late nineteenth century

One decorative file made by Hiram Younge around 1811, is some 30 inches long and two inches wide and depicts scenes in the file-makers' shop, including cutting, grinding and forging, as well as a view of Wentworth Castle and the city Coat of Arms (see Plate 44). The design, rendered as a frontal view, owes much to contemporary engraving and was probably worked for the owners of the factory for a particular occasion. The various scenes showing inside the file-cutters' shop and the different processes employed follows a popular tradition of work-related subjects. Again these confirm the pride and interest of workers in their own profession – a mixture of pride and respect for the processes themselves, despite the appalling conditions. Smaller, less grand files have more modest decoration.

Engineers, trained in building precise pieces of machinery, were particularly adept at working with and handling metal. Miniature models of larger pieces of machinery, many of which could work, were favoured. Notable examples were made by J. Robson of Gateshead, including the Overtype Semi-

Portable Steam Engine at the Science Museum in Newcastle (see Plate 45). The original was built about 1905; the scale model (1:32), which took several years to complete, stands only eight inches tall and was constructed using a minimum of tools. Robson also made a miniature working model of an inverted vertical engine, one and a half inches tall. Working model engines built by S. G. Friar of Wallsend between 1920 and 1965 involved the machining of all parts which was carried out on a treadle-operated centre-lathe with planing and surfacing attachments built by his father in 1896. The lathe and other tools from Mr Friar's workshop, together with 15 models, are now in the collection of the Science Museum in Newcastle.

The making of miniatures, whether depictions of workers doing their job or of tools and machines of the trade discussed earlier in the chapter, has a long history. During the nineteenth century there were new opportunities to form models in metals

Plate 47 Brass bobbin-stand assembled from factory-produced components, about 10 inches tall, c.1890

Plate 48 Tin lanterns made by tinkers in Scotland, about 12 inches tall, late nineteenth century

whether these were miniature coal-burning fireplaces (see Plate 46) complete with poker, shovel and tongs, brass tea urns, models of a metalworking shop in cast-iron or cartoon-like figures of workers in the factory. One factory worker made a decorative bobbin-stand, some eight inches tall, by ingeniously assembling various metal parts made in the factory. Cotton reel holders served both a decorative and practical function and the ornate example shown in Plate 47 reflects popular Victorian taste. Skilfully assembled and inventive in its use of ready-to-hand component parts, the cotton reel brings together both art and readiness for improvisation. Such pieces are in the People's Palace, Glasgow, and Beamish Open Air Museum.

A very different group of workers who made full use of the versatile qualities of metal and exploited its creative potential were the tinkers in Scotland, whose skills and inventive work are legendary; they turned their hand to a wide range of crafts to produce clever and intriguing designs, whether working with tin, silver (they made a fascinating range of jewellery using local rare stones),

wood or horn.

Some of their most effective work was done on tin lanterns (see Plate 48). Basic in form, they consist of a cylindrical body with a pointed top. Before shaping, the tin was pierced with holes in various designs so allowing light to pass through and thus cast different patterns. Designs varied and the effect achieved was attractive and practical; it was also a way for each maker to create their own designs.

Tinkers also produced small cup-sized staved vessels made up of strips of wood carefully joined together. Local woodworkers would occasionally make these containers too, but the smaller, more intricate ones were made by the tinkers. For the small vessels – known as quaichs, and usually used for taking a dram of whisky – the tinkers joined the staves by 'feathering'. On particularly valuable pieces, alternate staves of light and dark wood were finely meshed together rather like the edges of a feather and the whole form bound with cane. The quaichs had the added advantage over glass in that they would not get broken when carried.

GLASS

During the nineteenth century the glass industry became concentrated in particular areas, notably Bristol, Staffordshire, Glasgow and Edinburgh; though factories became larger and more efficient, many working methods and conditions remained little changed until after 1945. Hot glass, with its need for a suitable furnace and controlled cooling conditions, has always been handled in factories while some cold glass, such as stained glass, could be worked in the home. An 1835 Government Commission into the glass industry listed 106 glass houses in England and ten in Scotland. By this date glass-making had concentrated in regions where coal was readily obtained and in thriving industrial towns offering good communications and a ready market.

Working with hot glass is a relatively sophisticated technological process which requires complex, expensive equipment and is usually factory-based. Apart from production pieces, a range of individual items includes one-off factory commissions of spectacular objects made as special pieces to stimulate new orders and convey the pride glass workers felt in their achievement, as well as more modest-sized pieces known as 'friggers', made by workers for their own pleasure and satisfaction or for friends and family. In addition, objects such as walking sticks, working trumpets and top hats to wear as well as fancy pieces were made to be carried in processions and festivals. This latter group is discussed in Chapter Three.

Within cities and towns many small factories, sometimes known as cribs, opened and operated for a short time. They often made coloured liners for the inside of silver vessels which would contain condiments such as salt or sugar. Many shade-makers worked in similar ways. They used two types of glass, opal for lining and a transparent coloured mixture for the outside. Such factories were often small and lasted a relatively short time. In London small workshops known as 'little goes' operated, often melting down glass bottles to make items cheaply.

The removal of tax restrictions on glass in 1845 brought an expansion of business. Over two hundred hands were employed at the Holyrood Glass Works in Edinburgh, producing high-quality tableware with skilled engraving. In August 1866 the *Scotsman* recorded that:

> The glass-makers are engaged every alternative six hours from Monday to Friday, working regular hours but sometimes nearly eighteen hours in twenty-four when working extra time. (. . .) At ordinary and every-day work a good hand can make £2 a week and often more. What may be termed fabulous wages are occasionally made.

The *Scotsman* went on to admire the workers' skill:

> The glass-cutter, like the glass-maker, will turn out copies of any design submitted to him, depending little on pencil, but greatly on his wheel, keen eye and steady hand. It would be difficult to say whether the cut or engraved glass was most worthy of admiration . . . Representation of foliage, flowers, fruit, heraldry, architectural edifices and of animals meet the eye.

A glass-cutter's wage averaged thirty-four shillings a week at this time. Of all the extraordinary glass items, some of the most spectacular are the sets of glass furniture made in Stourbridge. The *Pottery Gazette* in 1844 reported on a

> magnificent billiard table, the entire framework of which is made of richly cut crystal glass . . . manufactured by the executors of the late Joseph Webb of Stourbridge, for a wealthy East India merchant. (. . .) The work is very finely executed, and the effect when lit up by brilliant light, is truly beautiful. This enterprising firm has been very successful lately in obtaining orders from India for crystal glass furniture and they have now another billiard table in hand, in addition to a suite of chairs, settees and sofas.

These professional *tours de force* were indeed brilliantly made, extending the use of the material into unlikely areas and demonstrating enormous skill. These were employers' pieces, commissioned to elicit trade or business; nevertheless, for the makers, able to defy the limitations of the material in size and scale, these items must have carried significant elements of pride.

In contrast, friggers, made by individual workers, were modest and unassuming though still enormously skilful. Such pieces were usually made during break-time, or at the end of the day, from any glass remaining at the bottom of the pot. 'End-of-days', 'walk-outs', or 'foreigners' are other terms given to this work. Friggers enabled workers to improve and demonstrate their skills and produce gifts for friends and family. Employers accepted the tradition but objected to the practice of selling these objects, no doubt seeing them as direct competition to the factory product. If a worker produced a particularly attractive or spectacular item, employers would consider incorporating it into the factory's production. Many manufacturers actively encouraged workers to make friggers as a way of practising skill.

Among the most common items produced were birds (particularly swans which could be fashioned relatively easily by pulling out hot glass), rats, crocodiles, pigs, horses, fish, crowns, gimmel flasks (which consisted of two separate compartments for different drinks) and bibles (see Plate 49). Whips and tops and teething rings were made for babies and presented to fellow workers who had become fathers. Other items include complex pipes, some over three feet long, with intricate tubing, and 'dog jugs' in the form of dogs, made in Bristol.

Some of the most intriguing pieces are flip-flops, which were usually bottle-shaped and the size of a large wine glass with a thin, flattened base and a long neck; the base acts as a slightly flexible membrane which could be made to emit a sharp, ear-piercing crack and these were often used as children's toys. Successful making required a great deal of

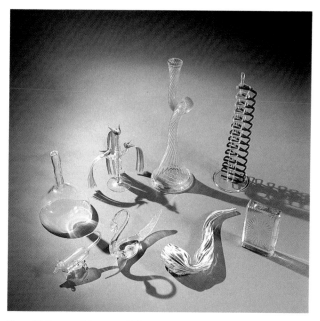

Plate 49 Group of friggers, FROM LEFT TO RIGHT: Flip-flop, mouse, peacock, swan, bugle, pipe, Jacob's ladder, bible, bugle about 12 inches tall, late nineteenth century

skill and finesse on the part of the glass-blower. A writer in 1893 described them as

a bottle about the shape but smaller than a mason's mallet, blown so thin at the bottom that the glass vibrates as you blow into it at the neck end, and as a consequence comes back again as you draw back your breath; the noise which resembles the sound by which it is called, viz, 'flip-flop'. In addition to this action boys used to put this thin part to their lips and sing upon it, when the vibration caused a sound consequent on their breath bearing upon the thin surface; it was then called a singing glass.[1]

Much of the skill and pleasure of glass-making is in its entertainment value whether fashioned into unlikely and unusual items or demonstrated as a technique. Lamp-worked tableaux of such scenes as fountains with birds of paradise, stag hunts and glass sailing ships are fine examples of the methodical use of delicate glass threads. An 1859 account of the Stourbridge fête reports that

Plate 50 Memorial mirror with incised decoration inscribed 'In Affectionate Remembrance of Margaret Ann McGovern who died April 21st 1905, And was Interred at St Helens Cemetery April 25th 1905. The Kind Mother Has Gone To Her Rest/Her Sorrows And Troubles Are O'er/Her Kind And Affectionate Breast Is At Ease/From The Pain That With Patience She Bore'

visitors were initiated into the mysteries of glass-making by Mr S. Edwards of Stourbridge, who manufactured all kinds of fancy ornaments or anything that was required by the visitor, by means of the lamp and pipe, with surprising facility and evident skill.

By the 1870s glass novelties were produced on a regular basis by larger glass-works and aimed at a more sophisticated market. Photographs of glass shown by the Richardson firm at the 1878 Paris Exhibition include two crowns, a cauldron and two flower-stands with hanging baskets in the shape of umbrellas which could be mistaken for frig-gers if seen in isolation.

Glass objects were often associated with superstitions, legends and good luck. Hollow glass balls, painted inside with bright colours, were hung in homes to ward off witches and the evil eye; a glass walking-stick, if hung by the front door and cleaned each day, was thought to prevent evil befalling the occupants. Rolling-pins, too, were regarded as purveyors of good luck; some were filled with salt or flour and decorated with painted designs and slogans. Rolling-pins were also part of commercial production though the decoration may have been carried out by individual artists and the finished pieces given as souvenirs or love tokens bearing such sentimental messages as 'Forget Me Not'. Sailors often gave them to their sweethearts. A more macabre form of memento were mirrors engraved to commemorate a dead friend (see Plate 50). Lettering and design were usually in ordinary script in a layout similar to that found on memorial headstones; these mirrors are associated with glass factories such as St Helens.

Glass objects were also made for more social and decorative purposes. When moulded forms became common at the end of the nineteenth century, among the most popular items were glass slippers. A Glasgow newspaper report of 1897 described a competition in a local dance to find the winner of the near life-size amber-tinted glass slipper in an up-dating of the Cinderella story. Glass-workers were adept at inventing different uses for the glass objects they made. At St Helens workers made a wide range of novelties by joining together cut sheets of plate glass to make tall ornaments in the form of Blackpool Tower and the Big Dipper. One particularly impressive piece shown in Plate 51 is a glass shade in the form of a tree made as a gift for a friend in the late nineteenth century. This has white glass birds with orange wings and tails and black beaks attached to the ends of the 'branches'. Many of the glass-workers lived in Milk Street, St Helens, where most of the men made glass objects ranging from small ornaments to models of sailing ships.

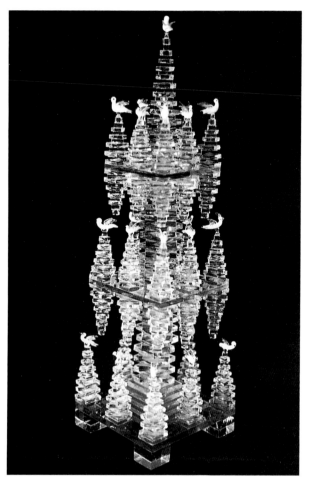

Plate 51 Glass shade in the form of a tower assembled from pieces
of twisted and plate glass, about 18 inches tall, twentieth century

The tradition of workers in glass factories making individual pieces in their own time continues. Some factories allow individual pieces to be made outside paid factory time with the stipulation that such work must not be identified as coming from the firm, though individual makers may exhibit and even sell it. In other factories friggers continue to be made despite official disapproval.

Talking to glass-workers gives a measure of the pride with which they see their work. Jimmy Marr, a glass-worker who retired in 1984 from Edinburgh Crystal, worked at the factory for fifty years. His leaving present, a set of cut-glass decanters made in the factory, is proudly displayed in his home. Mr Marr worked on the night shift, from 5.30 p.m. to 5.30 a.m., when friggers were usually made; most were gifts for friends and family, few were for sale. Particular makers were also mentioned, men who trained in the 'handmade' – John Irwin, Tony White, Peter Archer, Tammy White and Danny Urquhart. Items made included penguins, swans and elephants, birds of paradise, chess sets, ships, swords and helmets. Younger workers often produced friggers for sale, a practice frowned on by the firm who eventually forbade making them. Mr Marr regularly made small items though not being employed in the 'handmade' he had never learnt all the skills – something he had always wanted to do: 'I would have tried to open my own glass-works and friggered, not to sell but just for pleasure. It's marvellous, but you've got to have money.'

Among the items Jimmy Marr made were a group of polar bears on an iceberg

Plate 52 Model of bears on iceberg by Jimmy Marr, about 6 inches tall, c.1975

(see Plate 52), other animals, small glasses and 'New Year Glass' – a bowl with a small hand underneath it for a handle – which was for use on New Year's Day and could not be put down until the entire contents had been drunk.

STRAW

During the latter part of the eighteenth century straw was favoured for certain fashionable items which included hats and dress accessories. It was also used for decorative items in the home such as boxes, firescreens, pictures and picture frames, particularly in the form of straw marquetry (discussed in Chapter Four). During the nineteenth century straw-work moved from being a relatively small industry into a thriving business involving men, women and children working mostly at home; it changed from a rural-based activity serving the needs of a pastoral community to one which had adapted to become well organised and to produce goods required in a more sophisticated society.

In rural areas straw was used for thatching roofs of houses, barns and haystacks and the like and for stuffing such objects as horse collars. It was also made into decorative finials, often in the form of birds, for the tops of thatched roofs, and for such ritual items as corn idols or corn dollies. These carefully woven and constructed objects made at harvest time were associated with fertility and fecundity. Straw was also formed into continuous coils, known as lip-work, and built up into rounded containers, baskets or beehives.

At the beginning of the nineteenth century the activity of plaiting straw was little practised outside prisons and workhouses but the war with France brought changes to this industry: French prisoners of war introduced a tool for splitting straw, making the working of it very much easier, while the difficulties of obtaining imported items encouraged home industry. Production flourished and became concentrated in the south Midlands, particu-

Plate 53 Straw plaiting 'at the cottage door', at the turn of the century

larly around Luton. The vogue for straw-hats further stimulated supply and what had been a quiet country craft was transformed into a commercial and well-organised cottage industry. Some villages were dominated by the trade, such as Northall in Buckinghamshire, where 63 per cent of the female population and 33 per cent of the males were recorded as plaiters. Some men made plaiting their main occupation, while others augmented low farming wages by plaiting in the evenings, whilst tending animals or filling spare moments as did the woman in Plate 53, who is shown straw plaiting in the door of her cottage. An experienced plaiter could make 40 yards of straw plait in a working day of 12 hours. In 1870 such work would earn 7s.6d a week.

One of the advantages of straw-plaiting was that it could be carried on virtually anywhere – 'At their cottage doors in the summer or at their firesides in winter, as they

Plate 54 Straw-plait dressed dolls in the form of a tableau, about 10 inches tall, late nineteenth century

Plate 55 Model house made from straw plait, about 9 inches tall, late nineteenth century

walk round the village street, tend sheep on the hill side or pay a visit to the market town', as one writer records. It was, however, dull and repetitive work, requiring many hours of toil to eke out a living. Some plaiters improvised new designs though variations on established designs occurred from maker to maker. One plaiter, a Mrs Parsons, invented a series of different plaits and used a different one for the bonnets of each of her six daughters.

Plate 56 Basket made from straw plait, about 12 inches long, c.1930

Luton, the centre of the straw-hat industry, provided the main market for plait. As well as making hats and bonnets, hat-sewers and straw-plaiters in the slack times of the seasonal hat trade used scraps of many different types of plait to dress dolls and make inventive models of baskets and cradles. Straw-plait dressed dolls and models were sometimes shown in exhibitions (see Plate 54); when the Prince of Wales visited Luton in 1875 he was presented with 'two very handsome dolls both attired almost entirely in plait and dressed in Scotch fashion'.[2] Luton Museum has examples of straw objects which include tea-cosies, model houses built in great detail (Plate 55), shopping baskets (Plate 56), even a life-size cradle as well as figures. Some dolls, 12 inches tall, are dressed entirely in straw-plait, complete with straw baskets and straw flowers.

Fashioning figures and objects out of corn as emblems or dollies associated with harvest time is one of the most familiar known forms of folk art. It is often seen as a romantic pastime, such as that suggested by the image of John Tarlton in Plate 57, but

Plate 57 John Tarlton of Essex making a corn dolly, 1938

Plate 58 Cock dolly made from wheat straw which would usually be set on top of a rick or mounted on a pole or weather-vane, 18 inches tall, c. 1950

originally the purpose was seen as far more significant. Traditionally 'dollies' or 'idols', kern maidens or kern babies, were made from the last sheaf of corn and intended to ensure the safety of the following year's crops. Sir James Fraser in *The Golden Bough* suggests that the custom originates from early religious beliefs and is associated with myths like that of Demeter, the Goddess of Corn.

The shape of corn figures, as well as the names given to them, varied from area to area. In Essex the most common form was a long twist, called a 'neck', of barley. Near Tewkesbury the straw was plaited into a triangular shape. In some areas the whole of the last sheaf was adorned and dressed as a corn figure; in other places more explicitly sexual forms such as the cornucopia and the long twist of 'neck' were plaited from the corn of the last sheaf. Corn figures were carried in procession with the last load of the harvest, and were kept in the farmhouse until the following year. In Devon, a development of the mid-nineteenth century saw straw ornaments shaped in the form of a cross for church decoration made as ceremonial items to be displayed in the harvest festivals which started around this time.

Popular interest in corn figures was revived in 1951 at the Festival of Britain when a number were on show as part of a promotion of the idea of 'Olde England'. Objects included a straw lion and unicorn made by Fred Mizen of Essex. Notable recent work has been that of Alf Wright who made thatched eagles and swans in the 1970s. Examples at Reading Rural Life Museum illustrate a thatched crown and a straw effigy of King Alfred made in 1961 by Jesse Maycock, a master thatcher of Charlton-on-Otmoor, Oxfordshire, and an impressive cock dolly which was usually set on top of the rick or mounted on a pole as a weather vane (see Plate 58).

SLATE

Though quarrying slate has a long history, it was not until the great expansion of house building which started at the end of the eighteenth century that this material was mined in vast quantities for use as roofing. At Gwynedd, in North Wales, in 1780 there were 54 quarrymen; a hundred years later this number had increased to 14,000. The impact of the Industrial Revolution on workers who had been accustomed to rural, pastoral living was far reaching. Men, recruited in their hundreds, were housed in small, cramped quarters away from home and family, some coming from as far afield as Liverpool to fill the industry's labour needs. As well as extracting and preparing the slate, quarrymen also found time to carve and decorate slate objects and make items for use in their homes. A characteristic of slate is that it can be made to split with a perfect cleavage, a quality greatly appreciated by the workers. At Ballachulish Slate Quarry in Scotland, it was considered necessary to serve a seven-year apprenticeship before being qualified as a slate-worker, dresser and splitter.

Slate-carving in the Ogwen area served by the Penrhyn Quarry flourished between 1820 and 1850. Workers made fireplace surrounds (see Plate 59), fans, milk jug covers and many other objects for their homes. As they settled, many built their own houses and carved fireplace slates were considered an essential embellishment. Large slates, measuring some 8 × 2 feet, were finely decorated by low relief carving and incised patterning. The skills required were quite outside those needed by quarrymen in their everyday work but a sound knowledge of the material enabled accurate splitting of the slate and detailed working on the polished surface. Motifs included representational freehand incising of churches, houses, wine glasses, ships, neatly annotated music, the Menai Bridge (opened in 1827) and groups of stylised plants. Borders, varied and intricate, were made up of classical and timeless motifs such as zig-zags, hoops, circles and parallel lines, many incised with scribes and compasses.

Some of the finest and most elaborate

Plate 59 Fireplace surround with incised decoration, life-size, late nineteenth century

slates were made around 1837 by two brothers, Thomas and William Jones, quarrymen in Bryn Twrw. They carved designs which incorporated complicated astronomical data which they had been given by the self-educated mathematical genius William Thomas, who later became Supervisor of Greenwich Observatory. The undermantel

Plate 60 Model fish on stand, carved from slate, late nineteenth century

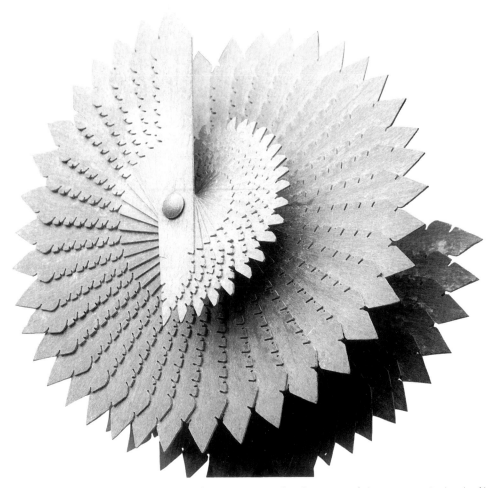

Plate 61 Fan worked in slate by a quarryman in his spare time — only a few pieces of slate were required and a file or light saw; late nineteenth century

slate depicts the zodiac and is carved with great wit and artistry; there is every reason to think that it was entirely the invention of the two quarrymen.

Objects made out of slate include such traditional items as fish on a stand (Plate 60), and elaborate opening fans of wafer-like thinness made of some 50 or 60 thin sheets of slate measuring roughly $12 \times 1\frac{1}{2}$ inches held together by a bolt through one end (Plate 61). Finely and intricately carved and etched, they were usually made as a home decoration. Some were entered in competitions in the local Eisteddfod. Less conventional were carved filigree trays displayed at National Trust Penrhyn Castle, Bangor, and a butter safe, a model stool and a harp on stand, which are in the Welsh Folk Museum, St Fagan, Cardiff. An elaborate model of

Bethesda War Memorial was made by William John Roberts who worked from 1920 to 1930 as a quarryman at the Penrhyn Slate Quarry. Roberts (1906–1982) carved the model of the war memorial after the death of one of his younger brothers at Chengdu, Szechuan Province, China, who had been captured by the Japanese and set to work building the notorious Burma Road.

Of particular interest are miniature items of furniture made as toys for children or as presentation pieces which often bore the name or initials of the recipient. Many were almost exact replicas of contemporary furniture, with neatly marked out drawers with brass handles and fine decoration. As well as grandfather clocks (see Plate 62), chairs and Welsh dressers, models of fireplaces complete with candlesticks and kettles were

Plate 62 Long-case clock, carved slate miniature, late nineteenth century

Plate 63 Book carved from shale, cut and painted to resemble leather binding with a tooled and gilded cover and spine, about 7 inches long; the front is inscribed 'History of the Oil Industry', the back 'Sample of Oak Bank Shale', 'Presented to John Gillan from John McCabe', the spine inscribed 'J. C. 1902'. The shale oil industry, based west of Edinburgh, was a source of oil in the nineteenth century

Ballachulish, commemorates the whole family of John McDougall, with his wife Rachel McColl and their children standing in a solemn row beneath the spreading wings of an angel. The gravestone of a gamekeeper bears a lively, flowing carving of a dog or a deer jumping effortlessly over the game-keeper's rifle. The low relief carving makes sensitive use of bold images to give a powerful and attractive result. On some tombstones the emblems of the deceased's trade were carved; examples are glovers' gloves and tailors' shears. In areas near the sea, ships are frequently found. At Sheringham, near Cromer, a low relief carving of an overturned boat is cut with a great economy and sureness of line.

worked. One model of a kitchen carved by quarryman Henry Williams of Garth Foel in Croesor slate (c.1920) is particularly impressive. Other carved items included inkwells, boxes, doorstops and fretted overmantels.

A similar material to slate is shale which for a period was mined in Scotland. This was used as a source of oil. One worker fashioned a book from the material to present to a fellow worker and engraved it with his name (see Plate 63).

Slate for tombstones was usually carved locally by stonemasons. Fine carvings on the burial island of Eilean Munde testify to local skills as do the slate gravestones decorated with drawings and fine lettering around Balla-chulish, carved by slate workers in the early or mid-nineteenth century. One memorial shows a dying slate-worker on whose brow a dove is about to place an ivy leaf (see Plate 64). In Kiel churchyard thistles carved in low relief were popular. Another slate stone, at

Plate 64 Carved slate gravestone commemorating a dying slate worker on whose brow a dove places an ivy leaf, Eilean Munde, Glencoe

STONE

Stonemasons, as skilled artisans, were among the better off within the working class, their home often slightly larger and their income above average. Their skill in handling stone

for building bridges and the like was often used for more expressive work. Flora Thompson in *Lark Rise to Candleford* records her father, a mason, setting up a small workshop

Plate 65 Carved stone chains and weight by David
Alexander, a mason from Montrose

in the 1880s where he carved decorative objects for his own enjoyment. These 'ornaments' included animals, heads and the like, which were kept around the house or occasionally given away. In the nineteenth century David Alexander, a stonemason of Montrose, carved such improbable technical feats as stone chains attached to a square 'ball' bearing the date 'Octr. 4th 1884' (see Plate 65). John G. Wilson, a stone-hewer from Brechin, carved a clock case inspired by neo-classical architecture in 1899. Made from local stone the clock, measuring 14 inches high and 12 inches deep, took the form of a classical temple with pediment and columns (see Plate 66).

Conventionally, when a mason built a bridge, a face was carved on one of the stones to serve as some special mark of its builder. The need for some particular identifying symbol provided other work for masons. When business was slack carvers went 'field ranging', whereby masoned stone was given carved decoration for embellishing the identical rows of terraced houses built in the late nineteenth and early twentieth centuries – an ideal opportunity for carvers to give full play to their imagination.

Gravestones were also carved by local masons. While memorial tablets and such like inside churches were likely to be the work of professional letter-carvers, work on gravestones was often carried out by a local mason for family and friends who had little funds to commission expensive work. They may even have been made by a member of the family, as were the slip-decorated grave-

markers made by potters in Staffordshire, for example. Popular motifs include the Christian symbols of winged cherubim, trumpets, wreaths, rays of glory, though the darker aspects of death were also represented, most commonly by human faces or even skulls. The faces vary in treatment but are usually simplified to a minimum of lines. The skulls range from mere scratchings to some which are deeply carved such as that on the tall stone in an Edinburgh cemetery shown in Plate 67. The deeply carved sailing ship with the crossed compasses, also in Scotland, is both a strong design and a powerful evocation of the mariner's life (see Plate 68). Innes Hart, researching 'primitive' tombstones, found remarkable examples in East Sussex, West Kent and parts of Surrey, putting forward the view that what was required for such work to flourish was good local stone, an established tradition of working and the encouragement of individual designs and skills.

Models of buildings made in stone

Plate 66 Carved stone clock-case in the form of
classical temple by John G. Wilson, a stone-hewer
from Brechin; made from local stone, 14 inches high
and 12 inches deep, 1899

Plate 67 Carved memorial stone with skull and crossbones, Edinburgh, late nineteenth century

could be dramatic and spectacular. Near Bradford a local mason built in his garden — in miniature — a castle, a public house, a lighthouse and a church with a nine-foot spire. All the stone was carefully cut and jointed. Ed Prynn, a former quarryman, has used rock to create his own miniature Stonehenge in the garden of his bungalow near Padstow, Cornwall (see Plate 69). The quartzite rocks, which came from the Falkland Islands, weighed about a tonne each and had to be delivered by crane. Prynn's intention was to erect the stones as a tribute to those who fought in the Falklands War; he asked the navy for a standing stone and the request was passed on to Sir Rex Hunt, then Governor of the Falklands. The consortium building Mount Pleasant airport quarried the stones and shipped them 8,000 miles to Britain. In exchange, Mr Prynn gave £200 to the Stanley Hospital Fund, preferring to spend his money on the temple rather than finish building his bungalow.

Plate 68 Gravestone with carved relief design of crossed dividers and ship in full sail, Eilean Munde, nineteenth century

Plate 69 Ed Prynn with his own version of Stonehenge made from rocks imported from the Falklands, 1980s (photograph by Roger Bamber)

COAL

Techniques of extracting or 'winning' coal by hacking with pick and shovel were virtually unchanged until the introduction of the mechanical coal-cutting machine around 1914. Sheer physical strength was, however, still needed and continues to be required. Industrial expansion in the middle of the nineteenth century opened up new coalfields such as those in Derbyshire, Yorkshire and Nottinghamshire, and these were deeper and more carefully planned than older mines. In 1851 there were some 216,000 coal-miners; 30 years later this figure had risen dramatically to 877,000.

As the demand for coal increased new shafts were sunk, with villages growing up within a few years virtually centred on a single industry. Until particular pits were exhausted there would be little or no movement of the population, and communities retained many customs going back to when the village was established. Scottish miners, in 1800, were in effect serfs bound to pits, while at coal-mines in Somerset the miners and their families were regarded as an alien community placed in unfamiliar and strange countryside. In many pit villages customs and traditions stayed more or less intact until well after the Second World War. In some areas this had been so for many years with village populations remaining static until the 1950s and '60s.

Daily life within coal-mining communities often combined both rural and urban characteristics, retaining pre-industrial customs alongside industrial production. Miners, skilled at extracting coal and trapped underground for their working day, used leisure time for outdoor pursuits such as breeding pigeons, training whippets or digging allotments. A few carved coal. Women and men pegged rugs to decorate the home as well as to help make it warm and comfortable.

Invariably most, but not all, coal-carving was done by miners who knew and could handle the particular qualities of the material. Many items, small and relatively simple in form, were suitable for displaying on the mantelpiece and often reflected the life of the miner – depicting his tools and the safety lamp, for example – while such items as shoes and boots took up traditional references to good luck. Some items, such as interlocking chains, were more intricate and detailed and served to demonstrate the versatility of the carver and the material. Relief designs, whether those depicting life below ground by Donald Lowe (Plate 70), or the stylised pose of a proud eagle (Plate 71), were a way round the problem of the tendency of the coal to split.

Fine-grained cannel coal, formed from sedimentary deposits of algae at the bottom of lakes, is ideal for carving. Seams of cannel coal – a bituminous type which burns with a very bright flame and was preferred by the coal gas industry – were exhausted by the end of the nineteenth century and this tended

Plate 70 Donald Lowe carving a relief showing miners at work below ground, 1982. Lowe, a coal-face worker at Seafield Colliery, Fife, carves coal and blae, a hard, slate-coloured material normally discarded as waste, to depict all aspects of the industry

to stop production of carved pieces. In Strathkelvin District Museum, Glasgow, a pair of boots carved by a local miner in the nineteenth century are very detailed and, in their black, smooth finish, have something of the appearance of ebony. It is likely that the carver worked in Anchenroich Colliery as this had the strongest tradition of carving in the area. Anthracite also has a fine grain and could be polished smooth.

Coal items were often carved following an accident or mining disaster and at the time would have been of great significance and relevance, not so much as works of art but for the feelings and emotions they represented. After the Wellington Pit disaster at White-haven in 1910, items carved included a low relief of a hand holding some sort of wreath and a plaque with the name and date of the accident. Following the Haig Pit explosion, also at Whitehaven, when four men lost their lives, a cross on a block base was carved (see Plate 72).

Particularly impressive examples of coal-carving, in Kirkcaldy Museum and Art

Plate 71 Coal carving in low relief of an eagle, anon c. 1900

Gallery, were carved from parrot coal (the Scottish name for cannel coal), and include ornaments made by a mason named Robert Nicol Key, using coal from Dubbie Pit in Kirkcaldy. Other examples are carved reliefs of the heads of a woman and a man. A woodworker, T. Williamson, carved a table

Plate 72 Group of coal-carved objects, including pieces commemorating the deaths of men who lost their lives in the Haig Pit explosion and at the Wellington Pit

Plate 73 Chair made from parrot coal by T. Williamson, life-size, 1855

and chairs from parrot coal in 1855, virtual reproductions of contemporary wooden fur-

niture (see Plate 73). With a deep black surface with a dull sheen, they resemble ebony rather than coal. Several pieces of coal have been joined together to enable the larger objects to be made. Detailed carved decoration adds to the effect. Fashioning such intricate and unlikely functional objects in so unfamiliar a material suggests that they were produced as show pieces to demonstrate skill and respect for coal – a material which dominated the economic and social life of the area. Such objects are as fascinating for their symbolic as for their aesthetic qualities.

Among some miners coal-carving continues today. Colin Telfor of Maryport, Cumbria, carves small table-tops out of coal as well as realistic sculpture which pictures the life of the miners – such as going to work, eating lunch down the coal-mines, poaching and so on. Alan Measures of Warsop, Mansfield, carves a range of small, fine items which include highly polished linked chains, animals, miners' helmets, picks, churches and fish (see Plate 74); Frank Pelt, who lives in Anselry Woodhouse, Nottingham, makes items of jewellery from coal.

Plate 74 Alan Measures with items carved out of coal, 1980s

IRON ORE

In small communities centred on one industry such as the mining of coal, slate or iron ore, there was often a unity between work, leisure and, in its broadest sense, culture. A vivid example of how this worked was given by the artist Conrad Atkinson in a catalogue essay in *Art For Whom* (Serpentine Gallery, London 1978). Atkinson, brought up in the iron-ore mining village of Cleator Moor, West Cumbria, was familiar as a child with the curious-shaped material, and the many uses found for it. Large lumps of kidney ore were polished with black lead and different formations used as doorstops; crystal 'spa' was used as a garden decoration for rockeries and the edging of garden paths as well as for making intricate installations known as cribs. The latter, though made for many years, became particularly popular during the 1930s when unemployed miners discovered that these decorative and educational objects had modest commercial potential. A small industry developed to produce such items for sale. Carefully chosen spa pieces were placed in glass-fronted boxes with mirrors at the back to create an attractive grotto effect in miniature. Most, however, were made for friends and family (see Plate 75).

Some grottos reflected their religious origins. Many families were descended from Irish Catholics and grottos using rocks from local mine workings were built outdoors on a large scale and dedicated to 'Our Lady of Lourdes'. Such decorative objects – made from inexpensive and readily available materials, carefully collected and chosen for their appropriateness – had important cultural and aesthetic significance within the

Plate 75 Crib made from wood and filled with different coloured spa and mirrors to create colourful grottos. Made by a miner, about 28 inches tall, 1930s

community.

The Manx Museum has several examples of 'Miners Grottos' as does Whitehaven Museum. Lead and copper as well as iron-ore mines in the area yielded a wide variety of rocks and, when carefully arranged in grottos, made popular domestic ornaments – a further link between work and home. Their basic form consisted of a small, glazed wooden case, about 15 inches tall and 10 inches wide, within which were mounted in ingenious arrangement small samples of colourful rock and minerals, forming an intriguing Aladdin's cave.

FABRIC

Before the Industrial Revolution the production of objects from textile fibres was largely carried out by individuals either singly or in small groups within the home. Most production units were family-based and had few guild regulations or old traditions. Machine production changed this as manufacture moved from home to factory. The cotton-weavers and spinners, particularly the head-loom weavers centred largely in Lanca-

Plate 76 Rug made from rovings (detail), mid-twentieth century

shire, were the first industry to experience the growth of factory production on a major scale. By the end of the eighteenth century ingenious machines gradually took over production. Employers, mindful of capital expenditure, only mechanised that part of the weaving process sufficient to meet the steady and known demand, whether working with cotton, flax, silk or wool, but factory production was firmly established and the ability to respond to market changes lay entirely in the hands of the owners.

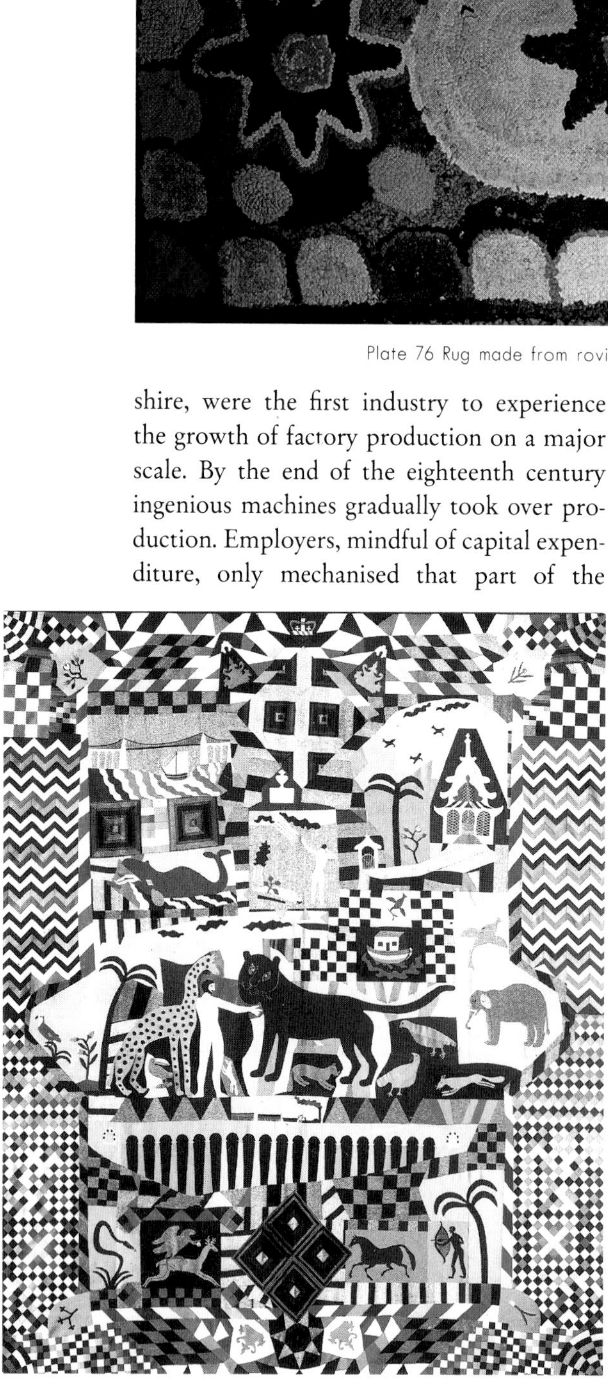

By 1782 nearly 90 per cent of the 20,000 stocking frames in use in Great Britain were situated in the East Midlands. Broadly, Nottinghamshire specialised in cotton goods, Derbyshire in silk and Leicestershire in worsted. Working conditions for the knitters were often appalling and piece rates were at an absolute minimum. 'As poor as a stockinger' was a common nineteenth-century saying. The industry had many middlemen, and wage levels, always low, were constantly depressed by changes in the market, by war and by changing fashion. Conditions described to the 1844 Government Commission were about as bad as they could be to maintain subsistence levels of living.

Against the background of hard toil, rock-bottom prices and terrible poverty within the framework knitting industry, there was little time or inclination to experiment or 'be creative'. There are, for example, few decorated power-looms in comparison to the number of hand-looms which were carved and decorated and turned into 'works of art'. Any ingenuity or inventiveness was as likely to be directed to the improvisation of different

Plate 77 Bedcover by James Williams, a tailor from Wrexham, showing animals, the Menai Suspension Bridge and the Ruabon Viaduct, 93 inches square, 1842–52

designs within the mechanical aspects of production rather than more artistic endeavours. A good example of this was the invention of new fabrics and patterns. Working in their own time, framework knitters produced decorative laces which were subsequently taken over and developed by larger manufacturers.

Nevertheless, opportunities were found for creative work. Though most patterns were handed down from generation to generation, sample books were prepared which demonstrated skill and inventiveness. Equally, the technique of clocking, that is embroidering on stockings, which went in and out of fashion throughout the nineteenth century, provided outlets for more inventive work. Shawls too, offered creative opportunities. They varied in design from one area to another and though most were made in traditional patterns, variations and elaborations were introduced. From the scraps of knitting cut-off from the ends of stockings, known as rovings, rugs were made for the home. Several are displayed at Ruddington Framework Knitters Museum in Nottingham (see Plate 76).

One-off creative pieces by tailors are described here because they were using their professional skills, while quilts and patchwork made within the home are discussed in Chapter Four. Tailors, like stonemasons, were likely to be at the upper end of the artisan class and would have had a certain respect in the community. In addition, they probably had more education and this is often reflected in the pieces they made.

Bedspreads, rugs, quilts and patchwork, the best known and most attractive examples of fabric work, offered makers a 'canvas', a two-dimensional surface on which to improvise designs and patterns. In this respect they come closest to the work of painters, and some, in the bold treatment of pattern and design, take on the appearance of tapestry. Unlike many spreads and rugs made in the home which tended to be elaborations and interpretations of familiar designs, albeit beautifully carried out, tailors' work often made use of representational imagery taken

Plate 78 Bedcover by David Robertson, a Falkirk tailor, with the words 'The American Clipper Ship, *Cobra* in appliqué work and embroidery, 51 × 60 inches, 1859

from a variety of sources, some being inventively adapted from popular prints and theatrical motifs. Because tailors had access to a wider range of fabrics than most working-class households, they were able to choose

Plate 79 *The Royal Clothograph* by John Munro, a tailor/artist from Paisley, 79 inches square, 1860s. In addition to the picture, Munro has embroidered the names of famous and intellectual men around the border as well as the following guidance: 'To gain the Grand End. We ought to keep in Mind 7 words. 1st Push 2nd Piety 3rd Patience 4th Perseverance 5th Punctuality 6th Penetrate 7th Please. Stop. Man know Thyself and others learn to know. Love God and Man. Amen'

materials for their suitability of colour and texture to enhance particular designs.

Daniel Owen from Mold used pieces of cloth left over from suits made in his shop to make a spread of geometric design. Another master tailor, James Williams from Wrexham, spent the ten years between 1842 and 1852 making a large and ingeniously designed bedspread, now in the Welsh Folk Museum. It includes representations of animals, the Menai Suspension Bridge (built in 1827) and the Ruabon Viaduct (built 1845) (see Plate 77).

In Scotland, Menzies Moffat (1829–1907), who described himself as a master tailor, artist and photographer, made an extraordinary patchwork, now in Biggar Town Hall, called 'The Royal Crimean Hero Table Cover'; the main Crimean leaders are shown in the border while in the central panel are medallions of Queen Victoria and the Prince Consort surrounded by ladies of the court. In all, Moffat's table-cover comprises figures from 81 prints, the woollen scraps of cloth joined together with consummate skill (see Plate 77). David Robertson, a tailor in Falkirk, Stirlingshire, worked several spreads, each with their own character. The pictorial coverlet, 'American Clipper Ship, Cobra', portrays the sailing vessel in calm waters, complete with a frame bearing a design based on sailors' knots (see Plate 78). In a more complex coverlet the patchwork has panels with chain stitches in silk. The figures, derived from popular and theatrical prints of the time, are neatly set into panels, the central one displaying a fully rigged ship with the royal arms above. John Munro, another tailor and self-styled 'Paisley Artist' (born 1811), fabricated an elaborate panel entitled 'The Royal Clothograph, Work of Art', which took 18 years to complete (see Plate 79). The seven scenes have geometrical pierced borders and include, among other figures, the nautical character of Mr T. P. Cooke based on a print of William in the popular melodrama *Black Ey'd Susan*.

WASTE

The relative low-level technology employed by the Scottish tinkers and others in making use of virtually any material to fashion it into something personal and of value occurred time and time again. Much of people's art is made from waste, whether fabric, metal, slate, glass and so on. Making a mark, whether by turning an industrially made object into an individual piece, or by using unwanted bottles or waste pieces of leather to fashion intriguing objects, produced fascinating work. No expensive machinery was required and they could be carried out either at home or even at work. Form and decoration need not be work-related.

The hand of the artist is particularly evident in the decoration on discarded commercially produced bottles and other low-priced glass forms. In Sunderland rolling-pins were decorated with designs based on popular engravings of Sunderland bridge literally chipped into the surface of the glass. Bottle production was mostly associated with Scotland or the north of England. Leith, a district of Edinburgh, was the centre of bottle-making, producing, when the occasion arose, oversized bottles of startling capacity.

Until the last 20 years of the nineteenth century glass bottles were blown individually by hand and all had a distinctive quality. This changed in the 1880s when semi-automatic bottle production – mechanically blowing bottles into moulds – was developed. Shapes became more uniform and regular and production costs were greatly reduced. In Kelvingrove Museum, Glasgow, a collection of bottles has particularly fine chipped and stippled decoration, which involved the use of a sharp-pointed hammer to produce a form of stipple-engraving (see Plate 80). These were probably intended as special souvenirs or mementos of a particular occasion, for the length of time each bottle took to decorate would preclude large-scale production. The considerable risk of breaking the bottle when being chipped suggests a skilled hand. Some bottles have designs and messages relating to weddings, others to the Salvation Army.

The finest of the bottles include delicate riggings of a bridge and may have involved some kind of acid etching. A chip-decorated brown glass bottle in the People's Palace celebrates the wedding of an Irish couple L. and M. Gilmartin in 1881. They had both emigrated to Glasgow in the late 1870s, met there and married. On the bottle is the date, entwined hearts, an Irish shamrock and the Glasgow coat of arms. This family later built up a successful stevedoring business.

Stippled as opposed to chipped decor-

ation has been used on a bottle on show in Edinburgh. The dark coloured glass of the bottle throws up the decoration in great clarity. The design may have been carried out by a 'hammer man' who worked with non-precious metal such as tin.

So-called waste material was used to make some of the most curious and mysterious leather objects. A group of hollow forms in the shape of figures, standing some 24 inches high, now in the Museum of Leather Design in Northampton, are, like similar pieces held in other collections, both sinister and intriguing. Each object is built up from overlaid pieces of waste leather, and while a certain amount of dexterity was required, it

Plate 80 Bottles with chip-engraved surface decoration. FROM LEFT TO RIGHT: Bottle inscribed 1886 'Capt. Lottie Jenkins' and the badge of the Salvation Army, 13 inches tall; bottle dated 'October 13th 1883, and inscribed with 'J. J. M. and I. B. Borthwick' and a view of the Scott Monument, Edinburgh; olive green shaft and globe bottle dated '19th February, 1839' and inscribed 'Andrew Robertson Grace Robertson'. Dark green shaft and globe bottle dated 1848 inscribed 'Isabella McLagan Stanley'

Plate 81 Seated figure made from pieces of scrap leather, about 24 inches tall

is impossible to assess whether or not they were made by a skilled worker. Their shape and the general stance of the figures recall the Toby Jug forms of Staffordshire but the leather figures are much larger and were probably made for display in public houses and inns as odd but fascinating 'conversation pieces'. Stylistically, the figures recall folk imagery, but, when rendered in leather, they assume an almost surreal quality which is both disturbing and threatening (see Plate 81).

Work skills and makers' concern and interest in their material prompted a wide variety of creative items: hat-makers at Luton, for example, employed waste scraps of the fine fabrics used in the trade to make a wall hanging entitled 'Made of Scraps from Luton Hats' (see Plate 82). Invariably well made and though often taking up established forms as

well as exploring alternative ones, the hat-makers added an individual quality which identified the piece as their own.

It is virtually impossible to place a value on such a work. It had little market value – either the maker would not part with it at any price, or else they may have given it away. When removed from the society in which it was made its value and relevance is utterly changed and can easily be seen as an 'art object'. Appreciation of such work does not depend on how well it fits the conventions of high art nor on how far it can be treated as an object separate from the context in which it was made but rather on its invention and skill as work serving a crucial means of individual expression and communication, conveying pride, skill and creativity.

Plate 82 'Made of Scraps From Luton Hats', wall-hanging made of pieces of scrap felt and other materials left over by hat-makers, about 60 inches long, twentieth century

Chapter Three

ART FOR ALL

PUBLIC CELEBRATIONS AND FESTIVALS – WORK AND PLAY

Public celebrations, fairs, carnivals, picnics, parades and religious ceremonies – so long a part of community life – took on a new and often dramatically different significance and form in the industrial age. Festivals in rural, pastoral communities marked seasonal changes and events; some continued in urban and industrial societies though their origins were often forgotten or replaced by political demonstrations, demands for votes, and celebrations of civic rather than religious occasions. In all these events the visual was as important as the verbal: costumes, floral regalia and decorated wagons involved whole communities. Union banners, sashes and specially made trade-related objects were meaningful representations of identity and pride, part of a cultural debate sustaining and confirming ideas of progress, even though the economic position of the workers demonstrating for better wages or working conditions was far from secure. In marches and parades workers celebrated their trade by carrying fine examples of their craft, displaying skills and asserting their status.

Street festivals and public celebrations also commemorated national or civic events: street parties were arranged by local communities, often on the smallest of funds, as an opportunity to celebrate and share food and entertainment with neighbours. Bonfires, Whit parades, well-dressing and harvest festivals occur across the land with some, such as Padstow's Obby Oss May Day festivities or the Rochdale Rushcart (see Plate 107), taking highly distinctive forms – celebrations with opportunities for visual display, whether in costume, street decoration or in more formal set-pieces.

Carnival has been a feature of life since the turn of the century, with decorated floats, homemade fancy-dress and the opportunity to relax and celebrate free from the restraints of everyday life. In the last few years carnival has taken on new importance within some working-class groups, whether centred around Chinese communities in Liverpool, London and Manchester or in the West Indian community of North Kensington, London, Leeds and elsewhere. These huge and popular occasions are, above all else, opportunities to create an effect, to make a visual display which is a crucial part of individual and cultural identity. Stylistically, the carnival has no direct equivalent, its theatrical excess achieving greater and greater heights of splendour as the years go by. Carnival also carries conflicting meanings: some are intended mainly as fund-raising activities for local charities, others are associated with religious celebrations, while a few are occasions for revellers to simply 'have a good time' – but all, to differing extents, are manifestations of class and cultural identity.

THE TRADESMANS FRIENDLY UNION, Instituted June 4th 1828.

CONCORDIA CRESCIMUS.

TRADE PROCESSIONS

As the Industrial Revolution gained momentum a network of well-organised trade societies sought to establish and maintain the rights of skilled workers. With membership a million-strong by 1815, they often had secret rituals and were rich in pageantry, affirming the sense of community and identity. The *Tradesman's Friendly Union* painting in Plate 83, depicting Britannia in a heraldic manner, makes use of classical allusions to convey strength and commitment as well as national pride. In 1802 the Preston guilds staged jubilee processions for a week, with woolcombers and cotton-workers colourfully dressed. In Bradford for the feast of Bishop Blaize in 1825 there were heralds, artisans and 470 woolcombers in wool wigs, 40 dyers in red cockades and a glittering display of craft work. After 1825 the unions marched openly, parading banners which identified

them at political rallies and the like. At Jarrow each colliery had its own banner. Until the 1840s union banners tended to be made locally and were embellished by signwriters, coachmakers, or talented branch members. Some were made communally by members of a family, others were the work of a gifted individual, but all served to effectively express professional pride.

In manufacturing industries highly skilled and relatively well-paid workers have a long tradition of parading objects as evidence of status and identity, proclaiming individual skill and collective strength. A Bristol procession celebrating the coronation of King William IV and Queen Adelaide in 1831 involved gardeners and nurserymen, shipwrights, basket-makers, glaziers, wireworkers, glass-workers, painters and confectioners, all of whom made special objects

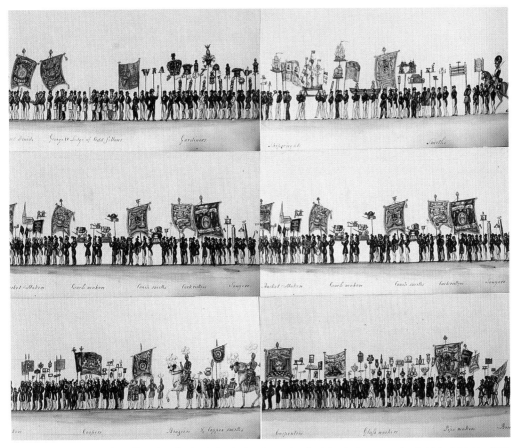

Plate 84 Pages from Robert Greethead's sketch-book showing a detail of the trade procession held in Bristol in 1831

Opposite: Plate 83 Tradesman's Friendly Union depicting Britannia holding a banner and standing by a lion, oil on canvas, 29¹⁄₂ × 20¹⁄₄ inches, early nineteenth century

Plate 85 Model firegrate, cast iron, c.1820 The decorations suggest that this was made for ceremonial purposes; these include the tools of the smith's trade and the religious symbols of their medieval guild. The eye of the Father looks down between the sun and the moon. Also included are Christ on the Cross, a book (possibly the Gospels), crossed nails, a ladder and lance, the lamb of God, the trumpet of the Last Judgment, and the keys which symbolise St Peter or the authority of the Church

bolic motifs such as the eye of God the Father, the sun and the moon, a model of the construction of a ship and a large stoneware jug (see Plate 85).

The 1830s saw peaceful demonstrations held to support such political causes as burgh reform, the extension of the franchise and the Ten Hours Campaign meetings. Various reform societies and the Liberal Party supported the demonstrations which were often arranged as pageants intended to show the strength and respectability of the reform movement. Programmes were worked out detailing the route and participating trades, what costumes would be worn, and the tools, products and banners they would carry. Participants saw themselves as part of a widespread historical struggle, and wanted to make their skills as visible as possible. They treasured their badges, aprons, banners and sashes, often passing them on to the next generation.

For the procession of 6 October 1883 to George Square in Glasgow, celebrating the laying of the foundation stone of the City Chambers, among the objects carried was a model blacksmith's forge. The Association of Blacksmiths was upwards of a thousand-strong, and, as the *Glasgow Herald* reported:

> the models displayed represented smiths engaged in different kinds of work – at the anvil, steam hammer, forge, etc. Anvils, hammers, tongs and models of tools used by the craft were displayed in large numbers. (...) A lorry from the Meadowside Works followed ... being a smith's fire in full operation, and a working model of a donkey engine.

A year later the great franchise demonstration to Glasgow Green included representatives from all major trades; Glasgow Upholsterers carried a full-size bed – 'the death bed of the House of Lords' – while potters from the Britannia Pottery held on poles a model kiln stuffed with smoking rags to give the illusion of a kiln in operation. A skilfully made model handwarping mill was paraded by the Glasgow Handwarping Society; their banner carried the slogan:

from the materials they used. These were carried aloft in the procession behind a banner identifying each group of workers. A local amateur artist, Robert Greethead, faithfully recorded the colourful event (see Plate 84). Illustrations by other artists record similar events in London and elsewhere; one depicts brass-founders holding jugs, coal-scuttles, candelabra and other related objects of their craft. In Bristol, among the objects carried was a cast-iron model firegrate bearing sym-

Plate 86 A section of the Royal Infirmary procession showing Edinburgh and Leith Flint Glass Works and depicting blowers holding items of their work on poles, c.1926

Plate 87 Model of glass chamber pot made in Couper's Glasgow Works, about 5 inches across, c.1870

Plate 88 Processional emblem of the tin-plate workers in the form of a painted eagle, carried in a Reform Bill
demonstration in Glasgow in 1832, about 30 inches wide

We warp the web
And will not stand
An intermeddling lordly band
Their web is warped, their leave is ta'en
The House of Lords shall not remain.

The Glasgow tobacco-spinners also carried a
banner proclaiming their attitude to the
House of Lords: 'TOBACCO AND THE LORDS
ARE EQUAL — THEY ARE BOTH WEEDS!'. A huge

pipe bore the legend 'SMOKE THEM OUT!'.

Processions and picnics were popular
social events in glass-making districts. At one
of the first recorded processions, in Venice
in 1268, water-bottles, scent flasks and other
graceful glass objects were carried to celebrate
the inauguration of the reign of Doge Lorenzo
Tiepolo. Similar processions were common
in Britain in the nineteenth century and
contemporary written accounts capture the

Plate 89 Metal processional banner of the Amalgamated Engineering
Union, about 84 inches wide, early twentieth century

Plate 90 Jug, Bristol stoneware, made for the coming-of-age celebrations of a worker in 1844. A similar jug made by W. & T. Powell was carried in a procession celebrating the city's take-over of the docks in 1848; about 36 inches tall

excitement of these events:

Today, September 28 1823, the workmen employed in several of the glass-houses of Newcastle and Gateshead made a procession through the principal streets, each bearing in his hand a specimen of his art, remarkable either for its curious construction or for its beauty and elegance. [The procession] was composed of workmen of the South Shields, the Northumberland, the Wear [Sunderland], the Durham and British [Gateshead], the Stourbridge [Gateshead], and the North Shields Glass Companies, arranged according to the seniority of their respective houses, and each distinguished by appropriate flags. The sky was clear, and the rays of the sun, falling on the glittering utensils and symbols, imparted richness and grandeur to their appearance. The hat of every person present was decorated with a glass feather, whilst a glass star sparkled on the breast, and a chain or collar of variegated glass hung

round the neck: some wore glass sashes round the waist. Each man carried in his hand a staff with a cross piece at the top displaying one or more curious or beautiful specimens of art, consisting of decanters, goblets, glasses, jugs, bowls, dishes, &c., the staple articles of the trade in an endless variety of elegant shapes and exquisite workmanship. A glass bugle, which sounded 'the halts' and played several marches, was much admired for its sweetness and correctness of tone. Many of the men wore glass hats and carried glass swords. When the procession arrived at the Mansion House it halted, while a salute was fired from a fort mounted with glass cannon to the astonishment of the spectators.

Parades continued in the twentieth century. In the mid-1920s Edinburgh and Leith Flint Glassworks took part in the Royal Infirmary procession with a decorated lorry on which sat female workers in white overalls with a table on which the finest wares were displayed. At the head of the parade were glassmakers with white aprons and jackets, each holding a staff on the top of which was

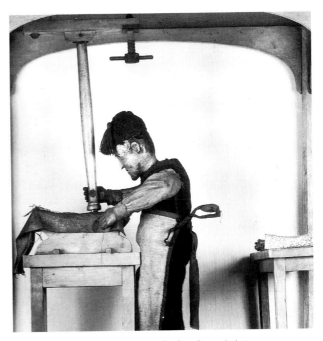

Plate 91 Model of chintz glazer at his bench, carried at the head of procession by Pullar's employees on their August holiday, late nineteenth century, about 17 inches tall

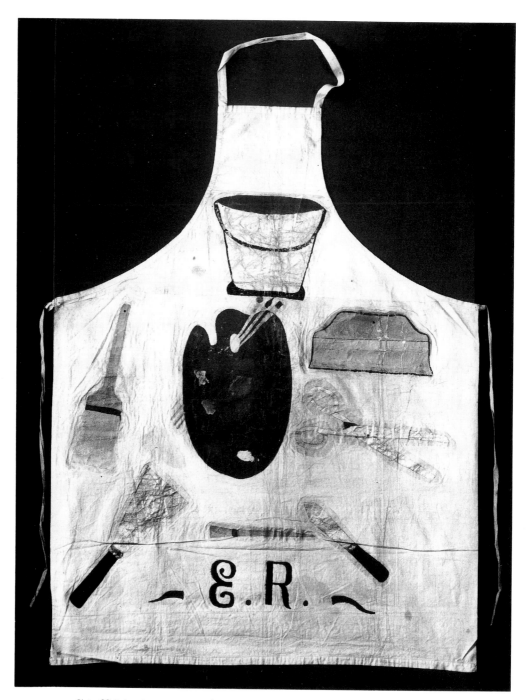

Plate 92 Painter's apron, cream linen painted with objects of the painter's trade, c.1953

Plate 93 Weaver's apron embroidered with the tools of the weaver's trade and the initials J. R., about 30 inches tall,
late nineteenth century

Plate 94 Salt arch, built of white salt lumps and rock salt to celebrate Queen Victoria's Diamond Jubilee in 1897 in Norwich

mounted a glass object such as a vase, bowl or goblet (see Plate 86). At the City Glass Works of James Couper & Co., Glasgow, Harry Cusick, a glass-blower at the factory, made miniature chamber-pots and glass crooks for the trades procession which were carried aloft mounted on the end of poles (see Plate 87).

In other processions carpenters bore tools of their work: bricklayers a giant-sized trowel; tin-plate workers an emblem in the

form of a painted eagle (Plate 88); and the Amalgamated Engineering Union created their own metal banner using silhouettes of lettering which not only proclaimed their name but visibly demonstrated their skills (see Plate 89). Potters made miniature kilns filled with smoking rags to give the impression of a firing in progress as well as magnificent examples of their craft. In 1844 at the firm of W. & T. Powell, Bristol, the potters made a huge jug decorated with applied relief decoration to be carried in procession (see Plate 90).

Chintz glazers carried a painted wooden figure of a man wearing a long apron and tasselled hat standing over a chintz glazer with a narrow wooden table supporting pieces of folding cloth (see Plate 91). This model was carried at the head of the procession by Pullar's employees on their August holiday. Also in this museum is a painter's apron (Plate 92) made of cream linen painted with the objects of the trade such as paint bucket, scissors, palette knife, paint brush, paint palette and the letters 'E. R.'. Weavers also made processional aprons embroidered with such objects as a shuttle and other tools of their trade. Beautifully sewn, the garment was likely to be a treasured possession (see Plate 93). More unusual are the salt arches in Plate 94 built by the salt workers in Northwich, or the coal arches constructed in Merthyr Tydfil for celebration processions, or the magnificent metal gate built for a royal visit by men at the ironworks in the town.

Village clubs, a feature of the West Country, carried insignia on poles, emblematic of their interests (see Plate 95). These were usually made of metal, though in some areas they were replaced by glass. Two such poleheads belonged to the old Nailsea Glassmakers' Guild. Shipbuilders in Bristol made large wooden versions of the tools of their trade, including axes nearly six feet tall with painted relief decoration on the head, such as those in Plate 96. More typical parade objects carried by glassworkers were glass top hats, trumpets, bugles (which were blown)

Plate 95 Insignia indicating the concerns of different local village clubs, late nineteenth century

and incredibly long rods some of which had the end curved to form a handle in the manner of a walking-stick (see Plate 97). Some rods had ornate spiral patterns down the centre and were over eight feet long. Items made specially for the procession were usually returned to the crucible and re-melted, though a few were kept. Glassmaking areas had special days reserved for glass-makers to parade their finest pieces, often with a prize awarded to the most original.

Plate 96 Shipbuilders' processional axes showing (right) Noah's Ark and (left) a model of ship; each axe is about 60 inches tall, late nineteenth century

Plate 97 Glass top hat, sword and bugle made to be worn, blown or carried in trade processions, life-size, late nineteenth century

Banners

As workers formed themselves into groups or unions to maintain craft skills and act as negotiating bodies with the owners, so visual emblems were needed to proclaim their craft and convey solidarity both within the group and with other workers. Trade banners perfectly served this purpose, reflecting workers' pride in their skills and a genuine concern for their profession. By the mid-nineteenth century most banners incorporated the tools of the trade and the products made as the basis for their design. In his book *Banner Bright*, John Gorman details the history and development of union banners, while Robert Leeson in *Trade Union Emblems* describes these and other related objects.

In the second half of the nineteenth century, banner-making became as much a trade and profession as the labour it was celebrating. Tuthills, the largest and most important of the makers, was founded by George Tuthill (1817–1887) in City Road,

Plate 98 Banner of the Tin Plate Workers Society depicting 'the all-seeing eye' taken from the Freemasons, the old Roman symbol of unity, a bundle of sticks bound together, and the allegorical figures of Hope and Justice. Ordered for the coronation procession of Queen Victoria in 1838

London. At the London May Day parade of 1898 some four hundred craft banners were carried, many made by the firm. All were elaborate, woven in silk and painted in oils, often in heroically conceived designs. At a May Day parade 70 years later, only six were on show.

The history of professionally manufactured banners has been well recorded by John Gorman in *Banner Bright*; here I concentrate on banners made or designed by workers or supporters in unions or in friendly societies. Early banners were unlikely to be designed in any formal way but adapted the heraldic tradition of strong, clear motifs which incorporated trade emblems to convey shared ideals. Objects in stylised form suggested qualities such as collective power, unity and strength. Banner-painters in the early part of the nineteenth century improvised designs, arranging them in traditional heraldic style.

A banner of the Tin Plate Workers' Society of around 1821, painted by a local sign-painter, provides a link, like many other banners, between the medieval craft guild and the modern trade union. The design, taken directly from the armorial bearings of the Worshipful Company of Tin Plate Workers, incorporates many of the components of the guild blazon (see Plate 98). All were adapted by sign-painters to contemporary needs and rendered more freely than formal designs. Hence the round ship's lantern, or 'rolling lamp', became a globe of the world, while the tinplate workers were dressed in down-to-earth but totally outmoded seventeenth-century craft-worker costumes.

Other unions were equally resourceful in adapting existing designs for their own needs. The Co-operative Smiths' Society, a small group of blacksmiths covering the area around Newcastle-on-Tyne, made a banner in the 1870s when the union was formed, showing the traditional 'uplifted hand', the proper sign of the blacksmith. Their motto, 'All Arts Do Stand', is a shortened version of that of the Worshipful Company of Black-smiths – 'By Hammer And Hand All Arts Do Stand'. Emblems used on a Tin Plate Workers' Society banner of much the same date also indicate the breadth of the design component. The 'all-seeing eye' came from freemasonry while the bundle of sticks denoting the strength of unity is an ancient Roman symbol. Not all emblems were historical but related directly to trade practice. In Whitehaven Museum, an 1838 banner of the Friendly Society of Sawyers shows workers at their profession; one holds a plumb line, the other a rule. In the background a sawyer is at work which is instantly recognisable to those in the profession.

One of the most popular forms of identification was holding and displaying the tools of the trade. A plane and a saw featured in the banner of the Amalgamated Society of Carpenters and Joiners, while more unusual items appeared in that belonging to the National Union of General Workers. A 1920 banner depicted union members by the Grand Union Canal, behind which was the gas-plant and saw-mill where many of them were employed. The central figure holds sounding equipment while others carry items such as boilermakers' spanners and sack hooks. A banner in the National Museum of Labour History, for the Amalgamated Society of Railway Servants for Scotland, made in the period 1872–92, features a steam locomotive. The banner, clearly homemade, has a charm that is direct and bold, both in the manner of its making and in its mottos. The outer border is stencilled on linen strips while the illustration of the railway engine and the lettering are hand painted (see Plate 99).

Professional banner-makers and painters were occasionally commissioned to carry out designs by union members. The Southall branch of the Associated Society of Locomotive Engineers and Firemen wanted the finest banner they could obtain and collected assiduously in the 1920s. Members devised a design to illustrate their militancy, showing a trade unionist breaking down the banners of capitalism and trampling underfoot 'secret reports' and private ledgers. A banner belonging to the United Society of Boilermakers, Shipbuilders and Structural Workers, designed by executive council-member John Happlewhite, includes a portrait of the leader of the boilermakers, a cockney born in East Ham who served his apprenticeship in the ship repair-yard on the Thames. The first and only banner of the Fire Brigades' Union was designed by a serving fireman and made by the firm of Toye (who made royal standards). Embroidered in gold and metal thread, the banner took a year to make, costing the impressive sum of £400 (see Plate 100).

Not all unions could afford to commission a banner (whether carried out to their design or using established patterns) and many produced their own. The National Union of Mineworkers, South Wales Area, made a banner in the 1950s during the Cold War. Not only does it proclaim the ideals of socialism and peace, but it also opposes the use of Castle Martin as a training ground for NATO (see Plate 101). The London Trouser-makers' Union made a vividly descriptive banner in the early part of the century recording the misery and sweated labour among Jewish workers in the East End of London. On one side a youth is shown lying exhausted over a sewing-machine while on the reverse a tailor points to the rising sun, an emblem of a better tomorrow (see Plate 102).

A truly collective effort was made by the Coventry branch of the National Union of Vehicle Builders in 1945. Arthur Ince, the chief shop-steward of the Standard Motor Company, organised the making of the banner; a car-trimmer made the leather straps and sockets, and George Plummer, a coach-painter, carried out the design. Although based on other National Union of Vehicle Builders banners, Coventry's design incorporated vehicles they made including in the centre the Mosquito aircraft built at Standard Motor Company during the Second World War. Like many other banners, the Coventry Vehicle Builders' one adapted Victorian design even though it showed contemporary vehicles (see Plate 103).

Plate 99 Banner for the Amalgamated Society of Railway Servants for Scotland made in the
late nineteenth century

Plate 100 Banner of the Fire Brigades Union, designed by a serving fireman and made by the firm of Toye, 1947

Some of the smaller banners, known as bannerettes, were created by particular interest groups. Suffragette banners were often beautifully sewn, making inventive use of such stylised flowers as lilies and roses to suggest both strength and tenacity in their struggle for equality. Local women's groups within the co-operative movement made highly distinctive banners. Visual images such as stooks of corn standing solid and upright conveyed both the importance of fertility and the strength to be gained by standing together (see Plate 104).

In the last 20 years banners have once again become important, effective visual images denoting presence at public gatherings. Trades unions, encouraged by social historians such as John Gorman, have restored their banners, while campaigns around broad issues which cut across particular trades, have prompted inventive and often witty home-made banners. During the 1984–85 miners' strike, numerous banners were made by different collieries and displayed at marches, meetings and on picket-lines, their message defiant and their effect rousing and encouraging (see Plate 105). Produced by the miners and their supporters, they included slogans as well as painted designs. Huntly House Museum in Edinburgh, the People's Palace in Glasgow and Manchester's National Museum of Labour History have material relevant to this struggle.

Pressure and interest groups have employed banners to assert their presence at large public demonstrations. Women have led the protest with a campaign against the presence of atomic weapons at Greenham Common; women also identified themselves as specific groups in the miners' dispute. Lesbians and gay men have asserted their rights in the 1970s and '80s, most noticeably against Clause 28 and Section 26, incorporating into the designs of their banners such symbols as the male and female genetic sign and the pink triangle to great visual success. The meticulously sewn Sappho banner paraded at the 1991 Gay Pride march denotes lesbian presence and makes inventive use of

Plate 101 Banner of The London Trouser Makers Union, designed by Israel David Goldman, the general secretary of the union, and painted by a local painter, 1924

emblems and the suffragette colour of mauve to make its point – examples of the art reflecting the movement reflecting the art (see Plate 106).

Plate 102 Banner of the National Union of Mineworkers, South Wales Area, depicting a coal-mining village, two miners and the legend 'Forward to Socialism', made in the 1950s during the Cold War when the South Wales miners opposed the testing of atom bombs and the NATO training area at Castle Martin, Pembrokeshire

Plate 103 Banner of the National Union of Vehicle Builders, a co-operative banner by different workers, 1945; the Latin inscription reads 'The sun rises after the clouds'

Plate 104 Bannerette, Chester Co-operative Women's Guild depicting a bound sheaf of corn, a dove and the wording 'OF WHOLE HEART COMETH HOPE', early twentieth century

Plate 105 Women with the banner of the South Wales Women's Support Groups GRWPIAU Cefnogi MENYWOD DE CYRMU 'Fighting for the Mining Communities', August 1985

Plate 106 Banner for Sappho Lesbian Feminists displayed at the Gay Pride March, London, 1991

CELEBRATIONS AND FESTIVALS

Celebrations in the forms of parades, picnics, street parties or public festivities have been and continue to be ideal opportunities to produce visual work, an intrinsic part of working-class life. Banners and sashes, specially-made costumes, straw effigies, the decoration of streets or factory workshops and shrines built in public places, express individual and collective identity. Christmas festivities or such civic occasions as coronations, jubilees or the coming of peace have served as a focus for communal activities.

Religious parades such as Whit walks, particularly in the Midlands and the north of England, involved decorated floats and have retained their religious significance although their origins not only relate to ceremonies of walking the parish boundaries – when participants were rewarded with a meal of bread, cheese and ale – but to earlier rituals of staking out territory. Other celebrations, such as the Grasmere Rush-bearings and the Rochdale Rushcart, combine both religious and secular aspects, evolving from the time when sweet-smelling rushes were strewn on the clay floors of churches and other buildings (see Plate 107). In the late nineteenth century the custom became more sophisticated,

involving the construction of complex structures often in the form of huge crowns made out of rushes and carried on a cart. The willingness of participants to take part in such celebrations is clearly recorded in photographs of the events. Well-dressing, associated with Derbyshire villages, is said to originate from the seventeenth century when wells were decorated with flowers to celebrate the provision of water in times of drought. Traditionally, subjects portrayed are biblical scenes, but in recent years more secular subjects have appeared as in the panel 'Take up the challenge', shown in Plate 108, even when displayed in a churchyard.

On important national occasions mills, factories and machines were decorated; ceilings were hung with garlands and streamers transformed the stark interiors. No matter how cramped and small the space, room was found to drape flags, trail bunting, hang huge bells and the like. The photograph in Plate 109 was taken in Bolton's Albion Towel Mill and records coronation celebrations on a patriotic theme. At Rishton Mill, decorated to celebrate the coronation of King George V, the tacklers' bench was trimmed up to look like a sideboard in the home; it was

Plate 107 Rochdale Rushcart with a structure made up of freshly cut, soft field rushes with floral decorations. The cart was part of a public celebration which combined elements of traditional church feasts with May Day festivities, c.1900

covered with a lace cloth, surrounded by swags of curtains bearing the motto 'Home Sweet Home'. Above it ran the slogan 'God Save The King'.

Patriotism, an ever-popular emotion, was particularly celebrated when a day was declared a public holiday. No matter how crowded the terraces and tenements of inner cities, given a suitable occasion, street festivals would be arranged. The street was free space, the basic social meeting place with public houses, shops and, in major towns, the music-hall, as focal points. Street parties were collective expressions of loyalty and part of a sense of identity, as well as a good opportunity for celebration. Local roads, such as Tenth Street, Old Trafford, were festooned with flags and bunting (see Plate 110), and shrine-like constructions were built to commemorate the monarch; and substantial meals were served on beautifully arranged tables placed along the centre of the street.

In these patriotic and civil celebrations, while local schools lent furniture, establishing a link between institution and community, the role of the church was less obvious, and in many areas the approach was totally

secular. For the 1935 jubilee celebrations in the East End of London the unemployed and the old were given vouchers which could be exchanged for half-crowns ($12\frac{1}{2}$p), a practical recognition of material need rather than a pious exhortation, and one which encouraged enthusiastic attendance. The official royal visit of King George and Queen Mary to the area provoked a variety of responses. While the socialist mayors were prepared to offer loyal greetings to the monarchs, they refused to do so in their official capacities or to wear official robes. No such restraint was practised by the participants of the street parties who wanted to celebrate royal occasions as fully as possible. Decorations were ingenious and imaginative and their complexity suggests much thought, time and energy was spent on their preparation, tangible evidence of a genuine feeling of affection and loyalty. Synonymous with the strength of the Empire, the presence of the monarchs evoked feelings of loyalty, opulence and international power.

Slightly gruesome mementos of such

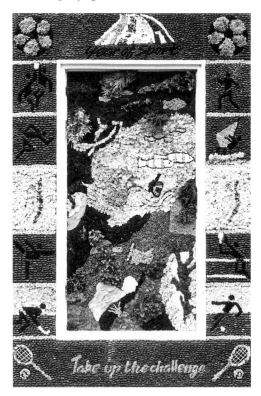

Plate 108 Well dressing: 'Take up the challenge'; made from flowers, leaves, beans and stones pressed into soft clay, Heath, Derbyshire, about 84 inches tall, 1991

Plate 109 Albion Towel Mill decked out with coronation decoration, early twentieth century

celebrations are the bones in Abingdon Museum, all that remain of the ox roasted on the coronation day of Queen Elizabeth II. Other bones carved with names in the same museum were saved from ox and sheep roastings; one notable occasion was when the Thames froze over in 1891, but there have been many other festivities since.

Each year Durham City plays host to what is one of the greatest working-class festivals in Britain – the Miners' Gala. In 1947 when the coal-mining industry was nationalised, a million pit-workers in the region celebrated. Forty years later that figure was reduced to 23,000, with only four working mines. Despite the contraction of the industry, however, the gala continues to be a huge and popular event. Men, women and children still march proudly behind the colliery band and the pit's union banner. Former mining villages now put on their own festivals. Local legend, myth or folklore is often the theme, something that is already a part of local consciousness. A variety of skills and creative

Plate 110 Tenth Street, Old Trafford, decorated for the coronation of Queen Elizabeth II, 1953. This street won first prize in a competition organised by the Manchester *Evening News*

Plate 111 Lewes Bonfire Society, part of one of the parades, 1983

energy go into making the event enjoyable and successful.

Of the longer established festival celebrations two are particularly notable. In Somerset the Glastonbury Carnival procession features floats which are highly detailed and carefully built. The planning and preparation involved in such activities is often daunting, demanding a lengthy and positive commitment. The 5 November bonfire parades of Lewes Bonfire Society are equally inventive and detailed, and attract wide local support. Made up of several competing groups, the society celebrates the Gunpowder Plot in lavish style. Each year different themes such as cowboys or Zulus are incorporated into the costumes, and floats are made accordingly. The processions, accompanied by musicians and blazing torches, are enlivened by flaming signs of the initials of the various societies, culminating in the burning of the floats in a dramatic gesture of pride and power (see Plate 111).

Fancy-Dress

Dressing up for special occasions has long been a feature of upper middle-class life, and many people went to great lengths to achieve complex and accurate designs for clowns and pierrots, fairytale characters and patriotic costumes. As leisure time increased at the end of the nineteenth century the opportunity to wear fancy-dress at local carnivals was taken up by the working class. These costumes had to be cheap and relatively quick to make. Despite the limited amount of money available, the urge to join in and participate in national and local celebrations encouraged improvisation. At the turn of the century carnivals were organised by hospitals in London's East End to collect money. Fancy-dress processions known as 'rags' included medical students, nurses and junior doctors in white overalls, long aprons and so on. Cockney helpers wearing crude home-

Plate 112 Mrs Beaver with Gerald dressed in pierrot
costume, c.1930

made fancy costumes representing Red Indians, clowns, comic policemen and Buffalo Bill also took part. Carnivals continued as local events, often collecting funds for charity.

Some of the improvisation and ingenuity required to produce special clothes is evident in photographs of the event, whether taken in a commercial photographer's studio or, more usually, snapped at home. The two figures in Plate 112, although dressed convincingly in a carefully made pierrot outfit, were happily photographed sitting on an upturned box in front of a very plain brick wall. It is the costume which is proudly displayed with little attention given to the setting or the social context it clearly describes.

Workers at factories also took part in carnivals, encouraged by their employers. At Wilkinson's liquorice factory in Pontefract one worker made an outfit out of strings of liquorice. The six young paintresses from Pountneys Pottery, Bristol, devised amusing outfits which reflected their work at the

Plate 113 Betty Paddock and other paintresses at the Bristol Pottery dressed for a carnival, c.1934. Betty Paddock
chose 'Old Bristol Basket' as her theme because she specialised in this particular pattern

Plate 114 'Wedding dress' made from paper and bearing such messages as 'Sweet Memories',
'Cracker', 'Have fun', 'Sex' and 'Stay Cool', 1970s

Plate 115 Pearly Kings and Queens, London, 1930s

Plate 116 'Paper Boys' or Marshfield Mummers wearing outfits made out of paper, Boxing Day, 1972 (Photograph by Brian Shuel)

Plate 117 Women supporters of Hull Rugby Football Club wearing specially made costumes for the Rugby League Cup Final at Wembley in 1983

factory for the 1934 carnival. These include hats in the form of cups and saucers and skirts made out of plates, all reflecting their own pride in their skill (see Plate 113).

Weddings – important occasions for friends, family and neighbours – were opportunities for the display of fine needlework and a chance for the bride to make a once-in-a-lifetime outfit, but they were also occasions for more earthy celebrations. At the Town Hall, Dagenham, women made a wedding dress out of paper for the bride-to-be, worn on the last day at work before the wedding amidst great celebration. A dress made in 1976 has a border of hearts and flowers with a series of slogans over the dress including 'Sweet Mems', 'Cracker' and 'This is the Big One'. A magnificent bonnet completes the outfit (see Plate 114). The tradition of making such dresses for a bride also occurs in other areas of the country.

Traditional figures, whether rural or urban, ancient or comparatively modern, are often associated with particular costumes. 'Father Christmas' with the ubiquitous red costume and snowy white beard, is a familiar example. More geographically precise are the Pearlies, the kings and queens whose ornate and visually magnificent costumes were derived from the Costers in London's East End (see Plate 115). The costume, which is covered with patterns and designs in pearl buttons, consists of a black suit for the man and a

long black dress for the woman. The tradition started in the 1880s when a road sweeper named Henry Croft became the Pearly King of Somerstown. Each area in the East End had its Pearlie royalty who played a central role in local activities, particularly active around fund-raising events, carnivals and the like when full outfits were worn. Each maker worked out their own arrangement of buttons, though typical 'good luck' motifs of horseshoes, bells, hearts, crosses, diamond crowns and boots were incorporated, carefully designed for a dramatic overall effect.

Equally remarkable costumes are those associated with either harvest or May Day celebrations. The Burry Figure of Queensferry, Scotland, is covered from top to toe with burrs stuck or stitched over the whole of the costume leaving only tiny spaces for eyes and mouth. At some points during the celebration the Burry Figure, holding sprays of flowers, moves amongst the crowd, a reminder of the success of the harvest and wish for success in future years. At Marshfield near Bristol, mummers who walk through the village on Boxing Day are known as 'Paper Boys' because they wear costumes made from strips of newspaper (see Plate 116). Like the Burry Figure, the Paper Boys are completely anonymous and the many layers of paper give them an exotic appearance. The costume also reflects concerns with waste and the environment.

Opportunities today for fancy-dress take many forms. Supporters' clubs for football teams, pop singers and rock musicians come up with inventive and clever designs. Items are carefully assembled to 'match', to be noticeable and to proclaim louder and more fiercely the allegiance of the wearer. Some are extravagantly assembled from ready-made items making full use of club colours – scarves, hats, huge rosettes and so on – but others are specially made. The two women supporters of Hull Rugby Football Club shown in Plate 117 made particularly detailed costumes when their club played in the Rugby League cup final at Wembley in 1983. Their outfits, in the team colours of black and white, combine Red Indian and oriental influences with fantastic and exotic headwear, one of which bears models of all the team members. Fans of pop singers make clothes and items celebrating their respect for the star. An admirer of the singer Barbara Dixon sent her three t-shirts painted with her portrait, and most fan clubs receive many handmade or decorated items based on the image of the star.

Fairs

Fairground decoration, whether on sideshows or rides, is one of the clearest manifestations of people's art, produced and targeted for a known and familiar audience. Consisting mainly of urban and low-paid workers, the unsophisticated, appreciative audience was an outcome of the cities and towns that grew up as a result of the second phase of the Industrial Revolution. Relatively well paid, workers from towns and cities wanted entertainment, and the fair, as we know it, replaced market fairs which had appeared on certain holidays in Britain since Roman times. Their character changed further as rides became more elaborate and colourful.

Showpeople themselves, like the designers of the fairings, painted easily understood and greatly appreciated imagery. Visitors continue to be thrilled, excited, amused, moved to tears and awe-inspired through the dexterous skill of painter-decorators, carvers and mechanics. Bold, inventive and colourful, fairground decoration is stylistically related to vaudeville and music-hall, pantomime, seaside amusement, external shop decoration and the personalisation of transport and advertising; it is a creative aspect of 'mass-culture' to which many of the examples in this book are related. At the same time it is readily identifiable as the product of a closely-knit community on the edge of urban life, an integral part of popular culture from which it draws its imagery.

During medieval times even quite small villages had a fair: old almanacs list fair-days on or near the village's festival of its patron saint. Gradually fairs lasted longer, tolls were introduced and even local trades people were obliged to close shop and bring their goods to the fair. Plays were enacted and great feats of endurance demonstrated with sideshows of 'freaks' — dwarfs, a spotted negro child, trained cats or a female child with two perfect heads. During early Victorian times fairs became the focus of violence and lawlessness; this, combined with changing social and economic habits, brought many to a close, with London's famous Bartholomew Fair ending in 1850. The excitement of early fairs is vividly caught in Charles Dickens's *Sketches by Boz* (1836) in his description of Greenwich Fair:

> Imagine yourself in an extremely dense crowd which swings you to and fro, and in and out, and every way but the right one; add to this the screams of women, the shouts of boys, the clanging of gongs, the firing of pistols, the ringing of bells, the bellowing of speaking-trumpets, the squeaking of penny dittoes, the noise of a dozen bands with three drums in each, all

Plate 118 Plaster cocks used for throwing sticks at after the custom of using live cocks was abolished, c.1860

Plate 119 Roundabout or Galloper photographed in central London, 1991

playing different tunes at the same time, the hallowing of showmen, and an occasional roar from the wild beast shows; and you are in the very centre and heart of the fair.

Fairs centred around trade, a useful

Plate 120 Decorated board for a fairground boxing booth, late nineteenth century

opportunity to present and sell different merchandise and break the usual pattern with amusement and relaxation. Local people and travellers came to buy and sell as well as to celebrate and enjoy the occasion. Some were principally hiring fairs where men, women and children came to make themselves available for work. Cattle fairs and horse fairs were staged in June and on St Bartholomew's Day (24 August). At the village of West Ilsley, Berkshire, a sheep fair attracted flocks from far and wide. Herds of Welsh ponies congregated at Blackwater in Hampshire. The Stourbridge Fair, held in an open field near Cambridge, was at one time the largest in Europe and continued into the twentieth century. Fairs were also associated with the sale of different, even exotic, merchandise not otherwise available.

Notable fairs thriving in the late nineteenth century included the Greenwich Fair, the Glasgow Fair (held in mid-July at the time of the feasts of Saints Peter and Paul) and Nottingham Goose Fair which continues to this day. 'Sleepy Market', a fair in the north of Scotland, was held in June when the nights were very short, starting at sunset and ending an hour after sunrise. St Giles Fair in Oxford was so popular that by 1850 the

Plate 121 Part of painted decoration for fair showing, 1991

Great Western Railway was running excursion trains to it from London, Cardiff and Reading. Reading Michaelmas Pleasure Fair was almost as popular.

Some old customs continued, others adapted to new forms. At Honiton, Devon, where the fair dates back to 1257, the town-crier announces the opening dressed in 'olde-worlde' uniform, carrying a pole decorated with flowers surmounted by a large gilt model of a gloved hand. Once the glove is up and the fair open, the local motto that 'no man can be arrested till the glove is taken down' comes into operation. The pole and glove remain displayed until the end of the fair. Many long-established fairs also had an official opening, usually performed by the mayor. The Mitcham Fair which dates back to the 1700s was, and still is, opened by a huge golden 'keye', four and a half feet long, referred to as the Chartered Key of Mitcham, and is made by a local carpenter. Still in use, the key is decorated with ribbons for the opening ceremony.

The game of throwing wooden sticks at stakes on which prizes were displayed probably originated from the barbaric practice of throwing sticks at live cocks to celebrate Shrove Tuesday. Legislation abolished this vicious sport, and imitation plaster cockerels, several of which are in Exeter Museum, replaced the living birds (see Plate 118). Today, the sticks have been replaced by balls, and the game is known as Aunt Sally or Aunt Mary.

A popular attraction at fairs and many other public celebrations is Punch and Judy. Operated by travelling itinerant performers, the puppets enact a traditional moralistic tale with unmitigated violence. Punch (abbreviated from the Italian Puncinello) is a grotesque humpbacked figure, partnered by an equally ugly wife. Showpeople themselves would carve the heads and hands of the puppets in wood with sufficient exaggeration to make the leering, caricatured expressions clearly visible to their audience. Often the carving is 'crude', in that individual cuts can be identified, but the expressionistic power of the characters is so forcefully conveyed – so unlike any other contemporary work – that the figures with their blend of ghoulish humour and gross characterisation command attention.

Today's travelling fair, with its compli-

Plate 122 Fairground decoration showing Concorde, 1980s (Photograph by Bernice O'Donnell)

cated, sophisticated mechanical rides and brightly painted decorations, came into existence when suitable machinery was available to power the rides, and when decent roads were built to cope with heavy loads. Road-building only started to improve following the Turnpike Road Acts of 1730 and 1780 and caravans did not become popular until considerably later when road surfaces improved. Only then could heavy sideshows, entertainments and elaborate rides be transported.

Throughout the nineteenth century the travelling fair developed complex assemblies. Early rides had been hand or animal-driven but with the advent of steam engines in the latter part of the century the machines were revolutionised as mechanical power was able to propel larger roundabouts and other rides. Steam also supplied power to transport equipment on the road. Later, electricity added bright lights while the internal combustion engine provided power. The modern fair, though with roots in early history, is a product of the social, economic and inventive aspects of the industrial period, the result of the rapid evolution of transport, the increase in leisure time and the demand for entertainment which met the needs of working people. The concentration of industrial centres provided a ready market for more sophisticated but still relatively low-priced entertainment.

Fairs became so popular that in some areas major factories, particularly in the Midlands and the north, closed for a week for the annual holiday. In some districts this was known by its colloquial name, 'Wakes Week'. The fair, in its new, mechanically driven, brightly decorated and brilliantly lit form, provided the opportunity for excitement and a different sort of entertainment. The principles that powered locomotives, factory looms, pumps and farm machinery also created the mechanical roundabout, one of the first 'rides' to be introduced. One of the most popular was the roundabout or 'Galloper', on which rows of hand-carved and decorated horses moved up and down as they went round, their shape and carving

giving the impression of speed (see Plate 119). Despite the fact that photography had revealed that horses do not run with all four legs off the ground, the convention of front and hind legs fully extended continues to this day. Roundabouts had existed many years before the 1860s, but the introduction of steam enabled new and more mechanically complex rides to be developed.

Stylistically, decoration on fairgrounds is a hybrid making free use of classical and heroic themes, academic presentation and composition, and commercial and pop art, incorporating the faces of national politicians, popular figures such as film stars and, more recently, television; it may include such diverse images as jungle exploration, boxing matches, space travel, the sleek lines of Concorde, the rough and tumble of the chariot races in *Ben Hur* to sexy, and sexist, images of female pin-ups (see Plates 120, 121 and 122). Though principally intended to attract and secure custom, fairground decoration also offered entertainment, instruction and creative expression, making inventive use of nostalgia and myths, the bold imagery of advertising, and the immediacy of topical events and personalities.

Representations of mock architecture with its evocation of grandeur through the use of carefully drawn detail and exaggerated perspective effectively creates an illusion of space. A superb example is Stanley Thursten's magnificent Ben Hur Ark built in the mid-1930s, and entirely redecorated by Fred Fowle in 1960. The Hollywood epic *Ben Hur* with its ornate dress and dramatic chariot race inspired the ride and its magnificent colourful and atmospheric decoration. More recently *Star Wars* has provided the stimulus for newer, more 'contemporary' themes. Both spheres of entertainment make use of all possible kinds of trickery and optical illusion – toy bikes are enlarged to a terrifying size, the two-dimensional surfaces are filled with shapes which seem about to burst into three dimensions. The colours and drawings are the devices by which 'magic' is transmitted to a machine, giving it life and helping create fascinating illusions.

The dulled patina brought on by wear and tear, with its faded, out-of-date image and suggestion of last year's style has little attraction or interest to fairpeople. At its best, fairground decoration is unsophisticated, brightly coloured and boldly executed with imagery changed to reflect popular social and political events. Like a mirror to society, fairground art reflects popular taste and attitudes, absorbing contemporary events and personalities into its range of motifs. Much of the painted decoration is directly affected by such industrial processes as colour prints, newspaper images and the like, a part of working-class culture employing few rural craft traditions save the skills of the wood-carver and coach painter.

Wood-carvers came from local carpentry shops, from toy-makers or from one of the few firms specialising in producing work for fairgrounds, but often much of the designing and making was done by showpeople, usually with great skill and expertise. Whether carving the head of a horse with expressionistic force, or the more sanguine and enigmatic features of a domestic cat such as that in Plate 123, carvers brought a great deal of freedom and interpretative qualities to their work. In the 1890s John Robert Anderson, a Bristol ship's carver, turned from making figureheads to fairground horses. Later, when his youngest son Arthur took over the business, the horses became more fantastic, remarkable for their individual character and frequently violent imagery.

Showpeople are often involved in designing and building their rides. In the 1950s Roy Presttney built and decorated a shooting-gallery constructed out of parts of a lorry. Raymond Armstrong is reported to have made an ingenious wagon out of a 40-foot container unit. He also decorated his Waltzer cars with the names of pop stars or television pop programmes. Matthew Taylor and his sons, who belong to the Scottish section of the 'Guild', built and decorated two machines, a 'Dive Bomber' and a trailer-mounted 'Paratrooper', for which they took

Plate 123 Carved head of a cat from a roundabout, a prototype for a 'Jumping Cat' by Savage of Kings Lynn, early twentieth century

out patents. Jim Noyce and Sons, based at Farnborough, bought and restored a set of horses or 'Gallopers' about 30 years ago when its condition had deteriorated.

Like canal-boat workers, showpeople live very different lives from the outside world; on the move for much of the year they are as self-sufficient and self-contained as possible. A report in 1926 in *World's Fair*, the showpeople's trade journal, recognised their diverse talents saying, 'they learn to be handy with the paintbrush, the joiner's tool . . .'. Commercially employed artisan painters, itinerant sign-artists or even scene-painters from local theatres occasionally carried out the decoration but much of it was produced by showpeople. Notable is the work of John Bell who spent time working with Fred Fowle, and Norman Fendick who developed a futuristic style of decoration. Describing how he went about decorating a ride, John Bell said that he devised and painted a single area as a unit, rather than section by section, and visual ideas came into his mind already complete.

Carnival

Carnival, an annual feature of many local communities since the end of the nineteenth century, and occasion for modest celebrations and for dressing up, has been mentioned earlier in this chapter. Floats are decorated, costumes made up and both are displayed in a parade through the town. Themes tend to be secular and reflect popular culture, much of it with a nostalgic element. Songs such as 'Somewhere Over the Rainbow', fairy-tales like Little Red Riding Hood, and the excitement of the Wild West or the Keystone Cops are created on the backs of lorries and trailers. Most involve the coronation of a local beauty queen who wears a long ornate dress and suitable jewellery and is surrounded by her attendants.

Over the past 30 years new sorts of celebrations have arisen, including carnival inspired by West Indian culture. Many public displays flourish partly because in the first place they spring from within the communities themselves and because they are part of an open assertion of cultural identity. Such occasions include the boisterous and brightly coloured and costumed Chinese New Year with its noise and crackers, and, in its more public aspects, Diwali, the Hindu Festival of Light. This festival, celebrating the victory of good over evil, may include the lighting of many sorts of divas (lamps), street decoration, patterns and designs painted on windows, the flower-like stylised rangoli patterns chalked on doorsteps, and the representation of Rama and the many-headed Ravana. Examples of the most personal decorations involve painting designs in henna on the hands (see Plate 124).

Some of the most spectacular carnivals and festivals are organised by the Afro-Caribbean and Asian communities. These have grown in size in the last few years to celebrate a culture that brings together traditional ideas — whether in dress, costume or floats — placed within contemporary set-

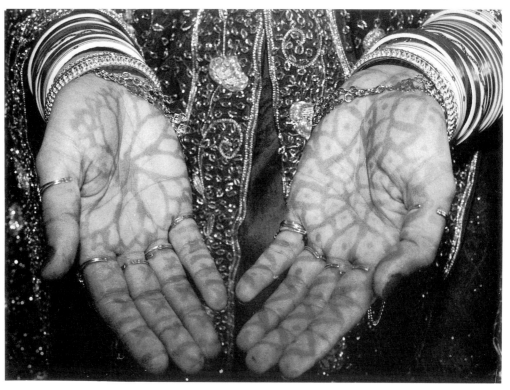

Plate 124 Asian Mehndi hand painting which takes place the night before a wedding, in this case a Sikh wedding. Mehndi is a henna dye paste which is painted on, and, the longer it is left before being washed, the more permanent the dye and the darker it will be. Photograph by Kulvir Kaur Mandair, Mount Pleasant Media Workshop, 1990

tings. One of the liveliest public carnivals takes place each August Bank Holiday at Notting Hill, London. The entire area is given over to the Afro-Caribbean community, many of whom have spent the best part of the previous 12 months making ornate and fancy costumes to wear in the Carnival. Each year outfits worn in the processions become more elaborate and inventive, celebrating skill, wit and an undiminished creativity. Themes may vary from issues of the environment to star wars, while costumes utilise anything from bubble wrap to painted fabric and netting.

The Notting Hill Carnival continues to be a particularly rich expression of people's art even though it has changed from its modest local beginnings into a major public occasion: it is still organised within a community drawn together around cultural identification and recognised as such; many people who take part in the Carnival are scattered around London, but the event and many of its organisers are centred in North Kensington, one of the poorer districts of the city.

The first Notting Hill Carnival was in 1966 but it was not until the early '70s that it attracted widespread interest. By present standards the early events were modest, but they nevertheless had enormous significance. In 1973, when a band of carnival performers led by Laurence Noel completed their Head Hunter costumes on Monday morning and travelled to Notting Hill from Leytonstone, the event was starting to attract national attention. The mainly West Indian crowd of three to four hundred people greeted them and the young Ebony Steel Band with enthusiasm and delight. It was a public expression of their own identity which they had created and of which they formed a significant part.

Over the past 20 years the Carnival has grown in strength, size and popularity, though its roots within the Afro-Caribbean community remain as strong as ever. The Carnival symbolises both ethnic pride and shared identity within a visual aesthetic which owes little or nothing to indigenous British culture.

Plate 125 Processional costume making reference to voodoo at the Notting Hill Carnival, 1991

Plate 126 An individual costume at the Gay Pride March, 1991

Its exuberant, almost anarchistic spirit embraces rebellion, religion and voodoo, aspects of which are often incorporated in the costumes (see Plate 125). As well as the fantastic costumes, stitched and created over many months prior to the event, the Carnival combines visual spectacle with sound and dancing, with much of the music created on or emanating from empty oil drums, and turned into musical instruments which form the steel bands. The materials, and the new sounds, are a product of the industrial age.

The origins of Trinidadian carnival, like that of many other countries, lie in a diverse range of traditional festivities – including paganistic rituals absorbed by the Catholic Church and accepted as an occasion for celebration and excess in the week before the more austere period of Lent. While much of the formalised pageantry associated with Roman Catholicism continues, there are strong undercurrents of darker rituals now well blended with social as well as political themes. The sense of exaggeration and ornateness, so vital a part of the visual spectacle, remains. The costumes, exotic, brightly coloured and many decorated with sequins, are larger-than-life fantasies created in wire and net, and often of enormous size and intricacy. Masks, suggesting a retreat from reality into anonymity and exaggeration, are a crucial part of the costume, whether worn as half-face coverings, or as whole headpieces extending two or three feet or more in any direction.

Dresses are often elaborate and ornate. When worn by men they explore the ambiguities of role reversal while women may become ultra-feminine. Many of the costumes are based on the crinoline and, in their over-the-top exaggerations, parody the genteel refinement of the middle and upper classes. Groups of people, disguised as reptiles, butterflies, flowers, comic-book characters, brightly coloured birds, and fantasies of all kinds, parade the streets, each group or individual seeming to out-do the others in their creative accomplishment and visual effects.

Festivals, fancy-dress parades and carnivals are opportunities for breaking the usual rules of decorum: men delight in appearing as clowns, monsters, stilt-walkers, transvestites, Vikings or Roman soldiers, while young women take the part of beauty queens, Arabian belly-dancers, or vamps bedecked in sexy underwear. Adults and children play an equal part and both can enjoy dressing-up fantasies. There is no direct equivalent with the more refined celebrations of the middle and upper classes, which are usually more private occasions. Examples such as race meetings at Ascot or the Henley Regatta – which employ professional entertainers and displays – are opportunities for the show of the latest high fashion, with little of the shared spirit and energy of a carnival or fair. Major differences lie in the behaviour of the revellers, with one group sedate and ordered while the other is energetic and lively, and in the visual effects achieved. Both epitomise different cultural attitudes.

In contrast to the high fashions of Ascot or Henley, carnival costume aims for theatrical excess (though intended to be effective at close quarters, and therefore carefully made, as well as at a distance), and parody; they make full use of bright colours with tones and shades creating almost luminous, eye-dazzling effects. Though usually finely sewn, intricately made and conceived as expressions of caricature, carnival costumes may appear loud and vulgar in comparison with more sober traditional taste – splashes of colour and exuberance which cannot be historically placed within the more controlled atmosphere of long-established festivals.

The handling of vulgarity and high camp is now a regular feature of London's annual Gay Pride march. Exotic and spectacular costumes incorporate elements of theatrical excess, questioning and exploiting conventional aspects of gender and dress while enabling gay men to parade wild fantasies on city streets. The figure in Plate 126 displays the fan-like dress with evident pride, opening out the costume to show off its ingenuity. Other outfits are equally spectacular, with figures with enormous beehive hair-dos and outrageous crinoline frames – parodies of extravagant taste.

From a strictly high art perspective, carnivals and other such events seem orgies of kitsch, with many of the costumes and tableaux little more than a pastiche of popular mass culture – the Notting Hill Carnival is a notable exception in this respect. But carnival is a collective as well as an individual expression, and the acceptance and use of other art forms subvert conventional values and are a means of appropriating aspects of middle and upper-class culture otherwise denied them. Carnival is an aspect of a changing society and the reality of its multi-cultural make-up, a part of today's society. The life and energy it conveys, and the pleasure with which the carnival is received, suggest that such events and all they represent are now an intrinsic part of working-class culture, changing and enriching it.

BLUFF COVE

FOX BAY

SAN CARLOS

FALKLAND ISLANDS.

1982.

Desire the Right

Q.E.2

Port Darwin

Royal Marines

Chapter Four

PRIVATE WORLDS: HOME, HEARTH AND HAVEN

In influencing and changing the way people worked, the Industrial Revolution also radically altered the way they lived, the money that was earned and, for the working classes, created a new aspect of their lives – leisure time. Much of this leisure was centred on or around the home, a place which varied in size and importance according to income and family status. The shift from working in or around the home to working away from it for the majority of the day had far-reaching effects on daily life. For many it meant fewer income-producing activities went on in the household: looms and spinning-wheels, which had dominated some homes, disappeared as production moved to factories. But some activities, including lacemaking or knitting, continued for many years to be major sources of income. As the nation's health improved, families became larger and, depending on the need of local industry for workers, children were either encouraged to stay at home and take a local job or to leave home to seek work elsewhere. For many the home was a sanctuary, a refuge from the world, a private place for individual and family expression. For others the home was merely a place to sleep, with social activity centring around the public house or the street.

Until the latter half of the nineteenth century, as far as the working classes were concerned, leisure was regarded as a luxury. The working day for men and women was long and holidays were few with little time left for activities which could be described as leisure occupations. Yet many people found time for self-help, to learn to read and write, to acquire new skills and make items for use and display in the home. This chapter discusses the range of home-based work, looking at it under three general but not discrete headings. The first, which usually pre-dates the other two, concentrates on the use of the home as a factory, a place where goods were produced for sale. The second, under the heading 'The Industrious Home', discusses the production of items such as rugs, bedspreads, clothing and pieces of furniture made for use within the home. The third area looks at the home as a centre of social life, a safe and secure 'nest' where many creative activities took place, whether the making of pictures or paintings, the fabrication of spectacular grottos, or generally helping to make the home comfortable, attractive and special. A final section discusses the impact of changing communities on people's art.

THE HOME FACTORY

Industrialisation in Britain at the end of the eighteenth century and in the first half of the nineteenth century had a profound effect on the home arts of the mainly rural communities. Out of these changes emerged different kinds of home-based activity to meet the needs of the new class of workers who, in the urban environment, needed some aspects of comfort in their home. Many householders could now buy inexpensively what they used to produce at home. As the factory system developed, people travelled to work at central

Opposite: Detail of Plate 139

production plants. Home and work became separate; although geographically located near each other until efficient and cheap public transport became available, they represented different environments, and the home became the haven to be made as comfortable as possible. Education was also profoundly affected by this separation. What had once been learnt within the home was now taught in schools.

Despite the general move of the work-place to the factory, in some trades and areas people continued to work at home, spinning or weaving, knitting, making lace and so on. The products were bought by agents or 'middle men' who, whenever possible, paid rock-bottom prices and demanded maximum output. The pressure to maintain output was enormous and though little time was left to experiment with new designs, or to carry out their own work, some did use their craft skills to produce pieces of their own.

Lacemaking

The industrial age brought major changes in the way lace was produced. Traditionally lace was handmade, the more popular methods involving pins, bobbins and threads worked on a pillow; it was made by twisting threads together in pairs or groups according to a pattern marked out by pins set in a cushion, elaborate designs requiring a thousand bobbins. Important centres were Honiton, Buckingham, Bedford and Ayrshire, all of which had their own sort of pillow and characteristic designs. The Great Exhibition of 1851 stimulated production and introduced new styles. Lacemaking continued in the home, but as a hobby rather than for sale.

The industrialisation of lacemaking started in the early decades of the ninteenth century. In 1808 John Heathcoat invented a bobbin net machine which involved the twisting motion essential to the lacemaking process, while five years later John Leavers invented a machine to make pillow lace. The application of the jacquard pattern process to Leaver's machine in 1837 enabled most types of lace to be made including trimmings, table-covers, wedding veils, dress fabrics and shawls.

The use of machinery was concentrated in the Midlands. At first production took the form of family groups in their own home, as often as not involving all the family – men, women and children. But like many cottage industries production changed beyond recognition as the Industrial Revolution progressed. Machine-made lace more or less ended the cottage-based industry though making did continue in some parts of the country, with Nottingham and the surrounding areas becoming the centre of the industry. Conditions were as hard as they were unhealthy. Lace was produced by the yard on a production-line basis – fixed patterns and designs, printed out on cards were used to guide the machines. Very little handwork was done. Making standards were high and Britain had become the world's leading manufacturer of lace by the middle of the nineteenth century. Ruddington Framework Knitters' Working Museum operates knitting and lacemaking machines in houses purpose-built in 1829.

The life style and living conditions of lacemakers were akin to those of other workers in the textile industry. Dwellings,

Plate 127 Yoke inset of christening robe, Ayrshire, nineteenth century

Plate 128 Border lace with pattern of church towers which was reputably designed by the wife of a local vicar in the Olney region who encouraged the cottage lacemakers. This was made for Elizabeth Bumfrey, c.1750

grouped around the factories, were similar in layout and design to those of workers in heavier industries. Little time was left at the end of the day to produce samples of lace in the factory because, unlike other processes which used small industrial units such as glass-blowing, lacemaking used heavy machinery and was produced around the clock on a rota-shift system. Some hand lacemaking continued in spite of the mechanisation, but the skill was handed down and taught within the family rather than on the factory floor. Very few early examples survive of lacemaking produced for leisure; only at the end of the nineteenth century and into the twentieth century did home-produced lace enjoy some kind of revival. This was largely due to the advances in the educational system whereby needlework became part of the curriculum, thus bringing a revival of interest in skills long since abandoned or overtaken by industrial processes.

Small pieces of handmade lace made by individuals using traditional methods to their own design do survive but these are rare; sampler size, many depict animals and flowers and were produced in the main by women who had retired from the factory-floor or domestic duties and who had sufficient leisure to produce lace for collars, cuffs, trimmings on curtains, pillow-cases and sheets as well as underwear. Many lace patterns followed traditional lines, such as the Honiton flower sewn on a dress, collar or wedding veil, made into a brooch or joined to others to make a larger item. Individual work was usually small

Plate 129 Lace in the form of a dog, about 5 inches long, early twentieth century (Photograph by Jeffrey Hopewell)

Plate 130 Lace bobbins with handles and glass bead decoration, late nineteenth century

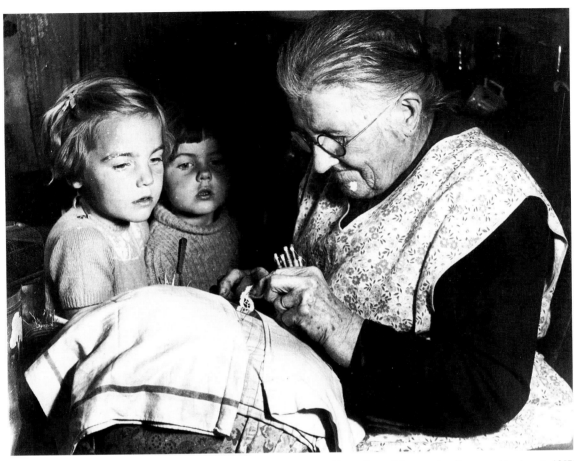

Plate 131 Mrs Dart of Branscombe, Devon, making lace in 1957

and fine. In Ayrshire highly detailed lace was made for such ceremonial garments as christening robes which were passed on from one member of the family to the next (see Plate 127). The example in Plate 128 of finely woven border lace from Bedfordshire incorporating a representation of a local church is both finely made and of particular local relevance.

Mrs Phoebe Lovell of Higham Ferrers made 'keepsakes' in the early years of this century by pricking over a picture in the local paper or a photograph; this would be worked in lace and then mounted on another material. Amongst her more unusual designs were a running deer based on a carving in the church, a motif of Rounds church, and a picture of Elijah ascending to Heaven in a chariot of fire. The standing dog ingeniously woven in lace in Plate 129 may have been made in this way. In more recent times, lacemaking has again become a popular pastime though the designs are often derived from commercial patterns. Notable collections are in London's Victoria and Albert Museum, Luton Museum and Art Gallery and the Cowper and Newton Museum, Olney.

Home-based lacemakers, like Mrs Dart in Branscombe, Devon, used traditional techniques which involved the use of lace bobbins to make their own work (see Plates 130 and 131). Individual bobbins carried a single thread and were made in a variety of distinguishing designs and patterns so providing endless opportunities for decoration and invention. Bobbins, a form of treen, are similar to knitting-sheaths, love-spoons and other small carved love-tokens in that they followed traditional forms, but each was made individual by the invention of its maker, embodying the same fascination for decoration and employing a variety of techniques and materials.

Bobbins became emblematic of the pride lacemakers took in their work and in the beauty of the tools of their trade; invariably home-produced, they were often made by male lacemakers for their sweethearts or wives. The long stem of bone, ivory or wood was decorated at the head with brightly coloured beads made out of glass or stones; small pieces of shell, bone, pewter and metals were often incorporated as part of the decoration. The long narrow body of the bobbin was sometimes incised with the maker's name, or with a date or an affectionate message. Like knitting-sheaths, bobbins display regional variations in their designs and methods of construction. Luton Museum has an excellent collection.

Knitting

The technique of hand-knitting was introduced into Britain some five to six hundred years ago. For many years fine knitted garments were imported for the well-off while most ordinary knitting was carried out with relatively unrefined materials. The invention by the Reverend William Lee of a knitting-machine in 1589 eventually led to the replacement of hand-knitting as gainful employment in all but some coastal and rural areas. Hand-knitting continued there because of well-established traditions and because this was a method of making warm clothing of a particular style which at the time could not be equalled by other means.

In the later Middle Ages the knitting industry had its own guilds and master knitters, and, while within the craft many designs were traditional, many others incorporated individual variations and elaborations. Long-sleeved gloves or 'gauntlets' were made, as were long woollen stockings intended to be worn by the knitter after his or her death. The pair made by Eliza Lewis in Wales in the middle of the nineteenth century incorporate her name as part of the decorative border (see Plate 132).

During the twentieth century hand-knitting once again became a popular and useful activity. The marketing of a wide variety of fine wools and cottons, together with the promotion of commercial knitting-patterns by wool manufacturers, aimed particularly at women, enabled a range of useful clothing as well as more special items to be made at relatively low cost. Ironically, through the careful instruction of various stitches and knitting effects, the levels of skill have risen while the ability to invent or adapt has been neglected in favour of following knitting patterns. Nevertheless, the great knowledge of hand-knitting skills has encouraged much creative and inventive work. During the miners' strike of 1984–85, for example, knitted 'coal-miners' were made in Scotland and sold to raise funds. On a more personal scale home knitters still adapt patterns and instructions for everyday garments, 'making it up' as they go along.

Since the Second World War, the manufacture of reasonably priced knitting-machines for use in the home has again made it possible to operate a small industry in domestic surroundings. Many knitters work piece-rate for suppliers, and some produce small ranges of lively and imaginative work they have designed themselves.

Traditional hand-knitted garments combined practical and aesthetic qualities. As well as being warm, wind and weather-proof and long-lasting, they were also a source of pride, a display of skill and invention. In addition to the stockings mentioned earlier, in ports the most common item was the woollen long-sleeved jersey or guernsey, usually made in dark blue wool from traditional stitches as well as invented patterns (see Plate 133). The garment was also an important identifying piece of clothing. Villages, even families, produced distinctive designs which adapted or incorporated their own subtle but significant variations into traditional work.

When attending fairs or celebrations the garment proclaimed the home of its wearer. And more importantly, in the tragic event of a fisherman being lost at sea, when the decaying body was washed ashore it could be identified by the distinctive sweater decoration.

Knitted garments, which took several weeks to make, were a source of pride, with the best ones carefully looked after and reserved for special occasions such as weddings and other celebrations. Women did most of the knitting though in some areas men also took part. Knitting groups were set up and the occasion would be social as well as productive. In fishing villages knitting groups would often meet on the beach, though women who worked as gutters preparing the fish spent every spare moment knitting. In winter the knitting would be done by the light of rush or tallow candles around a fire. Instructions for making the various garments were handed down verbally from generation to generation and traditional stitch patterns included combinations of anchor, cable, diamond, flag, hailstone, herring bone, lightning, moss, rope ladder and shell.

Stitch patterns themselves were often the knitter's interpretation of objects important in the fishing community such as tools, harvest and the weather. In some areas a future bride would knit her prospective husband an elaborately patterned jersey, known as the 'bridal shirt', to be worn on their wedding day. Its design would be made up of a combination of the traditional stitches of their village, so providing a recognisable and distinctive garment when it was worn at special events away from home. The 'gansey' was an essential part of the fisherman's trade, providing warmth and freedom of movement. By far the majority of the garments were made by and for the family, either by the women or the men, but for some knitters it was a means of providing secondary income. Most took some weeks to make, and, around 1900, sold for 3s.6d (17½p) each.

Some fishing communities in Scotland developed knitted pullovers which had more

Plate 132 Pair of stockings inscribed 'Eliza Lewis' and intended to be worn after the death of the knitter, made at Esgair-onnen, Cardiganshire, 1850

Plate 133 Fisherman's guernsey with Flamborough pattern

distinctive patterns. These were made either in a single colour, such as Arran, or with bright multicoloured designs as in the case of Shetland (where the wool is plucked or 'rooted' from the animal by hand and used in its range of natural colours) and Fair Isle (see Plate 134). The latter introduced the use of dyed wool before the days of chemical dyes, using plants, roots and berries to obtain colour. Decorative motifs are reputed to be derived from the patterns on the clothes of Spanish sailors who were in the vessels of the Spanish Armada wrecked off the coast. but this may be a part of craft folklore rather than historical fact. Such patterns are said to include the Armada Cross and the Rose of Sharon. Traditionally the grandmother knitted her grandson his first sweater, known as a Robe of Glory, to be worn when he became an adolescent. Within the design each pattern was significant, depicting a 'voyage through life'; it usually started at the bottom with the Water of Life, then came the Seed of Life, followed by the Anchor of Hope and the Star to guide him. At the shoulders the pattern ended with a Crown of Glory – the wearer's final reward for a 'good life'.

Plate 134 Shetland knitter wearing a leather knitting-belt working on a pullover with a traditional Fair Isle pattern, 1950s

THE INDUSTRIOUS HOME

Many of the objects used in and around the home were made by members of the family, and included various items made from fabric – clothing, a wide range of rugs, spreads and so on – and treen, the general name given to the variety of small domestic objects mostly carved or fashioned from wood. Not only were all these items useful, in that they had a particular function, but they also helped make the home more comfortable and colourful. Much of the work made use of recycled materials which cost little or were free save for the labour, and in this respect represent an economy of thrift.

Textiles developed faster than most other home-based activities as a creative form of expression. This was partly because basic materials were relatively cheap, partly because

such making could be done by men and women in the home, and partly also because the finished objects had a practical use.

The economic factor is important because it made the medium accessible. Whatever fabric was used, whether in the form of woollen garments, unwanted clothing, or yarns of various sorts, numerous ways of using it were found. Equally, the capacity for textiles to be constantly recycled made them available even to those lowest on the economic scale. Many of the creative processes could be described as a form of recycling, often of the most inventive kind. Textiles were re-sewn, re-shedded, re-woven and re-cut, with great imagination.

Until the introduction of nylon and synthetic fibres, the fabrics available remained constant, though changes in manufacturing textiles were nothing less than a revolution. Significant class divisions affected the work made. Working-class families could only use materials available or purchase scraps bundled up by suppliers for the purpose, while the better-off selected and purchased fabrics to give their work more 'style' and colour. Quilting and patchwork were practised by both working and middle-class people.

The need for home comforts was a major factor in stimulating the development of textiles both as a means of providing useful objects and as a medium of creative activity. Items made for home decoration provided opportunities to create visually pleasing designs, enabled colour to be used and allowed experiments with pattern-making. In the rapid change from rural to urban living and the even faster expansion of towns into cities, some established practices associated with rural existence were adapted to the rigours of urban life. In the shift, despite the often appalling conditions of industrial urbanisation, the home was able to retain in adapted form traditions associated with country life. Textiles (which included floor-coverings and bed-covers), whilst providing a link with the past, also took on new forms.

For many working-class people living in urban conurbations, poor conditions and the inadequacies of the most basic human needs made it difficult to accept the fact that

their dwellings could be regarded as homes of any sort. In some industrial communities a kind of 'village' life centred around a small number of streets, and within the larger cities individual areas emerged with a distinct character. This is significant because many items that survive are often from communities such as these which had a strong communal feeling. Rag-rugs from the north-east – which vary in pattern and even in colour depending on where they were produced – are good examples of such work. Regional variations existed but it is very interesting to find differences in designs in relatively small areas, sufficiently distinct to be understood and identified by local inhabitants as a way of establishing individual identity.

Sewing, weaving, tapestry, patchwork and so on provided a readily available means of expression, whether by individuals or groups. Magazines and how-to-do-it books promoted the making of traditional items such as patchwork, usually suggesting particular patterns and motifs rather than encouraging individual designs. As in canal-boat communities where styles of painting and decoration by various boat-yards could be easily identified by canal-boat people, so textile items produced within the home carried the individual mark of the maker. Clothing also developed significant regional variations, its decoration in particular being of considerable relevance to working-class culture.

Quilting and Patchwork

Quilts, patchwork and coverlets are some of the most expressive forms made in the home. Their utilitarian qualities and, often, the coarseness of some materials, suggests that by the beginning of the industrial age – and certainly by the mid-nineteenth century – they were a part of many households particularly in the north and south-west of England, and in parts of Wales, Scotland and Ireland, which, untouched by fashion, had retained a domestic art in cottages, farmhouses and colliery villages. Earliest known examples in

use in Torrington and Bristol by the 1750s were embroidered with stitches rather than with appliqué. Some of these were 'knotted', as were so-called rag flour rugs of the late nineteenth century where strips of cloth were tied through the weave of the background material to form a design. Many surviving rugs were made with homespun wool, coarse and nubbly, similar to the hooked rugs made more than one hundred years later when it became fashionable to put rugs on floors.

The technique of quilting, that is sewing

together two or more layers of material, came to Europe from the Orient; in Northern Europe advantage was taken of the additional warmth given by two or more pieces of fabric with a thin layer of wool between, joined with stitching to hold it all in place. No recorded dates for this kind of coverlet are known because they were rarely initialled or dated. Their simplicity of design – diagonal lines, basket weave or waffle – made them attractive to produce, although their main attraction was that they provided an effective and economical way of keeping people warm at night. The actual quilting was done in simple white thread, effectiveness of design being achieved by shadow and light. Quilted items of clothing such as jackets were worn by soldiers either beneath their armour or in place of it, to provide warmth and protection.

In the eighteenth century fine quilting was regarded as a suitable activity for the leisured classes, with patchwork used only as a backing. In the early years of the nineteenth century, as other forms of fabrics became available, quilted garments went out of fashion for the well-to-do, but were taken up by working-class people. Quilted waistcoats and petticoats were popular because they were so warm, and it was not uncommon to see wives of Northumbrian fishermen in such petticoats until the middle of the twentieth century. The craft was passed on from generation to generation, the youngest children beginning by threading needles for the more experienced sewers. One quilter of Brownley Colliery remembers being allowed to leave school early to thread needles for quilters at the Methodist chapel, and being given a free meal for his help.

One or two professional quilters adept at marking out patterns, such as Joseph Hedley (c.1745–1826), known as Joe the Quilter, produced intricate work of the finest quality. A chintz quilt made around 1815 has a particularly elaborate pattern typical of his work (see Plate 135).

Patchwork, originally a method of using up pieces of scrap material, became an art in its own right and was rapidly taken up by

Plate 135 Chintz quilt made around 1815 in the Haydon Bridge area; the fine quality and elaborate pattern, date and place of origin suggest that this was the work of Joe the Quilter who lived only a few miles away at Warden

working-class people particularly in mining areas around the north-east and Wales. Making quilts and patchwork also helped provide a meagre income for the less well-off. Widows of miners often sewed patchwork for others

Plate 136 White sateen quilt with border of printed material made in 1890 by miner's widow Mrs Sally Rason of New Seaham, County Durham

to help eke out a living, such as Mrs Sally Rason of County Durham who, after the death of her husband, raised a family of four by making quilts and running quilting clubs. An example of her work can be seen in Plate 136. Quilting and patchwork remained a popular way of providing bed-coverings well into the present century and more recently has been revived as a creative process.

Quilting, patchwork and appliqué, which flourished from 1765 to the early 1900s, was influenced by industrial development, in particular by the production of low-priced printed cotton at the end of the nineteenth century. This opened up the possibility of incorporating snippets of colourful printed fabrics into the spreads. Before the late nineteenth century all printed processes on textiles were slow and costly, making the finished fabric expensive. After 1880, faster mechanical methods of colour printing speeded up production. The invention of the roller and full industrial mechanisation enabled lengths of fabric to be printed cheaply and quickly, resulting in lower prices. Though relatively inexpensive and easily obtainable, especially in areas of cotton production in the north-west and Midlands of England, printed fabric was still beyond the means of many working-class families.

Traditionally, every young woman wanted a chest filled with quilts before she was married, while the culmination of her work and effort took the form of a 'bride's quilt'. In some areas, notably the north-east, it was customary for women to spend the day at the 'quilting bee', when all would work round the quilting frame. This ritual was also partaken of by men, who would join the women in the evening, making a social event of the occasion. A quilt survives that has the embroidered admonition:

'At your quilting, maids don't dally.
A maid who is quiltless at twenty-one
Never shall greet her bridal sun!'

Some quilts were only worked on in the evening and took many years to complete; for many women their whole life was reflected in the quilt with each piece of material, each part of the design relating to events or activities in their life. Popular designs based on geometrical divisions included Star of Bethlehem, Lemon Star, Octagonal Star, Sunburst, Sawtooth, Log Cabin, Diamonds, Triangles, Double Wedding Ring, Stair Steps and Patriotic. The availability of printed fabric influenced the design and visual effect of patchwork quilts. 'Crazy patchwork' became popular in the period 1870–1900 and had the advantage of being able to incorporate virtually any small-sized piece of fabric and hence may have velvet, silk, wool and calico placed side by side, though no particular pattern was followed (see Plate 137).

Some old quilting patterns were derived from familiar, everyday objects – fruit and flowers abound. In 1937 Elizabeth Hate recalled a West Country woman who remembered both her grandmother and mother coming home with sprays of oak leaves, ivy, clover and thistle to study in the evening as they planned their quilting patterns. In Northumberland some quilters have recalled how designs came from the sea: '. . . on the coastline they have had designs pertaining to the sea. Seaweed and shells . . . belonging to Seahouses down to Amble . . . the designs . . . near the hills . . . were all flowers and foliage and feathers'. One highly worked patchwork coverlet included panels embroidered with flowers, with an intricate outer border decorated with verses of the popular hymn 'Jesu lover of my soul'.

Appliqué quilts, whether sewn from cheaply purchased textile scraps or cut from old clothes, were very useful, and the making of them was seen as a thrifty occupation. Clothing that could no longer be passed on and was beyond repair could be cut up and used for quilts and rugs. Appliqué coverlets were created by sewing design elements cut from printed chintzes on cotton or linen spreads. These coverlets incorporated home-spun checks, 'India' chintzes, stripes and plain and printed cottons of every type and style. Sometimes designs for these quilts went

Plate 137 Crazy coverlet from the Whitley Bay area, c.1860

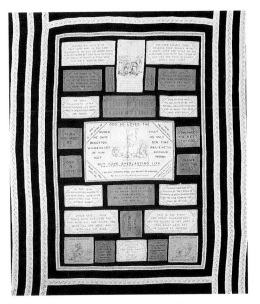

Plate 138 Quilt made up of printed biblical texts which have been machine-appliquéd to Turkey Red twill. Most panels are rough and utilitarian, but the panel bearing the words and music of the hymn 'The Ascension' has been wave quilted; 79 × 85 inches, c.1870

beyond the geometric shapes of patchwork quilts to more creative 'pictures' recording life and events, buildings and animals.

Groups also worked together on so called 'bible quilts', such as the one in Plate 138. Women's Institutes, chapels, Sunday Schools and such like sewed patchwork quilts which could be displayed or offered as prizes in raffles. Some were made up of different panels each bearing the embroidered signature of the maker which were then sewn together, while others incorporated panels bearing uplifting texts all set within a neat geometrical arrangement. In the inter-war years, as candlewick bedspreads and eiderdowns were produced cheaply and more women went out to work, there was a rapid decline in quilting. But during the Depression, organisations such as the Rural Industries Bureau encouraged quiltmaking as a way of bringing in income.

In the last few years there has been a revival of interest in quilting with classes set up and exhibitions held. Today, patchwork is used to respond to new and different conditions. A quilter in the Scottish Highlands has made a highly detailed patchwork in which each panel is based on an incident in the Falklands War, in which her son served as a soldier (see Plate 139). The finished work was raffled to raise funds.

Taking up the concept of the quilt as emblematic of the most intimate aspects of life – referring to such monumental events as birth, sex and death – the AIDS Quilt is a modern response to the tragedy of the AIDS epidemic. Started as part of the Names Project which began in the USA in the mid-1980s, the project now has local 'chapels' in Britain which invite people to make a panel 6 × 3 feet by stitching and appliqué to commemorate the life of a loved one who has died from an AIDS-related illness. Each panel bears the name of the deceased and a design which in some way reflects their life. Because the Names Project extends to anyone who has died as a result of AIDS no matter what the mode of transmission of the virus, both the making of the panel and the display of the quilt serve as a way of coming to terms with death. It is also an opportunity for people to meet and talk as well as to create a beautiful object. The quilt, made up from the assembled panels, is a powerful and moving statement about the epidemic, as well as a strong visual object made by many hands (see Plate 140).

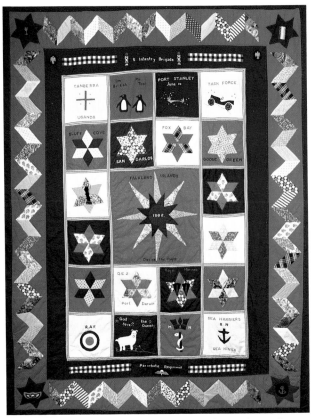

Plate 139 'The Falklands Quilt' by Elizabeth Boles, made up of ten
panels on which are appliquéd various badges based on different
events in the conflict, 68 × 88 inches, 1980s

Plate 140 Part of the UK AIDS quilt assembled from panels, each 36 × 72 inches, created by makers to commemorate
the death of a friend or loved one, 1991. The quilt is part of the NAMES Project, started to commemorate the 'lives,
loves, memories and, most important, the bravery of those who have died from AIDS'

Rugs and Weaving

The recycling of materials, so much a feature of the creative use of textiles, is no better expressed than in the production of rag-rugs. Like quilts and patchwork, they are excellent examples of what can be made from 'left-overs' and unwanted scraps. For most working-class homes these left-overs were all that could be afforded. The recycled materials were put to good use; the rugs not only served to keep out the cold but provided decorative and colourful floor-covering, a testament to the industry and creativity of the maker.

Historically, rag-weaving was associated with the production of coverlets, the earliest recorded being produced for this function and called 'tatter weavings'. Originally from rural parts of Scandinavia, they provided an inexpensive means of guarding against fierce winters. Though documented in the eighteenth century in Sweden, they may have much earlier antecedents.

In Britain, rug-weaving is first recorded around 1840 and appeared in America at much the same time, though Jane Austen refers (around 1800) to ladies being busily employed measuring lengths of worsted for rugs and of their doing 'carpet work'. Rugs were not woven but 'prodded' or 'hooked' through a hessian base. Jute imported from India in the 1830s was used to make cheap and strong hessian sacks which, when washed, made efficient bases for the rugs. The most common method was to prod or peg short lengths ($1\frac{1}{2} \times \frac{3}{4}$ inches) of cloth (preferably of non-fraying woollens, serge, worsted, even old socks) through hessian using a home-made pointed tool made from such items as keys, nails or wooden clothes pegs. For hooky rugs long strips of cloth about half an inch wide were looped through the hessian using a hooked tool. Some rug-makers worked on a frame, others with a material over their knee, but there were many local variations.

Very poor homes simply laid sacking on the floor: 'What is the good of back-pegging rugs when an old sack thrown down would serve the same purpose?' wrote Flora Thompson in *Lark Rise to Candleford* on the attitude of one villager. The Somerset Rural Life Museum records a poor village home *c.*1900 as having 'No carpets on the floor. Only the very "élite" had any carpets in those days. They just had one, probably that was a rug they'd made themselves, as they called a rag-rug.'[1] Certainly they were considered the poor person's substitute for the unattainable luxury of woollen carpets.

Primarily utilitarian, the newest rugs would be placed in front of the fire in the parlour or living-room; as they became flattened with wear and the colours became dirty, they would be replaced by a new rug – the old rug gradually working its way from living-room to kitchen, ending up in the porch or on the doorstep. Like quiltmaking, rag-rugs served a social function in bringing people together, sometimes to make a rug as a combined effort. An Ashington Group painting depicts such a scene in the late 1940s. Like quilts, rag-rugs contain references and memories about the lives and homes of the people who made them, and in their different fabrics is to be found a history of the kinds of textiles available to the less affluent, whether for clothing, furnishing or bed-linen.

The artist Conrad Atkinson describes

Plate 141 *Proggin the Mat* by Oliver Kilbourn, about 30 inches wide, *c.*1938. The warm kitchen atmosphere – the women progging a rug on a frame in front of a roaring coal fire with a kettle coming to the boil – is well caught in this domestic interior

Plate 142 Hooky woven rug with typical diamond
pattern in a frame made up of a half-circle, 1930s

how as a lad in the village of Cleator Moor,
West Cumbria, neighbours would gather in
the evenings to make hooky or rag mats. He
recalls them sitting round a wooden frame
some 5 foot square over which a length of
hessian was stretched, usually made up from
laundered potato sacks; old clothes and rags
were collected and cut into strips, sorted into
colours and then hooked into the hessian in
various patterns and colours. It was a scene
painted by such Sunday painters as Oliver
Kilborne in 'Proggin the Mat' (Plate 141).

Though practised in many parts of
Britain, rag-rug making, like patchwork
tended to be associated with the mining areas
of the north-east, Scotland and Wales. It was
also carried out by sailors: 'I came across half
a dozen pegging away sitting at the back
of an eating house in Lowestoft', recorded
Dorothy Hartley in 1939 in her pioneering
book on country crafts and industries, *Made
in England*. In industrialised areas food sacks
from the countryside and those from abroad
bringing sugar and grain from the docks provided suitable material for the rugs' backing.

Rag-rugs also reflected the working
clothes of the day. A typical material was
serge, often augmented by woollen stockings
and blankets. Since working clothes were
always neutral in colour and left plain,
soldiers' red tunics were particularly prized
by rug-makers to bring a splash of colour to
their designs. Other more fortunate rug-
makers could rely on 'hand-me-downs' and
clothing from more well-off relatives. Around

1855, a Derbyshire woman recollected that
'clothes were plain and home-made but
Grandma took a pride in her girls. She'd a
sister married well who used to send things,
and what a big one grew out of, a little one
would wear, and then every bit was made up
for a rag carpet, or a cushion for grandfather's
chair, and patchwork.'[2]

Identifying where or how particular
patterns and designs of such popular widespread activities as rag-rugs and quilting arose,
and what their origins are, presents almost
insurmountable difficulties; many of the
motifs and arrangements of patterns stretch
far back in history and occur, seemingly at
random, in different cultures. Some of the
most common decorative devices of the
geometric divisions of space (employing basic
forms such as squares, rectangles, diamonds,

Plate 143 Hooky rug with a central design of crazy
paving in random colours, set in a frame, about 96
inches long, 1960s

triangles and circles, often drawn using different-sized plates as a template or carried out freehand) are present in the rug in Plate 142. Other rugs may further incorporate the comma (signifying the soul), suns, radiating lines, broken lines, dots and so on. Pegged rugs, furniture reliefs, and patchwork are typical examples which employ such themes. An equally common recurring motif is the heart, either used as a three-dimensional shape or as a linear decoration. An evocation of love and affection, it appears on pincushions, on Scottish trivets, carved on furniture and in profusion on quilts.

Because many basic designs and motifs were widespread with similar sorts of patterns appearing across the country, particular motifs or styles cannot be accurately attributed to specific geographical areas. A dark border, for example, is a common feature and visually serves as a 'frame' for the colours and patterns within. Identifying particular patterns is further complicated by the fact that in the 1920s the co-op marketed hessian was already marked out with a pattern. The random use of colour is appropriate for pegged – as opposed to hooked – rugs as it allows almost any sort of fabric to be used, each piece being simply poked through without a pattern having to be followed. Marbling, or crazy paving in random colours, is equally common and again gives the weaver good scope for using up scraps (see Plate 143). For special occasions or as gifts, more ornate designs may be carried out. The floral rug in Plate 144 was made by a Miss Latimer who gave it as a wedding present in 1904.

Pictorial hooked rugs were almost exclusively made in Cumbria where patterns incorporated stylised representations of such animals as cats, cockerels and horses, many using geometrical patterned backgrounds. The bull in Plate 145 is set in a landscape made up of a crazy-paving design. The artist Winifred Nicolson greatly admired the rugs in the 1930s and encouraged the makers. Floral patterns occurred in many areas and some were based on commercially designed factory-made carpets, but greatly simplified

Plate 144 Hooked rag-rug with floral design by Miss Latimer who died in 1959 at the age of 88. The rug was given as a wedding present in 1904.

by being translated into home-made rugs. Commemorative rugs were also made, recording national events. One from the north-east

Plate 145 Pictorial rug with design of a bull in a field, about 40 inches long, 1930s

Plate 146 Rug made for the Durham Light Infantry. Despite the commemorative design, the rug shows signs of wear

celebrates the Diamond Jubilee of 1897 using a stylised crown in the centre while another bears the coat of arms of the Durham Light Infantry (see Plate 146). Though clearly special, the rugs were used rather than merely displayed. Overall, the effect of a newly made rug was one of thickness, luxury and colour before the tufts became flattened and worn, and the definition of the pattern dimmed by use.

Rugmaking, as with patchwork, provided a creative outlet, allowing the inventive use of design and colour when little else was available, and was also a shared activity as indicated by the two women in Plate 147 working on a rug in the early years of this century. In the north-east rugmaking would often involve the whole family, including the men. A Durham woman recalls how neighbours would help each other make rugs in their back yards on summer evenings, and that schoolgirls would sometimes get a free meal if they joined in after school (Newarke Houses Museum). The activity of rag-rug-making became fully self-expressive, if by accident rather than in any planned way, as has been the case with many popular arts. Flora Thompson's description of a cottage interior in Oxfordshire in the late nineteenth century may be typical of the more prosperous cottages in other parts of the country: 'Rooms were bright and gay, with dressers of crockery, cushioned chairs, pictures on the wall and brightly coloured handmade rag-rugs on the floor.' This theme is also evident in the description of a farm labourer earning 17 shillings a week in 1913: 'There is a bright fire in the living-room, but it is very obviously the abode of poverty. There is no carpet on the stone floor, but a good-sized hearth rug and a smaller rug, both of them made out of

Plate 147 Two women making a proggy rug on a frame, early twentieth century

clippings by Mrs Arthur, and two smaller bits of sacking. The place is clean and fresh.'[3]

Like patchwork-quiltmakers, rug-makers who lived in the vicinity of textile mills had a good supply of materials in the form of weaving off-cuts. It was also possible to obtain short lengths of waste yarn and tailors' off-cuts. Rag-rugs were the product of economic necessity and with the availability of cheaper carpeting the practice declined steeply at the beginning of this century. Only during the two World War periods did rugmaking revive as part of the spirit to 'make-do and mend' promoted by such bodies as the Women's Institute. In the post-war period greater affluence reduced the need for rugs, while kits to produce long-tufted woollen rugs to some extent satisfied the need to make home furnishings.

By the 1970s the skill of making rag-rugs had all but died out except in areas of the north-east, but interest in the technique as part of working-class culture has resulted in several large, popular exhibitions illustrating the range and variety of work made. This has led to a revival in making rag-rugs particularly in areas in the north of England such as Sheffield where there has been a long tradition of such activity. Classes in community centres have attracted much interest and techniques once learned in the home are being taken back and practised there again. Designs and patterns are individually evolved, some making inventive use of simplified abstraction such as the rug entitled 'Tulips' by Narcian Jenkins to make practical and decorative items for the home (see Plate 148).

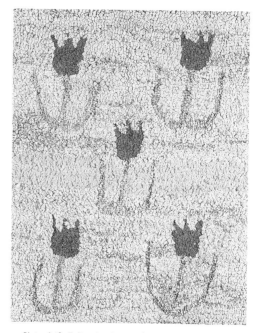

Plate 148 *Tulips,* hooky mat by Narcian Jenkins of Sheffield, about 30 inches tall, 1991

Clothing

The decoration and making of clothes roughly falls into three types, each of which is distinctive in its appearance and aim: occu-pational clothing, decorative 'fancy-dress' (discussed in Chapter Three), and clothes as a means of individual and group identity which are detailed later in this chapter.

This book is concerned mainly with clothes people have made themselves rather than those bought or purchased, except where individuals have adapted and transformed factory-wear. Above all, working clothes have to be functional, hard-wearing, warm, protec-tive and comparatively low priced. Yet they can also provide some recognisable identity with many clothes indicating at a glance a particular occupation. Some outfits were related to special trades while others were associated with specific areas or villages.

Some communities whether in cities, towns or villages, established their own form of dress with workers spending hours making such clothing. A major exception to this were the very poorest people, who wore clothes passed on from others. Often this was of superior origin but in the last stages of wear. One of the poorest groups, the London dockers, went about their work fitted up in worn-out tailcoats and old bashed-in top hats. Costers, highest in the ranks of street-traders, had evolved a distinctive costume by the 1830s which included such refinements as

Plate 149 Welsh fisherwomen with baskets of shrimps at Barmouth, 1904

pearl buttons on waistcoats. In London costers tended to stick together and much time was spent in dressing well. For women, this tended to follow fashion but included a dress of printed cotton, a clean white apron, a dark shawl and a small round bonnet set over a net cap. For men, a waistcoat was essential. Henry Mayhew's detailed and first-hand descriptions of coster dress in his comprehensive work *London Labour and London Poor* (1851) make clear the social importance of the outfits.

Working communities developed distinctive outfits. In Merthyr in the iron and steelworks, the 'coke girls' who stacked coal for coking in the pits, had outfits which, according to one nineteenth-century observer, consisted of 'coarse sleeved pinafores, handkerchiefs tightly bound over their heads, battered hats bristling with frayed feathers, blue stockings and in some instances masculine overalls.'[4] On one occasion an observer saw them at work on the mountainside in pouring rain which 'literally ran off their coal-bedaubed petticoats over their boots, in black streams, to the ground'.[5] The clothes were not only distinctive, but were highly serviceable for the toughness of the labour required.

Fishing communities such as those along the coast of the Firth of Forth and east of Edinburgh, also developed hard-wearing and strong outfits. Costumes worn by women varied from village to village, each one, though similar, having distinctive qualities in the chosen materials or in the cut. The tradition also provided scope for individual makers to introduce their own variations. Outfits worn while preparing fish or hawking it round the streets (stalls were not set up until comparatively recently), such as those worn by Welsh fisherwomen in Plate 149, were typical – heavy and well lined and usually made by the women themselves, handstitched and, later, sewn by machine. Working dress consisted of a skirt, blouse, apron, shawl, stockings and a purse worn rather like a sporran. The purse, more colourful than the rest of the costume, may have been an opportunity for the expression of individual 'taste'. Much of the costume was made from traditional materials – a woven dark blue with a pin-stripe, a black cape and a shawl in grey, white and black. These were for everyday use. For special occasions and celebrations, Sundays and holidays, the costume was altogether more colourful, and these continued to be worn well after the Second World War – though younger women showed little interest in them.

Smocks, the protective outer garments worn originally by country workers in England and Wales, are an example of a rural-based garment made by and for the sole use of workers, crossing over the boundaries of urban and rural society (see Plate 150). In addition to being worn by agricultural workers such as labourers, ploughmen, wagoners, gardeners, woodmen, gamekeepers, and shepherds, during the nineteenth century they were also used by tradesmen working in towns. These included butchers, fishmongers, tailors, cidermakers and brewery workers. Smocks were highly practical, the stout material providing an extra layer of clothing to protect against the cold and damp. They also served to keep undergarments clean, a particularly valuable asset in a messy job.

Styles of embroidery and the colour of the linen varied from area to area around the country; embroidered decoration included motifs representative of the profession or employment of the wearer, but often more abstract designs were created. The height of the popularity of the smock was reached in the middle of the nineteenth century when the garments were at their most ornate and fanciful. *The Times* (13 June 1851) records the appearance at the Great Exhibition at Hyde Park of 'nearly 800 agricultural labourers and country folk from the neighbourhood of Godstone in Surrey . . . The men wore their smartest smock frock, and the women their best Sunday dresses'.

There were, broadly, two types of smocks: those made for everyday wear and those for special occasions. Working smocks were generally made of coarse twill or drabbet in beige or fawn. Small manufacturers such as Messrs Brown and Crosskey of Lewes, made smocks for over one hundred years, though the majority were made by skilled women who supplied local needs.

Smocks made for special occasions were fashioned out of finer linens, usually in white,

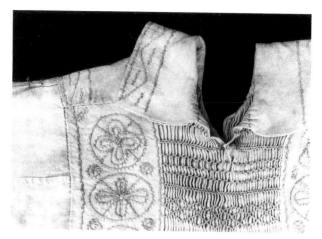

Plate 150 Detail of smock with traditional embroidered patterns, c.1900

and were generally made by a member of the wearer's family. Many had intricate stitching and embroidery and were often handed on through the family. Pattern and design varied, but the work of individual hands can be recognised. Some makers preferred highly stylised floral motifs, others sheaves of corn, ploughs, hearts and so on. Some designs incorporated such old rural sayings as 'God speed the plough'; others acknowledged a more business-based activity in the words 'success to trade'. Patriotic motifs were also popular particularly at national celebrations such as coronations and royal weddings. A smock in the Victoria and Albert Museum incorporates a design of Britannia as she appeared on the back of an old penny.

Towards the end of the nineteenth century smocks started to lose their popularity. New machinery took away some of the drudgery of work and such heavy protective clothing was less necessary. Equally, smocks could get caught up in the machines. Alternative and cheap factory-made clothing became available. Yet smocks and smocking influenced fashion: in the 1870s smocking became fashionable for women's and children's clothing because of its practical nature and its attractiveness. Among the supporters of this move was Constance Wilde, wife of Oscar, who was an active member of the National Dress Society. Liberty, the London store, opened a costume department in 1884 and had smocks made in their own fabrics.

Working with Wood

Traditionally, a central part of vernacular style has been defined by work in wood, whether for architectural detail and construction, boatbuilding or more modest items for use in and around the home. Wood is readily available at low cost and can be easily worked by such techniques as whittling, carving, sawing, planing or turning on the lathe. Home objects include items of furniture such as chairs, cupboards and sideboards, covers for radio sets, candlesticks, frames for pictures or childrens' pull toys such as the bull on tiny wheels in Plate 151, and the diverse groups of small objects known as treen. Like smocking, objects made from wood are examples of methods of working which continued in both rural and industrial communities to provide useful and decorative pieces. Over the years working methods and items changed as wider influences came to bear, new machinery became available and different objects were needed. In the last few years a range of efficient and well-priced electric power tools have made more sophisticated techniques readily available.

Treen, the general term applied to various small wooden objects, was usually made by hand either by the person who was

Plate 152 Snuff-boxes in the form of everyday items including a shuttle, a boot, a coffin and a woodworker's plane, each about 2 inches long, c.1900

to use it or to provide a simple tool or token to present to a loved one. Though much treen is associated with rural, pastoral communities rather than urban environments, during the nineteenth century there was a cross-over period when similar objects were made in industrial areas. Typical items include carved apple-corers, busk stays, snuff-boxes made in a variety of forms such as shoes or books (see Plate 152), loving-spoons and knitting-sheaths.

Some treen was made commercially (albeit on a small scale) and falls outside the scope of people's art. The extent and range of work produced is indicated in the impressive collection made by Edward H. Pinto and his wife, now in Birmingham Museum and Art Gallery. Assiduous and careful, they published their extensive research in *Treen and Other Wooden Bygones* (G. Bell and Sons, 1969). While Pinto made no attempt to distinguish between treen made within the urban industrial environment and that produced in rural areas, or between professionally made work and that produced as people's art, this is nevertheless a fascinating record of the range and inventiveness of the items made.

The custom of making useful objects and carving emblems of affection, such as love-spoons and love-tokens which often included in the decoration initials, dates, names and so on, has a long history. During the nineteenth century such objects were also

Plate 151 Pull toy in the form of a bull, soft wood, 18½ inches long, early twentieth century

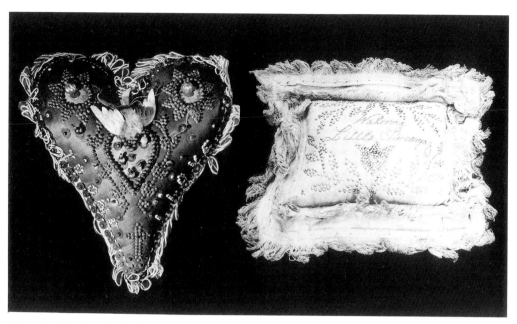

Plate 153 LEFT: Pin-cushion in the form of a heart with pin and bead decoration, about 6 inches long, late nineteenth century; RIGHT: Pin-cushion made to commemorate the birth of a baby, with 'Welcome Little Stranger' in pinhead decoration, about 6 inches long, late nineteenth century

produced for local sale and included heart-shaped pin-cushions worked in beads (see Plate 153), heart-shaped tablets of soap, jugs decorated with lustre from Sunderland, and painted glass rolling-pins. Small pin-cushions made to celebrate the birth of a baby were decorated with a design built up from pins pushed into the white fabric. Some, such as the one from Luton, carried the motto 'Welcome little Stranger'.

In Britain the pre-eminent love-token was the Welsh love-spoon: its aim was to record and convey a message of love and as such had to be as intricate and finely carved as possible. Equally fascinating is the fact that these carved objects transformed an everyday, commonplace item into something highly significant which had no practical function other than as an expression of love and affection.

Love-spoons such as those in Plate 154 were made from readily available local hardwoods and the most common carved motifs were single and twin hearts. During the nineteenth century the comma motif, representing the soul, often arranged in pairs, was nearly as popular. Sailors also carved love-spoons, incorporating anchors in their decoration. Messages such as 'we two are

one' were expressed literally and symbolically. Some tokens were linked by intricately carved wooden chains, suggesting the marriage bond and displaying the skill of the maker. A shoe or a boot was also a common motif traditionally associated with luck and marriage – a custom recorded in the Bible, when the taking off of a shoe denoted the confirmation of a contract and which is still acknowledged today by shoes tied to the back of wedding cars or ornaments on wedding-

Plate 154 Six wooden love spoons showing typical carving including a chain, small wheels and incised decoration; the longest is 12 inches, nineteenth century

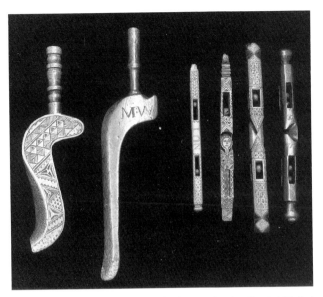

Plate 155 Wooden knitting-sheaths. One is initialled
M.W., and the goose-wing sheath has incised
decoration; the longest is 11 inches, nineteenth century

the bottom of the double-ended needle. Most were made out of wood and individually carved. Some were decorated by their makers to give as love-tokens, particularly in the Yorkshire Dales. Sheaths generally followed traditional designs and patterns, many specific to particular geographical areas but each one with the makers' individual variations (see Plate 155).

As areas in the north-east of England such as County Durham became more urbanised in the second half of the nineteenth century, traditional forms of wood-carving were replaced by cabinetmakers' techniques and sheaths were made which incorporated fine veneer with a highly polished finish, inlaid panels of mother-of-pearl and glass as well as rare, imported woods. Ivory and bone sheaths were usually the work of sailors, while tin, brass and glass specimens were sometimes used around Sunderland, reflecting local industries. In fishing communities wood for carving the sheaths may have come from an old boat, and the form was often adapted to the shape of the piece of wood. Surfaces were usually decorated, either by carving or incising, while a few were marked by burning with a hot tool.

cakes and the like. More recently, love-spoons have been produced commercially and such a popular item has long been made and sold by people with carving skills.

Like love-spoons, knitting-sheaths are associated with pastoral, rural communities. Traditionally, hand-knitters used a knitting-sheath to support one of the knitting-needles, worn on the right either under the arm or held in position by a special pocket. The sheath helped take the weight of the knitting as well as preventing the stitches slipping off

Whittling or carving was also used to make walking-sticks. Some made of thorn-wood in the early years of this century by an old man in south Leicestershire (now in Newarke Houses Museum, Leicester) had emblems encircled by panels of cross-hatching and spirals divided by bands containing hearts, lozenges and stars.

Woodworkers also made wind-powered tableaux depicting figures carrying out such activities as pumping water from a well, chopping logs or – in a more intricate piece, such as that in Plate 156 – being driven along in a horse and chaise. Single figures mounted on upright poles were often military in origin, showing sailors or soldiers painted in bright colours with arms on pivots so they could flail in the wind. Some, like the two sailors in Plate 157, are quite intricate, and would have required detailed making. Few have survived the damp British climate in good

Plate 156 Wooden whirligig in form of horse and
chaise, about 12 inches long, c.1900. As the wind blows
the legs move up and down

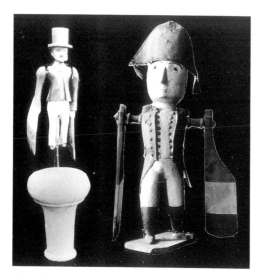

Plate 157 Whirligigs in the forms of sailors, soft wood with sheet metal, about 18 inches tall, early twentieth century; the arms go round as the wind blows

condition, as Thomas Hardy records in *The Trumpet Major* (1880), where one such whirligig is described as 'a vane in the form of a sailor with his arms stretched out. When the sun shone upon this figure it could be seen that the greater part of his countenance was gone, and the paint washed from his body so far to reveal that he had been a sailor in blue.'

For indoor amusement, figures with movable limbs were carved from wood and known as Jumping Jacks or dancing dolls (see Plate 158). Some were left plain while others were painted with bright and elaborate patterns. The loose limbs were attached to a string which, when pulled, animated the legs; variations included the use of a spring. In the hands of a skilled operator, the figure could be made to move quite naturally.

Furniture provided not only the opportunity to make practical objects for the home, but encouraged initiative in using available material. Until the development of industrial production methods in the nineteenth century, most furniture was made in the district where it was to be used. Materials were those available locally and making methods were traditional and long established. Country furniture was made from the native woods of oak and elm, and was rarely embellished with painted decoration. In addition to wood, furniture was also made from rush, osier and

straw. Chairs built out of straw rope (lip work) were made over much of the country, though these now tend only to be associated with the Orkney Islands and Wales. Straw was also used in Orkney to make the backs of chairs, which would add both warmth and comfort (see Plate 159).

While carpenters made furniture for the local community, individual makers built furniture for their own use. An excellent example is the child's tramp-work pine rocking-chair in Plate 160, probably made in Wales around 1850. The sides and back of the chair have carved and pierced designs of animals and figurative motifs. The style of the work and the choice of the designs suggest a close relationship with the decoration on love-

Plate 158 Jumping Jack toy operated by a string which, when pulled, causes the arms and legs to move; carved and painted soft wood, 12 inches tall, nineteenth century

138

Plate 159 Making straw-backed chairs in Orkney in the early part of the twentieth century

Plate 160 Tramp work rocking chair, pine wood,
probably made in Wales, mid-nineteenth century

spoons. Equally fascinating is the chair carved in a single piece from a tree-trunk shown in Plate 161, with the inset seat the only additional part.

In the Highlands of Scotland each area has its own tradition of making: in the West Highlands chairs were usually made from a slab of timber with the back and legs socketed into it, similar to a method found in Wales; more decorative and sophisticated chairs which tend to be built round a natural fork of timber were made in the Central Highlands; in the North, there was the use of a knee of timber. In treeless areas driftwood and other recycled timber could be made into chairs, as was straw or marram grass. Bog-wood buried in peat from primaeval times was also used to create remarkable seats. A skilful example of driftwood furniture is a dresser from Fochar on the island of South Uist. An imaginative use of the material not only result-ed in a functional object but created a visu-ally attractive effect (see Plate 162). The High-land Folk Museum in Kingussie has an impressive collection of this furniture.

In contemporary Britain, the work of Andy the furniture-maker (b.1958) is particu-larly significant. He started to build his own furniture quite simply because he needed

some. Without a job but with a flat in which
to live he scoured London's skips (the large
containers placed on the streets and in which
household and factory rubbish is deposited
before being carted off to be disposed of). In
these he found much that could be recycled
including wooden boards and boxes – even
unwanted market stalls. Though completely
untrained and with only a minimum of tools,
Andy collected suitable wood and started
making the furniture he needed for his own
flat – chairs, tables and a bed base. In the
early pieces Andy worked to a basic but
functional and strong design, while more
recent work has taken on a quality of its
own, resulting in a mixture of modern func-
tionalism with some gothic, almost theatrical
influence. Some wood is left with its original
markings – as, for example, a chair whose
sides are made from boxes which held Argen-
tinian corned beef (see Plate 163), constructed
during the Falklands War as a protest against
the military action – while others are stained
black and dark brown, creating an impression
of rugged strength within a functional style.

Plate 161 Chair carved from a single piece of wood,
about 60 inches tall, late nineteenth century

Plate 162 Dresser made from driftwood, Fochar, South
Uist

Plate 163 Chair constructed from wooden corned-beef
boxes by Andy the Furniture Maker, early 1980s

HOME, SWEET HOME

Save among the poorest people and the slum dwellers, the cult of the home in the 1870s and 1880s caught the popular imagination. The widely loved song at this time, 'Home, Sweet Home', despite the mediocre words and music, virtually became a second National Anthem.

> Mid pleasure and palaces though we may roam
> Be it ever so humble, there's no place like home;
> A charm from the sky seems to hallow us there.
> Which, seek through the world, is ne'er met with elsewhere
> Home, home, sweet, sweet home!
> There's no place like home! there's no place like home!
>
> *John Howard Payne (1791–1852),*
> *Home, Sweet Home*

Ruskin's phrase 'Home is the Nest', used to describe the contemporary vogue by professional artists for painting pictures of domestic scenes, became a motto framed in many working-class homes.

Having an immaculately furnished and polished parlour, even if seldom used, was an important sign of respectability. Among the less well-off, status and 'decency' were dependent on a variety of factors. In local communities it was considered highly significant whether or not a house had curtains at the windows, if there was a plant in the window bottom, and whether the doorstep was cleaned every day. On freshly cleaned floors patterns were trailed in different coloured sands or rubbed from softstone on washed steps and floors; these were seen as an essential part of home care and pride, particularly in some areas of the north and Midlands.

Plate 164 Donkey-stoning the front door step using soft sandstone, 1950s (photograph by Jack Hulme)

In Glasgow tenements, the common stair was washed once a week by each of the residents in turn who would then chalk down either side of the stair with different patterns. Executed in pipe clay, there could be loops, lines or zigzags or even chains of flowers. The art form ceased in 1968 when the last of the pipe works closed. 'Raddling' or 'donkey-stoning' are terms used in the Midlands and north of England to describe the rubbing of sandstone on steps and floors (see Plate 164). There was a general belief that decorative designs and motifs scoured on the doorstep and hearth averted 'the evil eye', and anyone entering the home saw the fresh decoration and the industry of the housewife. It was also thought to bring good luck. Today the tradition is continued in some areas by painting a frame on the edge of the step in red or yellow.

Flanders brick was a yellow version of hearthstone and sold well in the north and Midlands. Sculleries and passages which were only washed once a week would have an elaborate pattern worked around the wash tub which would last seven days. Sand was

Plate 166 Straw picture showing Conway Bridge, about 24 inches wide, late nineteenth century. Many such straw pictures were produced, each with variations on this scene

also used in the north particularly in public houses (sawdust was more common in the south), as William Smith of Morley records in 1886:

> To minimise the effects of dirt, which every visitor to or occupant of the house could not fail to bring in from the dirty roads of the village, handfuls of yellow sand crushed very fine were scattered over the bare floor. The hawking of sand for household purposes was a recognisable trade.

The sand – red, yellow or white – was likely to be arranged in patterns so intricate that it was said a clever barmaid could convey a message to her sweetheart in a sand pattern.

Within the home, treasures and personal possessions could be made, displayed and shown to friends and neighbours. The home was essentially a private world, though often an important part of community life, a retreat from 'work' where the outside world could be excluded. Neighbours and family were invited but strangers were often as not kept on the doorstep. In and around the home, individual as opposed to community traditions were followed and people were free to 'be themselves'. Objects such as love-tokens, favourite pots and pictures were displayed. Some were purchased but many were home-made. Workers in the salt indus-

Plate 165 Salt ship made by workers dipping the model into a pan of brine which dries to leave a covering of salt crystals on the structure, nineteenth century

Plate 167 *West Bromwich Sweep*, a vivid watercolour portrayal of the scene after a
boxing match, inscribed: 'As he appeared at george Holdens after his fight with fred higgitt
being waited on by Jem Parker through wose superior Generalship he won his Battle in
1 hour and 20 mineets on the 7 of January 1850'; 20 inches wide, mid-nineteenth century

Plate 168 *Two Boxers Shaking Hands*, embroidery, late nineteenth century

Plate 169 The Lord's Prayer, pen and ink drawing combining calligraphy and illustration showing many motifs traditional to the slate headstone carver including cherubs, angels with trumpets, hour-glasses. 'Our Daily Bread' is illustrated by drawings of sowing and harvesting. Portrait of Our Lord as the 'Superstar' of the period at the base. Signed and dated 'Syston Academy — Written by Charles Brown — Christmas 1849'; 24¾ × 19½ inches

Plate 170 *A Still Evening* by Hannah Lee, depicting a pastoral scene built up of coal ashes 'from my own grate',
22 × 33 inches, 1908

try at Northwich made 'salt ships' by dipping wooden models of ships into pans of shimmering brine: salt crystals formed on the models to give an attractive frosted effect (see

Plate 171 *Adam and Eve in the Garden of Eden* by Hannah Lee, a highly detailed scene of the naked couple complete with serpent, Eve picking an apple watched by the all-seeing eye in top left-hand corner; cut paper, 27 × 27 inches, 1874

Plate 165). At Christmas, decorations were made in much the same way, branches of holly and so on being dipped in the brine to obtain crystalline effects.

A great variety of materials were ingeniously employed to make pictures. In Wales cut sections of straw were used to make 'straw pictures', most of which depict the same scene of the Conway Bridge (see Plate 166). All include a similar range of motifs but each composition is slightly different. Pinprick pictures were a pleasant way of creating images often based on contemporary engraving. The tinted drawing in Plate 167 entitled 'West Bromwich Sweep' vividly pictures the cleaning up of a severe black eye received, presumably, in a boxing match. It is interesting to compare this with the bravado conveyed in the highly detailed embroidered picture, 'Two Boxers Shaking Hands' (see Plate 168). Probably based on a contemporary engraving, the stylised rendering catches the pre-fight mood of tension and expectancy. The illustrated picture of the Lord's Prayer by Charles Brown, dated 1849, is written out with a combination of calligraphy and illustration and incorporates many motifs

Plate 172 Fretwork mirror and calendar dated 1929, cut from plywood, about 8 inches tall. A note tucked into the frame reads 'To Winnie From Fred Best wishes I made this myself'

traditional to the slate headstone carver, including cherubim, angels with trumpets, and hour-glasses – a detailed and impressive work which serves as a reminder of belief and ingenuity (see Plate 169).

A series of large pictures – some 5 × 4 feet – made in the early years of this century by Hannah Lee of Leicester, also made ingenious use of waste material. 'A Still Evening' (1908) in Plate 170 depicts a pastoral scene built up from 'pure untainted ashes' using 'all ashes from my own grate'. The subtle colours and naïve perspective give the picture the romantic charm of the English countryside. Other pictures were made of butterflies, bones, flies, moths and onion-skins while 'The Old Homestead' (1921) was made out of cinders. A version of Adam and Eve in the Garden of Eden made in cut paper displays not only great dexterity in making the shapes, but an ingenious understanding of composition in which all parts of the picture are filled with detail (see Plate 171). Hannah Lee's wide range of materials was reflected in the diverse styles she used, which extended from pastoral landscapes inspired, perhaps, by the work of Samuel Palmer, to the more visionary approach of William Blake.

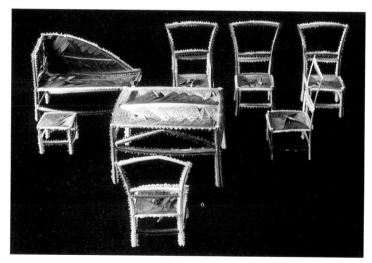

Plate 173 Feather furniture constructed from cut feathers, made around 1850 by 'an old man for a little girl at Mistley Essex'

Plate 174 Disabled ex-sailor with a model made of matchsticks, 1938

for radio sets were made in the late 1920s and 1930s, while letter and spill racks, mop-stands and decorative calendar-holders were also popular. The fretwork calendar frame in Plate 172 still bears the note written by its maker remarking on the fact that 'I made this myself'. A particularly elaborate example in Newarke Houses Museum in Leicester is the Lord's Prayer with sacred symbols made in 1904 by Joseph William Hughes, Glenfield, Leicester.

Working with common or everyday waste material encouraged initiative, inventively linking art and craft. Bones such as the vertebrae of a cow were painted and decorated to form amusing ornaments; apple-corers were carved from sheep shin bones. Miniature feather furniture was assembled from carefully slit feathers (see plate 173), while calen-

In the early part of the twentieth century the introduction of a simple but efficient fretwork machine operated by a foot pedal was a great success. Instruction booklets included ideas and patterns for a wide range of objects which could be made using the highly popular fretwork technique, either laboriously cut with a fine fret saw or using the peddle-driven fretwork machine. Covers

Plate 176 Dog woven out of Wills Wild Woodbine cigarette packets, 8 inches tall, 1950s

dars and belts were made from silver foil of sweet wrappings, matchstick models patiently assembled to create objects as diverse as Tower Bridge, gypsy caravans and Swiss chalets, all made with meticulous care. Some makers, like the disabled sailor holding a matchstick model of a Tudor house in Plate 174, used their skill as a means of eking out a meagre income.

Smoking and smokers' paraphernalia contribute a colourful range of images. In addition to the silver foil wrapping there was

Plate 175 Frames woven from cigarette packets, about 6 inches across. On the back of the one on the left is the message 'Belle and Sid – A Merry Xmas – happy New Year... Martha and Will'

Plate 177 Plate with cigar bands and other collaged images stuck on with a central figure bearing the slogan 'Socialism' beneath a coat of arms, about 10 inches across, early twentieth century

Plate 178 Broody or mosaic ware, made by sticking broken pieces of crockery and such like on a plain ceramic plate with putty and covering it with household varnish, about 10 inches across, c.1900

the attraction of the packet itself. Players Navy Cut cigarettes with their colourful image of a romantic bearded sailor and Wills Woodbine packets were cleverly fashioned into frames (see Plate 175). Bright and attractive to look at, these frames (some of which were round, while others were in the shape of hearts) were often made as gifts. A particularly ingenious use of cigarette packets is the weaving of animals. The dog woven out of Wills Wild Woodbine packets in Plate 176 has a direct simplicity which perfectly catches the essence of the animal. Though widely made, few such pieces were valued or cared for.

The richly coloured bands obtained from cigars were also highly prized and were often carefully stuck on pottery plates. One plate in Beamish Open Air Museum uses these and other printed material to make a colourful pattern incorporating into the design the slogan 'Socialism', displayed above a young woman in the centre of a border. A layer of varnish protects the final result which to some extent resembles brighly coloured and gilded porcelain (see Plate 177).

Equally fascinating is a group of objects known as mosaic or 'broody' ware, which consists of broken pieces of pottery, shells, coins, metal and found objects stuck on pottery plates or tin trays with a thick layer of putty. Among traditional seaside mementoes would be boxes encrusted with shells while home-made items included jugs and plates. First the surface was covered with putty or some similar material into which the objects were pushed as close together as possible. The plate on which shards of broken decorated pottery have been stuck gives a curious but lively effect which recreates rich pattern and colour (see Plate 178).

Similarly, a vase in Ironbridge Coalport Museum indicates how some factory workers reacted against prevailing 'good' taste. A bone china vase, seven inches tall, was covered in broken pieces of colourful pottery; clearly the plain white form had little attraction for its owner. The effect is bright and cheerful, particularly in comparison with the finely – but sparely – painted vases produced in the factory where great skill was used in the decoration. Blanks, freely available to factory workers, were decorated in a wide variety of ways suggesting that the extent and diversity of 'working-class' taste is as complex and involved as that of any other.

CHANGING COMMUNITIES

In the years since the Second World War the most significant changes within working-class communities have been the break-up of old established patterns of living as large areas of towns and cities have been pulled down and architect-planned estates built; different ways of working with new technology have replaced traditional methods. As manufacturing industries declined, service industries have been set up, and for the first time there has been considerable movements of population away from the centre of towns and cities. Traditional industrial areas where manufacturing jobs have been lost – such as Blackburn, Bolton, Gateshead, Halifax, Manchester, Oldham, Salford, South Shields and Wigan – have declined in population. Towns which have doubled their population include Blackpool, Bournemouth, Cambridge, Coventry, Luton and Southend-on-Sea. Large areas of the Home Counties have become suburban. Overall conditions of work have improved – working hours have been shortened and holidays made longer; but class divisions within society remain, as do large areas of poverty.

Today 'private worlds' seem more significant and important than ever before. When high-rise flats and anonymous estates provide little sense of community or of belonging, the need to create a 'nest' becomes even stronger, and some individuals have decorated rooms in highly personal ways. The artist Stephen Willats photographed interiors of homes in high-rise flats and included the pictures in his exhibition installation 'Another City' (Riverside Studios, London 1984). Willats wanted to show how individuals living in London use visual art to find a meaning when 'they can find none in the uniformity, listlessness, repression and violence which surrounds them'. Little wonder that Willats found rooms painted black and smeared with a mixture of paint and body waste, as well as rooms filled with religious icons and shrines. Titles of the installations ('Living Like Goya', 'A Difficult Boy in a Concrete Block', 'Night Painter' and 'Secret Prima Donna') give an indication of the lives he was describing. The installations explored the contrasts between the starkness of tower-block reality and the exoticism of the night world, the contrast between dependence and self-determination. Willats wrote: 'I want to make a direct connection between the createivity of young people's fight back against the passivity inherent in the dominant culture.'

Some individuals wanted not only to decorate their homes but to create an entire and complete environment. From the outside we can see only the appearance and very little of the meaning of this work, though the strength of the imagery is often visually powerfully and highly personal. Murals such as those painted by Cyril Smith, who died in 1975, covered much of the inside and outside of his house, Rose Cottage, as well as most of the furniture. Smith, a Londoner, worked in the printing trade among other jobs and soon after the end of the war moved to Somerset. In the 1960s he began to decorate the doors and walls of Rose Cottage, depicting recalled events in vivid colours. His style is a blend of caricature and naïveté, with wit and humour important ingredients, the intuitive and untutored images conveying intense conviction and personal vision. Many of the removable paintings were saved for the Western Museum and Somerset Rural Life Museum, Glastonbury, as were items of furniture and doors, before Rose Cottage was sold and renovated after his death.

Robert Tressell painted murals in St Andrew's Church, Hastings (now destroyed),

Plate 179 Detail of mural by Mr Chate painted on the walls of his living-room in his bungalow in Southampton; it shows the influence of epic cinema, ancient times and the power of the sexual drive, late 1930s

photographs of which are held in Hastings Museum, while a Mr Chate (1902–84) decorated practically every surface of his bungalow in Southampton, including the kitchen, hall and bathroom, and also transformed the garden by carefully landscaping and decorating it with concrete deer heads. After a slight boating accident in 1936 he had given up sailing to concentrate on decorating his bungalow. The walls of the living-room (see Plate 179) were first covered with second-hand canvas and painted with a mixture of house paint and artists' oils. Subjects include large-scale panoramas depicting the sea — with which he was familiar — as well as

Plate 180 Decorative shell work on a house in East Cowes, Isle of Wight, using flint pebbles, shells and whole and broken crockery, 1985 (Photograph by Eileen Lewenstein)

Plate 181 *Safety First* mural by George Edwin Davies urging miners 'Don't take risks' and 'I am waiting for you', *c.*1960

more imaginative compositions involving the opposing forces of good and evil, many of which reflected the influence of epic cinema.

In London an occupant of a council flat created a hanging-garden outside her window by making ingenious use of disused

Plate 182 Ron Hamilton tending the 'factory garden' workers built at the Sliphouse at the Ideal Standard vitreous china bathroom equipment pottery, Kingston-upon-Hull, in 1986

postcard racks. The effect of carefully selected pots of different coloured flowers covering up the supporting racks was highly attractive. Shells have been used in many parts of the country to create attractive surfaces. On the Isle of Wight, one householder has created a shell garden using stones, many sorts of shells, broken crockery and other oddments to create colourful and inventive series of wall pictures which depict local events and buildings, while another has made murals and patterns on the walls of the house (see Plate 180). All the surfaces are covered so making an almost complete environment.

Contemporary art and the wider, more diverse images of 'pop' culture have also been influential. Particularly significant are the murals by miner George Edwin Davies painted at the bottom of the Salisbury shaft at the Victoria Colliery, Stoke-on-Trent, which take references from the home into the workplace. Painted in the late 1950s and 1960s (Davies retired about 1968) the murals depict characters from television's *Coronation Street* with a portrait of Ena Sharples, portraits of the Queen and Prince Philip, as well as glamorous pin-ups. There is also a witty visual warning of 'Safety First', urging miners not to take risks down the mine; beside it, a naked woman stands by a bed, an incentive to return home safely (see Plate 181). What is visually so strong about the paintings is not so much the technical skill of the artist – though this is considerable – but rather the juxtaposition of images (painted on cast concrete walls) against the various pieces of machinery, and the position of the murals, which meant they would be seen only by fellow workers.

A similar art scheme was carried out by Ron Hamilton, a ceramic worker at Ideal Standard, Kingston-upon-Hull, in 1986. In a corner of the factory floor he created his own garden grotto complete with a fountain jet and a pool. Behind it he painted an 'idyllic' landscape which appears to merge with the garden to create the illusion of vast space (see Plate 182), again crossing the boundary between home and work.

Plate 183 *Masters of the Universe* mural by Stephen Harrison, painted for his son's bedroom, early 1980s

Plate 184 Billy Gofton with life-sized figures in his garden, early 1980s

A more private home-based world is that painted by Stephen Harrison, a gardener living in Walton, Chesterfield, who painted one wall of his son's bedroom with a 'He-Man' mural to celebrate his sixth birthday. The 'action-packed' scene, showing superhero He-Man and his trusty pet Battle Cat fighting off 'baddie' Skeletor, is based on a popular cartoon character; the change in the scale, from small to huge size is confidently carried out and has resulted in a particularly powerful image (see Plate 183).

The enjoyment and pleasure of creating art was experienced by Billy Gofton, a South Shields shotblaster who started to paint in oils while studying engineering and who subsequently covered his home with giant murals. The urge to work in three dimensions came when he began using cement to make raised beds in his garden. To add interest to

walls made of large, smooth beach cobbles, he placed a few beer bottles stuffed with gold or silver foil and sank them deeply into the cement so that only their bases showed. The foil reflects the light, breaking up the surface and giving a mysterious effect. Surplus cement was used to build up menacing life-size figures. A method of forming the figure on a chicken-wire frame supported on a skeleton of mild steel bars was devised and the mixture of cement applied to this. Before it had fully set, the cement was carved and the final form created. Billy Gofton's garden is now full of expressionist figures, including life-size blind men, fishwives, pop groups and madonnas (see Plate 184). Gofton thinks that anyone with a bit of imagination and a rudimentary ability to co-ordinate hand and eye can make satisfying sculpture.

New Communities

One of the features of people's art, particularly since the Second World War, has been the growing awareness of making art for the home and creating private worlds, as well as art concerned with the community. As the difference has widened between home and work, much creative energy has centred on the smaller, more personal 'community' of the home or interest group. Post-war society has seen long-established, geographically-based communities broken up: schools have become bigger and more centralised, drawing pupils from larger areas; many local hospitals, too, have closed as larger institutions take over; urban transport systems have made travel quick and efficient, thus enabling people to travel long distances to work, further adding to the split between home and work.

In the 1950s and 1960s new working-class youth cultures, outside trades or professions – and certainly not 'fancy-dress' – emerged as a means of establishing individual and collective identity in a rapidly changing society. Social attitudes and events in this period were shaped above all by the memory and aftermath of the war and by a rapidly changing society; despite austerity and rationing, the country as a whole moved towards economic and social recovery, with prosperity for all apparently on the horizon.

The 1950s brought a new surge of affluence: the economy was expanding and there was little unemployment. Immigration was encouraged. But though economic expansion brought full employment and reasonably good pay, many jobs were dull and repetitive, offering little interest to the work-force. Future prospects were equally limited. Though Prime Minister Harold Macmillan insisted that 'most of our people have never had it so good', the reality for working-class youth was dead-end jobs leading to boredom, frustration, disenchantment and alienation, rather than involvement or concern. Prosperity also saw the start of huge rebuilding schemes and the break-up of many working-class neighbourhoods as old houses were pulled down and families moved into new homes. Anonymous estates and homes without gardens or easy access to outside space helped foster restless and unsettled communities.

Rockers and teddy-boys were the first identifiable groups to come out of specifically working-class districts in London. Their clothes proclaimed personal choice at a time when clothes were still regarded as 'right' or 'wrong' (suits signalled best wear for all classes while work clothes were strictly defined). As in the early and mid-Victorian period, the social centres once again moved from the home to the streets. Homes were seen as belonging to the parents and family, while small local cafés – or 'caffs' – and streets were made their own. Teddy-boy outfits, based on the dandified cut of Edwardian men's suits, were a parody of decency, a distortion of Savile Row style originally created for the upper middle class (see Plate 185). Trousers were tight 'drainpipes', jackets had large shoulders and were loosely cut in the 'drape' style, with velvet collars. Thin 'boot-lace' ties were worn. Shoes were suede with thick crêpe soles. Hair, compared with the accepted fashion of the time, was worn long, well-cared-for and swept round at the back into a DA. Sideburns were full and low. The influence of US popular culture was also important in introducing style and attitude.

Rockers, often confused with teds but actually very different, drew more heavily on American culture, in particular the freedom implied by the archetypal cowboy hero and motor-cyclists. Outfits, exaggerating masculinity, featured denim jeans, white t-shirts, leather jackets, studded belts and boots, all carrying suggestions of sexuality and hints of violence. Many rockers owned motor-cycles and were members of unofficial groups identified by painted or studded decoration on jackets in imitation of heraldic devices used by medieval knights (see Plate 186). The skull and crossbones, emblems of death, were often featured, though eagles and such like were

Opposite: Plate 185 Ted holding a tobacco tin decorated with matchsticks bearing a caricature self-portrait and the lettering 'Kev', 'St Albans Teds', the names of rock stars such as Jerry Lee Lewis, and the initials 'C.S.A.' (Confederate States of America), c.1980 (photograph Gus Wyllie)

Plate 186 Rocker's leather jacket with studded design of an eagle and a Maltese Cross, and the lettering 'Rockers', c.1980 (photograph Gus Wyllie)

also popular as were the brand name designs of motor-bikes such as Triumph and Norton. In the 1960s rockers adopted the name 'greasers', originally used as a term of abuse; Hell's Angels, an equally emotive description, dressed in a similar fashion but often wore Nazi helmets and insignia such as the swastika, not because they necessarily supported Nazi policies but because these were universally detested emblems.

In contrast mods, or modernists, conveyed an impression of affluence and relative conformity. They originated in East London and the working-class estates in the suburbs of the city. Mod style was characterised by short hair, smart, well-cut suits and an obsession with a neat appearance; many drove motor-scooters fitted out with fancy trimmings. Sunglasses ('shades') were favoured, as were pork pie hats. Most had respectable semi-skilled or unskilled jobs. By closely emulating but exaggerating the praiseworthy values of neatness and a well-tailored look, the mod style was entirely alien to it. By the mid-1960s, in the face of growing economic decline and rising inflation, mods had started to wane as other groups came along.

Changing conditions brought new, harsher styles. Towards the end of the 1960s

skinheads emerged as an identifiable subculture, first in the unskilled working classes in London's East End closely followed by other urban centres (see Plate 187). Puritanical, chauvinistic and aggressively proletarian, skinheads adopted modes of working-class dress as a clear and explicit 'uniform'. Skinheads drew on two apparently contradictory sources – the culture of West Indian immigrants, especially on the 'rude boy' subculture of black delinquent youth, and the hard look of the white working class. They congregated on the all-white football terraces and consorted with West Indians on street corners and at local youth clubs, aping their mannerisms, adopting their curses and dancing to their music. Their style – aggressive, tough and macho – consisted of close-cropped hair at a time when flowing romantic locks were in fashion, tight-fitting jeans or sta-pressed trousers worn at half-mast and held up by braces, with 14-hole Doc Marten 'bovver boots'. The entire outfit was both a reassertion of the solid, male, working-class, tough look and at the same time an intimidating caricature of it. Most skinheads were unemployed, part of the economic recession.

Skins tended to congregate around particular pubs, to support local football clubs and to hang about favourite streets or specific areas. Many held traditional 'working class' conservative values, associated with maintaining jobs and life-styles, a few expressing them violently. A hatred of 'Pakis' or 'queers' was often combined with a jingoistic patriotism. Most striking of all was the almost total commitment to being a skin, manifest in thick tattoo markings over the face, neck and shaved head. This 'back-street' tattooing (professional tattooists often refused to work on the face) was sometimes done by the wearer or by another member of the gang using a needle and ordinary ink pricked into the skin; a design of a cobweb stretched over the entire head is common. Some designs incorporate large Union Jack flags or slogans such as 'Made in England'. The style was an expression of anger and alienation.

In the mid to late 1970s, punks arose first in London and then in other large cities, as much a response to the prevailing values and conditions of society as to the high levels of unemployment and inflation. Punks rejected such traditional values as wealth, property and mind-numbing jobs in favour of an anarchistic suspicion of imposed values,

seeing themselves as outsiders living only for the present – the future did not matter. Convention and tradition were rejected as punks sought to create their own alternative subculture. Clothes were emphatically do-it-yourself; principal colours were black and white and the more rips and tears the more expressive it became. Almost any cheap or obviously trashy product was worn. Black plastic bin-liners, lavatory chains, zips, safety-pins, dyed hair, torn t-shirts and bizarre school uniform were chosen precisely because of their perversity and downmarket 'value'. The wearing of rubber items, fish-net stockings, bondage suits and leather straps, belts and studded jackets suggested sexual and social perversity (see Plate 188).

Though essentially working class in origin, punk later drew on middle-class influences particularly from art schools and conceptual art, and had connections with middle-class hippies and student anarchists. More recently the boundaries between punks and skinheads have become less easy to identify with the enormously complex variety of costumes and hairstyles which include Mohican cuts, partly shaved heads and dreadlocks.

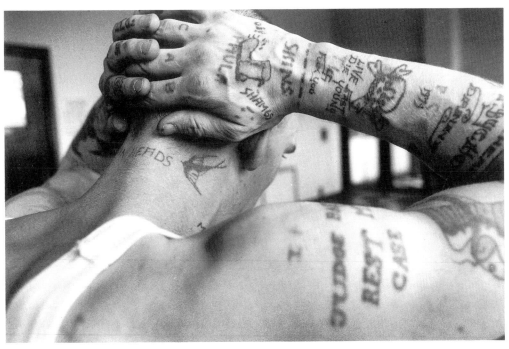

Plate 187 Pete, skinhead with self-made tattoos, 1991 (photograph Jon Jones)

Street anarchists, punks and skinheads today are related to each other by poverty rather than any common ideology: squatting was easier in the 1970s while today it is virtually impossible. As gay and lesbian identity has become more public many of the styles of rockers and skinheads have been taken over and subverted as political statements about sexuality, making any easy reading of such outfits a more complex task.

A major feature of the 1980s was the high levels of unemployment (a word first used in the 1880s), rising from 1.5 million in 1979 to a peak of 3.4 million in 1986 and this continues to fluctuate at relatively high levels. Ironically, while unemployment provides many hours of free time, workers have little or no money to spend and most regard the unavailability of suitable work as an imposition and resent being pressed to take banal, repetitive jobs at low rates of pay. While a national policy of reduction in the number of hours worked would create more useful and rewarding employment and thereby enable more workers to have access to income, this idea has found little political support. Indeed, there is pressure to work longer and longer hours to gain necessary overtime payments. With a proper income and satisfying work more people would be able to choose their leisure activities.

Nevertheless, some individuals have responded with ingenuity and creative energy. Pictures have been painted, furniture built and a range of schemes set up, often in association with local community centres. Unemployment has also influenced youth culture particularly among working-class groups. Rockers, mods, hippies, skinheads and punks reflected their distinctive identities and their political beliefs in their dress and costume.

Immigration, too, has brought new cultural influences and changes which have affected such art forms as music and theatre. There have been long-established Chinese settlements in Liverpool, Swansea and the East End of London. Since the war immigrants from the West Indies, Pakistan and other countries have brought their own cultural forms, much of it street-centred. The Notting Hill Carnival, discussed in Chapter Two, has inspired similar events round the country. Some community and arts centres have put forward schemes aimed at attracting black people and immigrant populations, such as the Crypt Association of Wolverhampton, which seeks to meet the needs of 'the underprivileged, unemployed, disabled and ethnic groups within the local community', with practical help and assistance, paying particular attention to developing leadership and technical skills within the ethnic and black indigenous community. In the early 1980s the Crypt Association launched the Arts Training School at Wolverhampton Civic Centre, to provide opportunities to learn and experience all the arts, organising an exhibition entitled 'Art on the Dole', showing work by local unemployed people.

The history of people's art in the late twentieth century has been one of rapid change: while much traditional work has disappeared, new forms have replaced it and continue to challenge any ready definition. Some aspects of the culture have been appropriated or substantially modified, particularly in the realm of musical entertainment. Professional artists have drawn on the direct styles of the 'untrained' eye. Writing in Italy in 1975, Pier Paolo Pasolini thought that today's consumer-orientated society had brought about 'the most complete and total genocide of restricted popular cultures'. He went on to say that, 'the sub-proletarian youth of Rome . . . have lost their "culture", that is, their way of life, of behaving, of speaking, of judging reality'. Such an impression is even more clear when comparisons are made with the nineteenth century, but despite all the odds, people continue to find creative and inventive ways of asserting their own personality. As communities change, so art finds new and diverse forms.

Opposite: Plate 188 Punk with Mohican haircut, and jacket decorated with studs and painted slogans, c.1980 (photograph Derek Ridgers)

Chapter Five

HOME FROM HOME

With time on their hands many take the opportunity to 'be creative', to make decorative and useful objects for personal pleasure or for friends and family. This is particularly the case where distance, separation or confinement provides ample time, if not unlimited resources. Sailors aboard ships, canal people, members of the armed forces, or prisoners constitute particular groups who create a 'home from home', whether by choice or force.

A characteristic of these objects is the intimate relationship between the maker, the working and living conditions, and the subject and form of the work. Prisoners tend to depict their cells, sailors their ships and the sea, while members of the armed forces make inventive use of such scrap as bullet cases, discarded propeller pieces and such like to form an integral part of the objects they make. Where space is confined and materials limited, objects tend to be small in size but intricate in detail. Ingenious use is made of a variety of 'waste' materials, whether shrapnel fragments used by soldiers or whalebone by sailors, and much time is spent working on the material prior to use. Before engraving whalebone sailors laboriously prepared the surface by endlessly smoothing it with fine abrasive powder. Sports and pastimes such as chess, cribbage or darts, which take on special importance in prisons and aboard ships, require score boards and the like which can be effectively handmade. As sea voyages became shorter and a wider range of leisure pursuits became available, much 'home from home' making abroad has ceased. In recent years it is prisoners who have increased in number and who now produce much creative work.

For canal workers the situation was different. Though not isolated by distance or imprisonment, they led lives quite separate and independent from other groups in the community. In the cramped living and working quarters of the narrow boat, space was at a premium and interior and exterior decoration extended to practically every surface – including buckets, jugs, cupboard doors and furniture. Patterns and designs, though part of a recognised and accepted convention, were seen as an important individual expression of pride. A freshly painted vessel with bright decoration had great significance for the owners of the craft for, while it offered little practical benefit, it was a central and major part of their lives.

Away from the powerful influence of middle and upper-class 'taste', people follow their own ideas and inclinations, calling on a wide variety of ideas. Some borrow freely from different aspects of high art, making use of images taken from engravings, or employ stylised 'gothic' lettering, a form popular on work by prisoners though invariably altered in some way. Many makers ignore altogether the refinement and subtlety of high art in preference for bright and gaudy colours, for patterns and designs which, from the academic perspective, may seem unduly romantic in feeling and appear to be in bad taste. Canal art is part of a tradition which has come from the continent of Europe, but which has taken a particularly 'English' form. Like fairground operators, canal people think decoration is at its best when freshly painted with the colours and surfaces undimmed by time and wear. Coming to terms with work which so clearly reflects 'taste' outside that

Opposite: Detail from Plate 206

defined by the middle and upper classes is a direct challenge to the idea that 'good taste' transcends its own contexts and conventions so as to be widely accepted.

SAILORS, SHIPS, SCRIMSHAW AND CUSTOMS

During the nineteenth century maritime trade greatly expanded; ships became larger, were built from iron and later steel, and were powered by steam-driven, coal-fired engines rather than sail. The East India Company lost its monopoly and other shipping lines vied for trade. Speed became increasingly important: fast clipper ships developed and steam was introduced, first with paddle-steamers then with screw propellers. The nature of the merchant trade also changed. Coal-carrying, for example, became a possibility as steam power replaced sail. Whaling, a major occupation which reached its peak in Hull in the 1830s, was in severe decline 20 years later. Ironically, while petroleum oils were replacing the needs for whale oil, it was found that the hide of the walrus, when tanned, made excellent belts to drive industrial machinery. Amid all the change, the life of the sailor, though different, maintained many old customs whilst developing new ones.

Sailors' Art

Though the popular image of the sailor was romantic, reality was very different: working and living conditions were often appalling; seamen had few rights and some were enticed on board by bounty payments, others were virtually press-ganged while many were reluctant volunteers seeking an escape from an unsympathetic environment.

Until the abolition of the press gang in 1815 and gradually improved conditions thereafter, life in the Royal Navy was much harsher than in the merchant service. Conditions were probably at their worst for ordinary seamen during the American and Napoleonic wars. Admiral Lord Nelson spent two years on HMS *Victory* without going ashore and Admiral Collingwood was at sea for 22 months without even anchoring. Below decks sailors lived in cramped, crowded spaces with hammocks slung only 14 inches apart. They had time on their hands only when there was no storm to weather or battle stations to attend, and periods of intense activity would alternate with weeks or months with little taking place. After months at sea, food was barely palatable and on occasions fancy articles were fashioned out of salt pork and salt beef, the flesh of which was reputed to be able to take on a polish like close-grained wood.

Just as there was a hierarchy above decks, so there was below decks; the most privileged were the bosun, carpenter, sailmaker and cook, all with specific responsibilities. They did not 'keep watch', were paid better wages and were often known as 'idlers'. Beneath them were able and ordinary seamen who had to be skilled and dexterous in a wide range of practical tasks such as handling the tools of the craft.

In the middle of the nineteenth century the art of seamanship was at its zenith. Muscle and skill reigned supreme: strength was needed on the capstan-bar or halliard or in picking up or muzzling a fighting sail. Generally it was considered to take five to seven years to make a first-class seaman during the age of sail. On the east coast a man was not allowed to ship as A.B. until he had passed an oral examination conducted by an experienced leading seaman of the local sailors' guild. Though with few possessions save the clothes they stood in, most sailors had a sea-chest and a ditty-bag or ditty-box which contained amongst their possessions such sea tools as a marline-spike, prickers, palm and needles and a bullock's horn of grease. The sailors' duties included cleaning the ship, steering by compass, splicing rope and working with the sails and rigging.

Whether in the Royal or Merchant Navy or on whaling ships, sailors had ample spare time. On sailing ships a voyage could last weeks, months or even years. Most sailors were illiterate, alcohol was forbidden or strictly controlled and pastimes such as handicrafts or music were encouraged. The scale and details of the work made related to the difficult and cramped living conditions below decks. No large objects could be stored, the constant movement of the ship meant that nothing too fragile could be made, and, by and large, the only tools and materials available were those already on board. Hence sailors' art is small in scale, intricate and complex in detail, with much time concentrated on one piece of work. Makers of ships in bottles, such as the two men in Plate 189, often had a set of special instruments, but others employed the everyday tools they had to hand.

Creative ideas came from two major sources – the ship itself and family life. The appeal of the ship image was universal amongst seafarers and, when ashore in shipping offices, building yards or dockside pubs, sailors saw expertly-made builders' models of ships and sought to try something similar. Captains and mates often commissioned paintings of their ship from professional pierhead artists, but on the lower deck sailors had to create their own images, copying and learning from each other. Standards were self-imposed and, while traditional designs and motifs were to hand, there was constant improvising and invention.

Models of ships, either made in scaleddown versions or as flattened relief pictures (see Plate 190), were perhaps the commonest objects made, most dating to the nineteenth century and depicting a great variety of merchant ships. Model-making reached its peak between 1850 and 1880 with the most popular subjects being sailing ships, in spite of the increasing use of steam. Many were displayed in cases with the model on a stand

Plate 189 Two sailors making models at sea; the larger vessel is a barque and perhaps a model of the ship on which they were sailing; the smaller one has threads attached to the rigging to enable the masts to be collapsed so allowing it to be placed in a bottle; late nineteenth century

so the entire profile could be seen or, for waterline vessels, set in a painted or low relief modelled panorama. Some create a vivid impression of a working ship rushing through the water under a great spread of canvas while others show the vessel peacefully at anchor waiting for the pilot. Some scale models are correct in virtually every detail.

The low relief image known as the diorama was an equally attractive way of making a ship portrait. This involved placing a half model of the ship in front of a painted or modelled background which often showed a coastline and such features as a lighthouse or rocks. The whole was placed inside a shallow box and given a frame. One diorama features the *Brynhilda*, a vessel built around 1886 and though made almost entirely out of pieces of tin, shows the vessel in full sail, capturing the romantic image of life at sea. In some, the entire ship was modelled and set in a sea of coloured putty or plaster, carved wood, cotton wool or, occasionally, paper.

Almost as popular was the detailed and precise technique of marquetry in which woods of different colour and grain size were laid together. This involved two skills: one was the pleasure of working with wood and adapting designs to the marquetry techniques; the other was to use woods from different countries which served as souvenirs of voyages made and places visited. The highly detailed

Plate 190 Diorama of half model of sailing-ship placed in a sea and landscape with the attendant small vessel *Bee* made by a sailor; about 24 inches long, late nineteenth century

marquetry picture 'Three Sailing Ships' (see Plate 191) makes clever use of patterns of the grain in a composition which depicts the vessels side and end on. Carving and whittling wood, whether for love-spoons or Aunt Sally and Jumping Jacks, was a way of producing useful as well as decorative gifts for friends and family (see Plate 192).

On board ship crew's quarters were basic and cramped. Seamens' belongings were stowed in their chest which also served as a seat. Old sea-chests had sloping sides which, with a base wider than the top, gave them a firm stand when the ship was rolling. In some only the two longer sides were sloping since this was enough to give them the necessary stability. They were about three feet long, 18 inches wide and 18 inches high. Chests from the last days of the sailing ships usually had

Plate 191 Marquetry picture of sailing vessels, the central ship complete with funnels issuing smoke; about 24 inches long, late nineteenth century

straight sides and were often made from cheaper pine woods compared to the old chests (see Plate 193). They were strongly built to withstand rough treatment and were usually painted brown on the outside, sometimes rust or a handsome bright green. Overlapping lids were fitted with two strong iron hinges. Locks were rare; a simple hasp and staple were considered enough. The lid was covered with sailcloth and generally painted black. The two rope handles, one at either end, were much easier to grip than the screwed-on iron or brass handles which were used later.

Plate 192 Wooden dolls in the form of an Aunt Sally and a Jumping Jack, carved from soft wood by sailors on board ship, tallest about 7 inches, late nineteenth century

These rope handles were rarely simple rope knotted on, but were often 'grafted' and decorated with Turk's-heads.

Sailors who could afford it chose teak for their chest and got the ship's carpenter to build it; this was not only extremely strong but needed no painting on the outside. The inside of the lid, however, was usually painted white and decorated with such devices as flowers and garlands, flags, symbols of faith, love and hope, or at least the owner's initials adorned with countless flourishes. Many sailors decorated the insides of the lids with

Plate 193 Seaman's chest with two stars and painted ship in full sail, about 36 inches tall, late nineteenth century

paintings of ships; although similar to ship portraits or votive pictures they are depicted more simply, partly because the paint on board was of inferior quality and partly because they were not intended as portraits but rather as emblems of good luck. Vigorously depicted ships were sometimes painted on canvas fixed to the top of the chest. One owner has written on the back of the canvas, 'Ship, Henry Reed, 1868'. Individual sea-chests expressed the identity of the sailor in otherwise stark and impersonal quarters. In order to provide a tidy stowage place for buttons, tapes and other small objects, the chest was often fitted with small compartments, some with folding or sliding covers. These were occasionally decorated with coloured inlays.

Building ships in bottles is by far the most well-known sailors' art, though it only became popular after clear glass bottles became readily available at the end of the nineteenth century. The apparently impossible task of assembling a ship complete with sails and rigging inside a narrow-necked bottle took ingenuity, skill and care. All parts had to be carefully prepared. The hull, masts and spars, lifeboats and so on were carved then painted and the sails cut out of thin paper. The hull and rigging were then assembled with the masts lowered and pointing aft. The standing rigging, that is the stays and shrouds, were made of thin thread, with the stays being sufficiently long for their ends to protrude from the bottle when the ship was inside. A coastal landscape with neat little houses and a lighthouse, or perhaps a patch of sea, was modelled from putty inside the bottle and painted with oils. Once prepared the ship, with masts lowered, was carefully inserted into the bottle and pressed firmly into the soft putty. The masts and sails were then erected by pulling on the shrouds with the spare lengths removed by burning them off with a long piece of red-hot wire. Finally the bottle was corked and sealed with wax (see Plate 194).

Though placing ships in bottles became popular as bottles were produced cheaply, the technique probably derives from the nativity scenes and similar miniature tableaux built in the eighteenth century. Early votive offerings were made in thanks for a safe return or a successful voyage. From before 1800 there were depictions of the crucifixion, street scenes, masonic symbols and ships built by sailors and others in carafes, which stood upright; these predated ships in bottles which were intended to be laid down horizontally. In the early part of the twentieth century ships in bottles became something of a cottage industry for retired sailors as well as for small businesses in seaside towns, and sold as souvenirs.

Images of ships were not only created inside bottles but depicted in a great variety of materials, including wool and paint and in relief. Woolwork pictures, some of the most distinctive, were more likely to depict naval rather than merchant vessels. Most were made in the second half of the 1900s with the most popular vessels shown being early iron-clad steam-ships, introduced around 1860. Sheathed in metal and heavily armed, these vessels carried a great spread of sail.

Generally, the outline of the ship was shown in a design which was flattened and stylised, though major identifying features were usually included. The stitching worked on ships' canvas (occasionally silk was used) was beautifully laid in long and short stitches with its direction adding to and enhancing the textural richness of the composition. Neatness and careful execution are typical of sailors' work. There was little attempt at perspective, and ships were invariably shown in side view so enabling size and shape to be fully demonstrated. Typical subjects are the magnificent woolwork 'HMS *Serapis*' show-

ing vessels fully dressed with all flags displayed. Nelson's ship HMS *Victory* was also popular and in some versions appears, improbably, with a funnel (see Plate 195).

Some woolwork pictures are winningly sentimental, showing scenes of sailors off on their travels while others are patriotic: these may include a crest flanked by eight banners, a crown and a motto such as 'My God and Wales', and the four national emblems of shamrock, leek, rose and thistle may also be shown. Others feature heroes such as Nelson and include the Union flag, Britannia, the lion of England and piles of cannonballs arranged in ordered symmetry. Most woolwork pictures were made in the Royal Navy in the second half of the nineteenth century, many produced as souvenirs and mementoes. As sailing ships disappeared so the art of woolwork ceased in the early years of the twentieth century.

Work with fabrics took many forms. On whaling ships which sailed from Hull – where crews were chiefly drawn from Orkney and Shetland with a few mainland Scots and only a sprinkling of English seamen – a frequent pastime was knitting, usually with the aid of a knitting-stick stuck in the belt or a sheath made up of a bundle of bird quills. The needle supported by these devices was manipulated with the right hand, allowing freedom to move about or smoke whilst turning out a sock or sailor's 'gansey'. All sailors had to repair their clothes and some even made them, one American writing: 'We have both been working on the cabin boy's suit of clothes. Sailor-like we made double seams, same as we used to when sewing sails', an attitude unlikely to be different to the British experience. Before the days of standard dress, embroidered embellishments were freely added. Some sailors also embroidered small items such as scarves, purses and pouches. Handkerchiefs with the name of a loved one were carefully embroidered and often had intricate edging.

On sailing ships sailors were adept at sewing, handling and working with rope. Part of a sailor's duties consisted of remaking rope as it came from the ropemaker into items needed as part of the ship's gear and rigging. They had to unlay and separate strands of ends of rope and 'splice' ends together. There were also a great variety of knots to be made for different purposes, eye splices or ends of rope to be 'whipped', and rope to be 'grafted', that is covered with weaving of thinner line.

Nautical literature records how simple tasks gradually inspired more complicated and refined techniques. Knots and splices were turned into new and attractive shapes which sailors called 'fancy-work', an appropriate term, since most of it was unnecessary from the point of view of seamanship. This occupation, which had its heyday in the second half of the nineteenth century, was based on definite shapes in which the knot proper, flat, raised, round or sometimes cube-shaped, was the starting point. There were also cylindrical shapes in which the strands were rove like a spiral, a turban (Turk's-head) or in a herring-bone pattern. Imaginative designs were also used in the making of mats, handbags, covers and net curtain, some being embroidered. Occasionally a flower — or fruit — basket was made entirely of rope, knotted, grafted and spliced. The manila or hemp rope was painted in various colours and often incorporated as part of designs. In the Second World War the crew of a submarine made a Christmas tree of rope, demonstrating that vestiges of this art survived in the Royal Navy long after sailing ships had disappeared. Knots were also assembled into decorative arrangements and framed, such as the print in Swansea Maritime Museum shown in Plate 196 of a sailing vessel surrounded by an arrangement of knots.

During the second half of the nineteenth century sailors made macramé using string and rope to create edges, fringes, nets and mats. Nets and mats were needed in places where the sails chafed against the mast or ropes and could have been damaged. A more important use of nets was as a safety precaution under the bowsprit and other places where men were in danger of falling off and would need to be caught. Such rope

work had a practical value, but other, less functional 'fancy-work' was employed to adorn objects of everyday use. The handles of buckets, water casks and sea-chests, and the D-shaped handles on duffel-bags, which could be locked, were also ornately woven. Rope ends were grafted with 'nettles' to make it easier to reeve them through blocks. Turk's-heads were applied to sounding poles, oars and the like. Railings were often grafted along their entire length to improve their grip. Varied and attractive designs appeared on bell ropes and on the handles of canvas bags sailors carried to hold their repair kit when they went aloft to make good damaged sails.

Scrimshaw, the general term used to describe bone and ivory objects carved and decorated by sailors, was most commonly carried out on board whaling vessels. Whether this skill started with American sailors carving the teeth of sperm whales caught in the South Seas or whether it was practised by sailors from other countries at the same time is not known, but the technique was used by many British seafarers. Travelling north to Greenland, they worked on baleen, the 'whalebone' of the eighteenth and nineteenth centuries. These pieces of horny material with hairy edges act as a huge sieve in the mouths of the baleen or 'right' whales, separating their food from the sea water. The baleen, when scraped and smoothed, provided an excellent surface for decoration.

The origin of the word scrimshaw is uncertain. Whaling captains set their crews to 'scrim shandering', probably during periods of enforced idleness, and hence the generic name. Some sailors, more gifted than others, were persuaded to make items for other seamen as this account by the carpenter of the *Duncombe* in 1820 indicates:

I was often employed in what the sailors dignified by the title of 'bone-carving', which art consisted in cutting on the bone, with the pen-knife, divers cyphers of the initials of their sweetheart, with borders of diamonds, squares or vandykes or 'tooth ornaments'; the interstices were filled up

Plate 194 Ship in bottle set within a wooden frame so making a picture out of the work, total length 14½ inches, 10 inches high, c.1900. The fine detail on the ship suggests this is a model made by a sailor for his own use; the ship touches the bottle top, bottom, front and back while tiny beads are used for blocks in the rigging. The wood surround has been made from an old tea chest

with chalk and oil, which brought out the patterns; in addition to the given round of ornaments, I could add panels of whales, ships, birds and the Prince of Wales feathers – the latter was a stock ornament at that period; besides, if it had not been so, what tar in 1820 could be so disloyal as to forget the Prince Regent, afterwards George the Fourth, of 'pious memory'? For these ornate decorations I received sundry mess-pots of grog.

In *Moby Dick* the American writer Herman Melville mentions the jack-knife as the main tool for scrim shandering, but improvised files, converted chisels and gimlets fashioned from nails may also have been used. The sailor's needle was the most versatile tool: it could be used for piercing and boring as well as pricking and scratching. Some whalebone could be worked while 'fresh', but older material had to be softened by soaking in brine. Whalebone and teeth and walrus tusks were considered to be the best

materials. As late as 1906 a young apprentice on board one of the last sailing ships recorded making and decorating objects at sea.

Once prepared and fashioned, designs were engraved in the surface with a sharp needle using a combination of lines and dots. Rubbing with a mixture of black ink and soot brought out the fine decoration on the creamy white background. Some were extremely delicate, exploiting the qualities of fine engraving. Designs, stylised to suit the medium, often had a naïve quality. The most popular subject was life on board ship and fond memories of home. Teeth were likely to be decorated with female figures or whaling scenes. Life on board ship provided a directory of ornaments: knots in the rigging, stars in the heavens, the figurehead and the stern board of the ship, fish of the sea, birds, boats and casks, bells, the anchor and so on. Some of the finest and most elaborate work was often based on drawings or engravings in books or illustrated papers, and often included patriotic motifs and symbols. The

Plate 195 ABOVE TOP: Woolwork picture NELSON carried out in the
patriotic colours of red, white and blue, late nineteenth century, about
30 inches wide; ABOVE: Woolwork picture by a sailor, of HMS
Serapis showing the vessel fully dressed with all flags displayed, about
30 inches wide, late nineteenth century

busk, with its more personal connotation,
attracted sentimental imagery. The flat, ruler-
like 'stay', made of plated whalebone some
two inches wide, was worn in the corset of
the nineteenth-century costume and prepared
by sailors for wives and loved ones (see Plates
197 and 198).

Other practical objects made on board
ship involved a great deal of ingenuity. Pastry-
cutters, needlework tools and walking-sticks
were common examples. Recreational activities of the nineteenth century included games
of cribbage, chess and dominoes. Often the
pieces for these were carved from bone, whale
ivory or walrus tusks. Some were also carved
from wood or cut from scrap brass.

Skilful and inventive, sailors improvised

Plate 196 Sailor's ropework arranged to form a
decorative frame round a print of the *Cutty Sark*,
15 × 15 inches, 1965

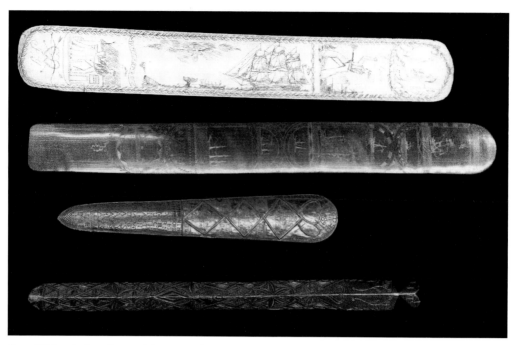

Plate 197 Stay busks with incised decoration, longest 15 inches. LEFT: White whalebone engraved with whaling scene, Britannia, a sailor and the sailor's return, inscribed 'J. Dare', nineteenth century; CENTRE LEFT: Whalebone inlaid with pique, inscribed 'To a valued Friend 1821'; CENTRE RIGHT: Whalebone engraved 'John Young August the 2 1789 mary Mays/When the ship does safe return let the church join the hearts in one. Benjamin Mays Mary Mays Samuel Mays'; RIGHT: Chipped and carved wood, inscribed on the back: 'The Gift is small but Love is All. Marey Oran, 1788' with an anchor in the centre and the initials 'I.T.'

Plate 198 Scrimshaw, engraved on pieces of the lower jaw of a whale; each about 6 inches long, nineteenth century

different materials to produce a wide range of objects; these included sail rubbers, paintings, drawings and patchwork. A carpenter on board the aircraft carrier HMS *Indefatigable* at the end of the Second World War made a bowl 12 inches across and inlaid it with eight different types of New Zealand woods. Other objects include a variety of decorated brass tobacco boxes intended for snuff, their lids painstakingly decorated with a punched design, some of which incorporate the sailor's own name. One design shows an early iron-clad vessel, similar to HMS *Warrior*, sur-rounded by a laurel-wreath motif with the name of 'Rt. Giddy' and the date 1864. Dolls and Jumping Jacks fashioned out of scrap pieces of turned wooden oars or spars were also popular. These simple but evocative figures have a powerful, almost magical qual-ity conveying good luck, and were given as presents to families and children at home. Carved and scratched decoration on such exotic items as coconut shells and ostrich eggs invariably had a nautical flavour.

Not all sailors' work was made as gifts,

however. A retired whaler named Johnny Harrison decorated the outside of his Shetland croft some years ago using a variety of shells. Patterns, arranged in panels, were made up from scallop, mussel and limpet shells used to colourful and attractive effect.

Customs and Ceremonies

Ceremonies such as 'crossing the line' or 'selling the dead horse' provided opportunities to dress up and were occasions for music and dancing. For 'crossing the line', when the ship went over the equator, novice members of the crew were subject to special rites by a sailor dressed as 'King Neptune'. 'Selling the dead horse' occurred after a month at sea when a symbolic wooden horse was thrown overboard denoting the end of the period in which sailors, in practice, often worked for no wages. The first month's pay was often pledged to an agent who had got them on board and the casting off of the 'dead horse' had practical as well as symbolic significance.

The whaling trade had a curious variation on the May Day customs celebrated on land. At midnight on 30 April each year a garland was hoisted in the middle of the main top gallant stay by the youngest married man on board. This May Day emblem took the form of a circlet wound around with ribbons given by wives and sweethearts as love-tokens and charms to bring luck to the fishery. The garland, usually surmounted by the silhouette of a sailing ship, was left hanging from the rigging until the vessel returned to harbour when there would be a race with the Trinity House navigation school to clamber up the mast and compete for possession of the weather-beaten trophy. In the painting 'The *Harmony* Of Hull' in Plate 199, a garland can be seen hanging between the fore and main masts.

The hoisting of the garland was followed, in the early hours of the morning

Plate 199 *The Harmony of Hull*, attributed to W. J. Huggins but probably a copy by Wheldon. An American-built barque, the *Harmony* was a typical whaler, and is shown here with whale jaw bones tied to the masts as a sign of a successful voyage and a May Day garland suspended between the fore and main masts; 37 × 49 inches, c.1860

(which in northern latitudes was almost as bright as day), by a ceremony paralleling that performed when a vessel crossed the equator. 'Neptune' appeared on deck, accompanied by other members of the crew dressed as his wife, a barber and two policemen. Men making their first visit to the Arctic, known as greenhands, were taken captive by the two 'bobbies' who ensured that their faces were well daubed with a mixture of grease and tar before being scraped by the 'barber' wielding a large mock razor made from hoop iron. Presents of sugar, tea, tobacco and spirits, to ensure gentle treatment, were shared by the crew. Insufficiently generous sailors were roughly handled before being dumped in a tub of water. A fiddler accompanied the revels.

The sailors' May Day garland recalls the Maidens' Garland, once common in parts of England. Maidens' Garlands were usually made in the form of a circle or crown of bent hazel rods (first-year hazel stems without blemish were specially cut). The rods were bound in white parchment and decorated with circular white parchment flowers painted with black crosses; some had white gloves cut out of parchment. The garlands were hung in church to commemorate the death of a parishioner who had been born and baptised in the parish and who had led an unblemished life. Such tributes were often paid to young and unmarried girls but boys and older people were also celebrated. The garlands were carried in the funeral processions and hung for three Sundays under the church gallery when in theory objections could be raised to the award. They were then hung from the roof of the chancel, where they remained untouched until they fell to pieces.

In some areas the garlands were originally of actual flowers – lilies and roses – and the gloves of white kid. By the later 1830s, however, the practice was already dying out and the garlands were imitative rose and lilies wreathed round a bough of peeled willow – a pair of gloves cut out in white paper and a white handkerchief, also of paper, on which was written a text. The use of garlands to signify a celebration of some sort dates back many hundreds of years.

TRENCH ART

Objects produced by members of the armed forces, particularly during time of war, served not only to pass the time but was a way of enhancing the often hard and bleak conditions. Objects such as knitted scarves (RAF Museum, Hendon) were practical, others were decorative and celebratory with an emotional and morale-boosting value for those involved. The decoration of the nose cones of aircraft, for example, asserts a resilient spirit demonstrating that at times of war artists could be witty, skilled and observant. Cartoon images of St George slaying the dragon or film star pin-ups were part of a desire to 'personalise' anonymous craft and make them their own.

Trench art, the general name given to objects made by members of the military forces, and presumably derived from items made in the trenches in the First World War, has been extended to include items made by all serving members of the armed forces. It also covers items made by British prisoners of war held overseas who were not necessarily members of the forces, and 'cone art' – the decoration of aircraft in both the First and Second World Wars. Prisoners of war, despite their highly restricted living conditions, produced skilful and imaginative objects, with some of the most detailed made by French prisoners of war held in British jails during the Napoleonic Wars. Bone and finely carved wood was fashioned into intricate models of ships, toys, games and so on, but fall outside the scope of this book because they were made by overseas prisoners. Examples are held in museums at Luton, Hull, Whitby and Peterborough, and the National Maritime

Plate 200 Vase, button-hook and letter-knife made
from shell case, spent bullets, parts of machinery and
shrapnel, and brought to a high polish by Percy Roberts
Thomas, about 6 inches tall, made during the First
World War

Museum in London.

Excellent work was made by members
of the British armed forces as well as by
British PoWs held overseas, particularly in the
Far East. In addition to the large collection in
London's Imperial War Museum, there are
examples in the Army Museum and other
collections. The work was usually carried out
in quiet-time either on leave or in camp and
typical materials used were those which
related directly to contemporary experience.
Shell-cases and spent bullets, parts of machinery and shrapnel, assembled, filed and polished to give a high finish were all used. The
brass vase, button-hook and letter-knife in
Plate 200, made by Percy Robert Thomas of
HMS *Nicator*, are fine examples of objects
made on shore leave. The knife handle is
built up from bolts and washers polished
smooth.

Objects were also made as toys for
children or souvenirs for loved ones at home.
A small aeroplane constructed out of an
empty bullet cartridge-case would have the
simple attraction both as a toy and, for the
marker, a memento. Models of tanks and
aircraft were also common. When raw
materials were in short supply during wartime, imaginative use was made of discarded
materials: cigarette lighters could be fashioned

out of brass buttons or model aircraft built
out of matchsticks.

For prisoners of war, one of the biggest
problems was to while away the hours at a
time of great uncertainty and deprivation.
Yet given the scarcity of materials and the
lack of proper tools the detail and skill
of work using available material is often
remarkable. Newspapers were produced
complete with illustrations, while objects
made included handbags, trophies, souvenirs
and jewellery. Plate 201 shows a teapot made
in a PoW camp from recycled food tins which
is a highly decorative object as well as a
functional piece of work. Unfortunately,
there is often little recorded information
about the makers of these objects and many
items donated by families to public collections
carry little detail other than the name of the
maker.

Like much other home-from-home
work, trench art is characterised by its self-
referential nature, whether in choice of available material, subjects depicted (such as aircraft or tanks), in the decoration or inscriptions which may include the names of fellow
soldiers or prisoners, company badges and so
on. It may be that particular subjects and
decoration referring to war and the experience
of individuals in wartime make these objects
of particular interest to such official organis-

Plate 201 Teapot made from recycled tins of Cow Bell
whole milk powder in a prisoner of war camp in France
in the early years of the Second World War, about 6
inches tall

Plate 202 Two solid wooden pipes carved with the badge of the Durham Light Infantry and the names of soldiers, about 6 inches long, Second World War

ations as museums. This may explain why so many objects on this theme are in such collections, given by friends and relatives keen to preserve a memory. The objects and the memories they record are in stark contrast to official histories for they embody real and vivid personal experiences. In official collections they are a reminder of the individual history in collective action.

Carving and fashioning wood was one of the most popular skills and many hours were spent on some pieces. During the First World War a common practice was to fashion small boxes from damaged aircraft propellers. Many such boxes have survived, some made out of laminated mahogany and American walnut, all varying in size and curvature of outline according to how far from the hub the section was cut. The making of souvenir trinket-boxes from damaged blades was a favourite occupation of mechanics with the Royal Naval Air Service and the Royal Flying Corps. Sometimes the actual hub was converted into a clock or barometer case.

Plate 203 Darts trophy 'Mark Time' in the form of a shield about 15 inches tall, inlaid with aluminium, inscribed 'No 3 PoW Camp Bandoeng, Jarva 1943', designed by F/O Scales and engraved by Gunner Lightfoot

In London's Imperial War Museum two solid carved wooden pipes are embellished in low relief with the badge of the Durham Light Infantry, together with the names and rank of soldiers; the maker carved the pipe as a souvenir recording the comradeship of shared times (see Plate 202). More practical objects were jewellery-boxes with a marquetry top, often fashioned from discarded cigar boxes, and cigarette boxes with poker-work decoration. A mah-jong set made in the

Plate 204 Mess tin about 7 inches long engraved with an image of St George Slaying the Dragon and the badges of different regiments by R. G. Dumas, a prisoner of war in Sumatra 1945

women's PoW camp in Sumatra 1942–45 has survived with all 144 pieces intact, the traditional flowers replaced by national flowers of the British Isles. In PoW Camp No. 3, a wooden darts trophy 'Mark Time', in the form of a shield and inlaid with aluminium, was designed by F/O S. Scales and engraved by Gunner Lightfoot (see Plate 203).

In the Second World War aluminium was one of the materials to hand in the form of mess tins (a lid and a base) and eating irons (knife, fork, spoon). From these, prisoners made boxes, soap-dishes, cigarette cases and the like with punched decoration on the lid. A decorated square mess tin engraved on its base with an image of St George slaying the dragon, by R. G. Dumas, a prisoner of war in Sumatra in 1945, is a particularly effective use of material and technique. Around the edge an ornate arch of oriental origin adds an exotic touch (see Plate 204). During the war St George appeared on gold coinage and on the George Cross; the oriental arch could have been based on a design seen on a cigarette packet. A private in the Army Service Corps, 35 Div. 1914–18, Algernon George Daiker, fashioned a metal salt spoon, probably from scrap material. Other spoons were engraved with the regimental badge and the names of members of the company.

Only occasionally have items of jewellery survived, though it is likely that many such pieces were made. In the Imperial War Museum an aluminium finger ring with an inlaid cross in copper, made from German

materials, is a gruesome memento. From PoW camps came a variety of small jewellery items including a black and white pin carved from the handle of a toothbrush.

Embroidery, appliqué work and knitting were also popular. Soldiers in the nineteenth century, recovering in hospital, sometimes made patchwork coverlets from the pieces of heavy cloth used for uniforms, as shown in the painting in Plate 205, 'A Crimean Casualty' (1856). A bedspread or rug made from soldiers' uniforms by David Hill (1838–97) is in Buckinghamshire County Museum, Aylesbury. Hill, a soldier, was wounded at the Siege of Lucknow in 1857 and made the cover whilst recuperating. He lived at Cheddington and later at Whitchurch where he kept the Chandos Arms. So popular was the activity that various manufacturers

Plate 205 *A Crimean Casualty*, by T. W. Woods, 1856. The painting shows Private Thomas Walker sewing a bedcover from pieces of army uniform as he recovers in hospital from a fractured skull he received during the Battle of Inkerman. A similar patchwork bedspread of tunic material made in Glasgow's Maryhill Barracks in the 1880s by Sergeant M. R. Cumming, Highland and Light Infantry, is in the city's Kelvingrove Museum and Art Galleries

Plate 206 Bedcover made from military uniforms by retired soldier. It has a central design of flags and the initials V. R.; late nineteenth century, about 96 inches long

Plate 207 Soldier's woolwork picture with a design based on various campaigns of the Second World War, about 15 inches tall. It shows the regimental badge of the Royal Artillery, African Star, Italy Star, Defence medal and Campaign medal, suggesting that the piece was finished after the war was over

sold bundles of pieces that could be used for this purpose. A brightly coloured patchwork with a design of crossed flags surrounded by an elaborate border makes effective use of traditional motifs and the material available (see Plate 206).

Embroidery was a time-consuming, skilled activity carried out by both men and women. The soldier's woolwork picture in Plate 207 incorporates emblems relating to different campaigns of the Second World War arranged in a neat geometrical design. A fascinating group of embroideries are beautifully sewn regimental badges carried out on cotton squares. Detailed and intricate, they are thought to be the work of members of the armed forces, made either during or after the First World War, possibly carried out as occupational work in hospital. They may have been intended either to be framed or made into cushion covers. Equally intriguing is an embroidered and appliquéd felt handbag. The scenes of war and protest slogans which make up the design were carried out by prisoners held as suspected aliens on the Isle of Wight at the outbreak of the Second World War. Other items include a tray cloth embroidered with the autographed names of prisoners from Yangchow. These can all be found in the Imperial War Museum, London.

Many examples exist of painting and drawing. In the collection of the Imperial War Museum, sketchbooks by soldiers record activities in camp, as well as scenes of life overseas on active service. An excellent example of a painted canvas kitbag by Private M. E. Brooks, bearing his name and a painting of Japan's Mount Fuji probably based on a picture postcard, can also be found in the museum.

Nose art decoration was carried out by airmen on the nose cones of aircraft, particularly in the First and Second World Wars, and was very much a collective effort. In the First World War and for the ten years following, there was little official restraint on how aircraft could be decorated or on the range of designs. Training instructors, for example, had their own aircraft and decorated it with a variety of geometrical and stylised

Plate 208 Martin Baltimore and crew, No. 13 Squadron, with the painted decoration 'Glamour Pants'

designs which had a practical as well as an aesthetic function – the plane of a particular pilot could be quickly identified and the aircraft more easily seen in the sky. The Wireless Training School at Biggin Hill also had particularly distinctive motifs.

In the Second World War aircraft were generally assigned a permanent ground crew of a rigger and a fitter. This crew would maintain the craft mechanically and repair the fabric; and it was they who would paint on any designs or decorations. The pilot and aircrew would usually have the aircraft for a limited period and on landing would hand it back to the ground crew. Aircrew would discuss the decorations but had no materials to apply it, and it was left to the ground crew to paint on the design. Fitters and riggers, unlike pilots, were usually non-commissioned and chosen for their technical and practical skills rather than class or social background. A favourite recruiting source of skilled technicians was from among railway workers who had served an apprenticeship of several years making precision parts, learning machine-modelling and hand-fitting. They qualified as

some of the finest engineers of the day and their skills were needed to build and repair the complex engine and airframes of aircraft. A strict hierarchy prevailed in the Air Force which divided manual workers, who got 'their hands dirty', from officers.

Decoration on aircraft was usually limited to tail-fins or the cockpit and imagery was often taken from a wide range of popular motifs including the cinema, music-hall and comic books. The film *Cleopatra* with its exotic images, the cartoon character 'Old Bill' and, from music-hall, 'the Flapper', were all featured. Other motifs include a fanciful dragon accompanied by the word '*Hofook*', Chinese for 'hello'. In the inter-war years official rules were passed defining more rigorously the regular markings on aircraft and restricting what was acceptable. From 1932 only the number of the squadron was allowed and individual endeavour was restricted to badges within which various motifs could be painted. Though popular cartoon characters were occasionally used, the stylised markings of chequers, lines and stripes were most common.

Plate 209 Avro Lancaster I with painted insignia 'Old Fred', referring to the aircraft code F for Freddie; the 49 roundels indicate the number of sorties made to targets in Germany and occupied Europe

The Second World War brought a relaxing of these rules and ground crews once again gave aircraft individual decoration celebrating and recording the success of the aircrew. Such decoration was largely carried out by bomber crews whose aircraft tended to last longer, rather than fighter aircraft which normally survived only a short time. Often there was an unofficial squadron artist chosen through aptitude rather than training whose job it was to carry out the decoration. The crew posed in front of the aircraft *Glamour Pants* are clearly proud of a design which incorporates an image of Mickey Mouse (see Plate 208).

On bomber aircraft the motifs, arrangement and presentation recall in size and composition the heraldic markings of medieval knights. There is just such a feeling to the roundels and caricature on *Old Fred*, a bomber which flew in the Second World War (see Plate 209). Just as those armour-encased warriors needed to be clearly identified, so the most impersonal aircraft could express the hopes and achievements of the airmen.

A particularly skilful example is St George slaying the dragon. Bomber aircrews, permanently attached to one particular aircraft, would discuss marking the plane with a name for the craft and a 'history' of the raids undertaken as well as a bomb symbol indicating a raid. On bomber aircraft such as the Lancaster and the Halifax, markings were confined to the nose panels.

For more formal, heraldic squadron badges rough ideas would be worked out by the aircrew and their ideas fitted into an acceptable official form by the College of Heralds. A well-known popular example is the 617 'Dam Busters' Squadron. Their badge, devised by the crew, describes vividly their most acclaimed achievement by showing a dam blasted in the centre, three lightning flashes and a flood pouring out from the breach.

Just as the regulations about aircraft decoration were relaxed in the Second World War, so a greater flexibility was allowed between various jobs. The Air Force, at the forefront of technological change, selected pilots and crews based on their ability to carry out the job rather than on their education and background. In the middle of the war aptitude-testing was introduced to identify airmen who could do the job best. A pilot, never lower in rank than a sergeant, need not be an officer. The end of the war brought this flexibility to an end and with it the freedom to 'personalise' aircraft.

The art of making objects was con-tinued by National Service conscripts, a favourite item being a decorative calendar on which the whole of the two years was marked in days. As the days passed, they were duly ticked off. Not all decoration was confined to aircraft. A tank used at the end of the First World War in the Imperial War Museum has an eye painted on either side, adding to its frightening image.

PRISONERS' ART

Like serving members of the armed forces, prison inmates have many hours in which to make objects, and this section is concerned with art produced in such circumstances (rather than objects produced by prisoners of war). Prisoners' backgrounds and training vary greatly but much of the work, made mostly by untrained working-class men and women, often reflects their status as prisoners who have few rights and privileges and access to only limited facilities. Much of the work made is time-consuming, laborious and detailed, carried out to fill empty hours with some sort of satisfying creative work, and ranges from matchstick models and ceramic pots to paintings and drawings. In more recent years prisoners have been able to make use of a wider range of materials compared to the nineteenth century, when only those locally available could be used. Slate, used for roof-covering, is easily workable, its softness providing a good surface on which to work complex and ornate designs. A slate roof-tile in Portland Museum, engraved with a formal rococo design by a convict in Portland Prison, commemorates the death of Chief Warder Brooks who died of 'apoplexy' while on duty in 1881. Detailed and intricate, the design is painstaking in its precision, recalling the decoration on gravestones (see Plate 210).

A relief wood-carving in the style of medieval work showing two figures in old-fashioned dress, now in Ipswich Museum, was made in the middle of the nineteenth century by a prisoner (see Plate 211). Skilfully carved and coloured with matt pigment, the piece appears to be the work of a trained carver. Such objects are relatively rare; only in the post-Second World War period have prisoners been given more opportunity to explore individual expression with official recognition of its importance. It may be that earlier work exists but has not yet come to

Plate 210 Engraved slate memorial to the memory of Chief Warder Brooks, HM Portland Prison, 'who died of apoplexy' in January 1881

Plate 211 Carving of David slaying Goliath with a stone in a sling, carved wood with coloured pigment, mid-nineteenth century

Plate 212 Head of Christ carved in sandstone by Hugh Collins in Barlinnie Prison, about 12 inches tall, 1970s

light. In some progressive prisons adequate and full provision has been given to enable prisoners to explore different forms of expression. Not all prisoners' work is made purely for creative reasons, however. In 1980 two prisoners, William Boardman and Vincent Mason, at Fetherstone Prison, Wolverhampton, during pottery classes held there, made pots imitating the work of the well-known potter Bernard Leach. These were successfully sold in London auction rooms before being recognised as fakes. In most cases prisoners use available facilities for more innocent pastimes.

At the Special Unit of Glasgow's Barlinnie Prison, prisoners have had the opportunity to work with a variety of different materials. Several modelled clay or carved stone producing excellent creative pieces far beyond any therapeutic value involved in the making of the work. With instruction kept to a minimum, there were no set art classes but materials and facilities were provided which prisoners were encouraged to use. Inmates saw other prisoners at work, or talked to visiting artists, but there was little formal teaching. For firing ceramic pieces and glazing, a certain amount of technical expertise was required but this did little to hinder the flow of ideas or to inhibit work.

Tom Galloway, a prisoner at the Barlinnie Special Unit, worked almost exclusively with clay. By the standards of academic work the modelling appears 'crude' but the power of the pieces and their ability to communicate deep and passionate feelings is clear. Titles such as 'Rejection', 'Down and Out', 'Man in the Electric Chair', 'Rock Bottom' and 'Frustration' testify to the autobiographical concerns and the almost desperate need to express and hence share these feelings. 'There is,' wrote Cordelia Oliver, 'something absolutely stark and basic about the few works I have seen by Tom Galloway; something which reminds me of the crude, but often frighteningly expressive figures, symbols and incidents carved on the backs of medieval gravestones in ancient churchyards.' Another prisoner in the Special Unit of Barlinnie

Plate 213 The *Mary Rose*, a scale model galleon made from matchsticks with painted decoration, about 120 inches tall, 1980s

Prison, Hugh Collins, carved a large-scale sculpture of Jesus Christ with explicit anatomical detail to which some took exception (see Plate 212). Hewn from ten tons of sandstone, it was a commission intended for the Church of Columba. The members of

Plate 214 Matchbox model of a prison cell, complete with minute detail including bed and window frames, about 10 inches tall, 1980s

the church did not accept the statue but its forceful carving has been widely acknowledged as a 'major piece of work'.[1]

Throughout the prison service there is a recognition of the value of arts and crafts, even though opportunities and facilities vary greatly from prison to prison. The efforts of the Koestler Awards in promoting and displaying prisoners' creative work (which includes arts and crafts, writing and music composition) has brought it to the attention of a wide number of people. Founded by the writer Arthur Koestler in 1962, the award, a registered charity, operates in conjunction with the Home Office which organises exhibitions of work. Annual shows in London are large in size and illustrate well the levels of skill, the range of materials used and the themes and subjects followed. The 25th Anniversary Exhibition of Prisoners' Art (October 1986) in London had nearly 250 visual art

Plate 215 *My Cell*, about 12 inches long, 1980s

entries from male and female prisoners across the country. Only the name of the prison is given so the artists remain anonymous.

Work made includes paintings and drawings, thrown and handbuilt pots, ceramic models, calligraphy, textiles, knitting, embroidery and, perhaps most impressive, matchstick models ranging from tiny boxes, miniature prison cells to huge sailing vessels. The 1986 show was dominated by the eight-foot galleon the *Mary Rose* in full sail shown in Plate 213 (from Leyhill); also on

Plate 216 *What Will I Do Now?*, watercolour
depicting an atomic explosion and the prison walls
topped with barbed wire, as seen through the bars of
a cell, about 12 inches high, 1980s

Plate 217 *Glasgow the Dear Green City*, picture made
from tacks and silk thread in support of the football
club Rangers against rivals Celtic, about 14 × 14
inches, 1980s

show was a model of a Harley Davidson motor-cycle (Wakefield), a snooker table (Kingston) and several traditional 'gypsy' caravans, each constructed in great detail. The model of a prison cell shown in Plate 214 is carried out with chilling detail.

Throughout these exhibitions two main themes recur. One is the self-referential nature of the subject, concerned for the most part with scenes and details of prison life; often these are presented in a straightforward representational style, such as 'My Cell' (Plate 215) but some follow more abstract or expressionistic modes as in 'What Will I Do Now' (Plate 216). Prisoners lying in beds in small brick-walled cells, the prison routine and so on, capture the feeling of forced, closed community life, or attempts at privacy and at efforts to sustain individual dignity. Others reflect specific interests; one ingenious piece made from pin-tacks and coloured satin thread, used emblems of two football teams to encapsulate the clash between Glasgow's Celtic and Rangers (see Plate 217).

Against the 'I am here' images can be contrasted the theme of freedom, the world of the romantic free-wheeler, who without a care can travel freely, having adventures without hindrance. They suggest a deep-felt yearning for an 'innocent' life, often based on vivid but remote mythology in which reality has little part. Themes such as a horse ranch or gypsy caravans shown in the most detailed way and faithful to traditional design, galleons in full sail on the high seas and the highly stylish Harley Davidson motorbike, are all highly symbolic of a desire for freedom and escape. At the same time such objects present an excellent opportunity for detailed, painstaking work, requiring many hours of labour-intensive industry to collect match-sticks, build up the models, devise construction methods and even produce working drawings. 'Matchstick models' combine a useful occupational therapy with a creative element. The models are 'real' but also evoke a powerful element of a romantic fiction.

CANAL BOAT ART

Canal boats, or more correctly, narrow boats, are long boats used to transport goods on the canals. Almost since they were built in the second half of the eighteenth century and throughout much of the nineteenth and early twentieth centuries, the boats have been highly decorated with traditional and improvised scenes. When around 1830 the railways started to compete with canals, many canal boatmen found that the only way they could survive financially was to have their families living and working with them on board. Life in the small cabins, measuring only ten feet or so long was cramped and unhygienic, but, like travellers' caravans, the living space was carefully organised with no inch wasted.

The interior was usually ornately decorated with elaborate paintwork and graining; fine crochet-work curtains screened the sleeping quarters and space was even found to display ornamental plates and glass pictures. The boat itself was painted both inside and out as were most of the implements used on board such as water-cans and pails, dippers and stools. Typical decoration consisted of painted pictorial scenes of castles, bridges and lakes, picturesque landscapes in the tradition of European high art but rendered in a broader and more colourful style.

Decoration on narrow boats had evolved by the mid-nineteenth century. It was described as 'landscape in which there is a lake, a castle, a sailing boat and a range of mountains'[2] and similar decoration continued to be used throughout the commercial life of canals. Other motifs included roses and symbols of good luck taken from playing card designs such as the ace of clubs and the ace of diamonds and so on, as well as elaborate and ornate lettering. All was painted in four basic colours of green, black, red and blue. Items like seat boards and bread-boards often received special treatment in terms of composition because they offered a 'canvas', but all the objects used were decorated including buckets and water-cans (see Plates 218, 219 and 220).

Boats were painted at yards around the country, including ones at Rickmansworth, Leighton Buzzard and Northwich, with one of the workers specialising in painting the traditional styles. A skilled eye could recognise where the painting had been carried out. Painters were known and were highly respected for their skills, including Frank Jones of Leighton Buzzard whose work is on show in Luton Museum and Art Gallery, and Isaiah Atkins of Polesworth boatyard (Stoke Bruerne Waterway Museum). In addition to the need for a sound knowledge of the craft of painting in which many coats were required to obtain the correct surface, the painter had

Plate 218 Seat board by Frank Jones of Leighton Buzzard, about 24 inches long, 1946. The board has a central painted landscape of a castle and a river which is framed by two groups of roses on a dark green ground. Seat boards were used at meal-times to provide additional seating

Plate 219 Water can with painted decoration of roses from Mr Townsend's narrow boat which operated along the
Thames from a wharf at Abingdon from the 1880s until the early years of this century

to follow the traditional manner of carrying out each motif so that the desired effect was achieved.

The painted designs and the actual structure of the cabin are thought to derive from different sources. The organisation of the 70-foot narrow boat had to allow the greatest space for cargo and the minimum for living accommodation. Cabins on board ships traditionally made efficient use of the space but the narrow boat's cabin, which had to house the entire family, is particularly intriguing in its ingenuity. Its ornateness and skilful making may have originated from the Romany Gypsies who settled in Britain in the mid-eighteenth century from Eastern Europe, though quite how this happened is not known. It is unlikely, however, that this is the source for the painting designs on narrow boats.

In his unpublished article *The Picturesque and Popular Taste*, Philip Pacey points out the absence of any picturesque paintings in gypsy caravans and the similarity in subject matter between narrow boats and the designs used on such popular items as japanned tin trays, enamel boxes, clock faces, wallpapers and window-blinds. Many were decorated with picturesque scenes: some were highly detailed, others were rendered in simpler, broader styles. In the early decades of the nineteenth century engravings after paintings were popular and relatively inexpensive. A relevant example is an engraving made around 1793 after J. Farington showing the Thames and Severn Canal at its junction with the Thames, with a circular lock house which is typical of this canal. The picturesque, both in painting and in landscape gardening, popular in the late eighteenth century, attracted a much wider audience in the following century. Castles, grottoes and ruins were being built, and there was a new awareness of 'history'.

Plate 220 Bread-board with a painted figure of a soldier on horseback from Mr Townsend's narrow boat which operated along the Thames from a wharf at Abingdon from the 1880s until the early years of this century

Nathaniel Whittock's *The Decorative Painter's and Glazier's Guide* (1827) illustrated picturesque landscape designs. Transfer patterns in earthenware pottery also include a range of landscapes.

Boat painters have continued to work in traditional styles up to the present day. Their work seems particularly bright and new when compared with older examples which have darkened with age, but it is the owner's desire to have the craft looking as fresh and gleaming as possible and this necessarily involves regular coats of paint. It is yet another example of how 'taste' is perceived within different groups of people. More muted decoration, which has the patina of age, is more likely to be preferable to the eyes of twentieth-century collectors than the apparently gaudy results of freshly carried out work which was the choice of workers who operated the boats – a further illustration of the importance of recognising and acknowledging 'taste' as a relative rather than an objective phenomenon.

Chapter Six

PICTURING THE WORLD

During much of the nineteenth century the fine arts of painting and sculpture, the two main areas of high art, were virtually the exclusive concern of the middle and upper classes. High art assumed great importance in validating the cultural values of society and was seen as expressing its creative and 'civilising' aspects. Painting and sculpture, and later photography, was shown in private and public art galleries, illustrated and discussed at length in the new art magazines and reviewed by critics in the popular press. High or academic art called on particular sensibilities and accepted conventions: it was produced mostly for sale to a knowledgeable and discerning public; it operated within an art market and was supported by a complex structure of galleries and writers who stressed its technical skill, its uniqueness and its creative and spiritual qualities.

Though very different from the paintings and sculptures produced by working-class men and women high art had a profound effect on many working-class artists; illustrated in magazines, displayed at fairgrounds, circuses, museums and art galleries (Sunday was known as 'people's day'), it informed and stimulated the imagination, presenting evidence of a particular sort of artistic genius and the uniqueness of the artistic vision. 'Art', it implied, could only be the product of refined and cultured minds.

How could working-class men and women even think of competing? Yet many did, finding their own styles and modes. A few, such as Elizabeth Ratcliffe and Joseph Browne whose work is discussed later in the chapter, emulated the style of high art but others found their own voice and way of working. Some translated the three-dimensional world and their experiences of it into pictures of their own imagining and making, devising their own way of showing space and handling colour. Others rivalled the skills of their more sophisticated peers with technical virtuosity. Many just enjoyed the activity of painting or modelling, driven by a desire to picture the world in a manner to which they could relate.

Practical, cultural and ideological factors helped shape painting, sculpture and photography by working-class people. Practical considerations include the availability of materials and equipment, their cost and the space in which to work. Few working-class homes have the luxury of a studio, a special room in which to paint, sculpt or take and develop photographs, so other means of carrying out these activities have to be found. This requires a great deal of improvisation, affecting the quality of the work. Culture refers here to the social and artistic background of the working classes with its emphasis on the practical, its enthusiasm for waste or found materials, its handling or even adaptation of familiar imagery, and of work produced for a particular group of people. Ideological factors are important because although they are dominated by the powerful influence and aesthetic criteria of the middle and upper classes in which great importance is placed on the artist's individual vision and the uniqueness of the work, working-class artists also act on the values and appreciative response of their own class, which may be in conflict with this sort of assessment.

Dominating aesthetic judgments are the

formalist considerations of art, the contemporary mode for assessing and analysing artworks. Formalist analysis places great emphasis on the form art takes, which may include style, its physical embodiment and the technical methods; subject, or content, is seen as a secondary consideration. Though form and content cannot readily be divided, the two aspects of art make up separate considerations. A formalist approach takes art out of its social, economic and cultural context and places it in its own autonomous sphere, giving it a special language and significance.

For working-class artists both form and content have particular meanings and importance dependent on cultural values quite different from those of the middle and upper classes. Usually the subject matter, the content, is more significant than technique or method. Painters and sculptors who study at art school or similar institutions learn the methods and techniques of art such as how to use paint to achieve particular effects, the rules of perspective and the considerations necessary to achieve successful compositions. They are also taught the 'language' of art which includes its code of classical, mythological and religious references, which are part of the conventions of easel painting. Equally, and perhaps most importantly, students at such established institutions as art schools have already been given one of the most privileged and special accolades of society – to be told they are special and unique with gifts of creativity and self-expression which can serve themselves and society. Working-class artists have no such recognition.

Some artists from working-class backgrounds found they could prosper in the art world by adopting accepted modes, and there are many examples of this in the past. William Blake trained as an engraver before establishing himself as an artist in his own right. Occasionally, artisan painters became established as fine artists, moving up the social ladder as they gained respectability. John Crome (1768–1821) was first apprenticed to a coach and sign painter before gaining a national reputation as a landscape artist, and George Morland (1763–1804) painted inn signs before his success as a painter of rural scenes. Other coach and sign painters who later became Royal Academicians include Charles Catton (1728–1798) and Richard Smirk (1778–1815).

But throughout most of the nineteenth century and the early part of the twentieth century fine art was almost exclusively the terrain of the middle and upper classes. By and large, artists who did attend art school, from whatever social and economic class, lie beyond the scope of this book which concentrates instead on art by working-class artists with little or no formal art training.

This brings up the controversial issue touched on in Chapter One of whether or not working-class men and women who produce art for their own or their friends' pleasure and enjoyment can accurately be called artists, and whether the work they produce can usefully be given the label 'art'. It is a question fundamental to this book, for even its title – *People's Art* – suggests the attribution 'art' is justified. But if the aesthetic conventions of high art are accepted and its largely unspoken codes understood, then it would appear that all artists must be taught in the academies and institutions which represent that point of view. Fortunately, such a mechanistic argument, though clear-cut, need not concern us for too long, for otherwise much of the world's greatest art can be dismissed because it was produced outside the academic tradition.

There are, however, difficulties in distinguishing in a non-pejorative way between high art and people's art. If the former is tutored, learnt, moulded, directed and unique, and the latter largely intuitive, self-directed and with no generally accepted form, then these are major and significant differences. But both are part of the spectrum of art for they are about the expressive and creative qualities of the individual. This is one of the central criteria for defining art.

Like all aesthetic and artistic critiques

there are no hard and fast rules upon which decisions with regard to quality, creativity, inventiveness, expressiveness and so on can be measured. Though each area needs to be considered, there is unlikely to be general agreement about why one piece of work is thought to be better than another. This is principally because the qualities which make up art are, in the last resort, undefinable rather than mechanical and measurable, and we have to trust the evidence of our own eyes.

Technical development and education

The development of painting and drawing in the period since 1750 is closely linked with the increasing availability of prepared paints, canvas and watercolours and the growing amount of leisure time. Painting and drawing could be carried out in relatively small spaces, materials were not bulky and it was an activity which could be done out of doors as well as inside. In the last decades of the eighteenth century the artists' colour suppliers Reeves & Son put manufactured watercolour cakes on the market, making well-prepared pigment generally available. By the 1840s tube paints, both oil and water-based, were in production. For the first time artists, freed from the need for a full technical training in the preparation of colours, had access to good – and portable – materials.

Publication of art periodicals and journals at the end of the nineteenth century also promoted and encouraged people to take up painting and drawing, as did manuals explaining various techniques. In the twentieth century local and national art societies (some factory-based or with specific mutual interests) were set up, providing a means of showing work as well as opportunities for like-minded people to meet and exchange views. More recently, programmes on television discussing practical aspects of visual art have attracted large audiences and stimulated new interest.

Towards the end of the nineteenth century cameras were produced which needed a minimum of equipment, were relatively simple to use and were sold at a price which was not prohibitive. Also at this time more people were able to enjoy greater leisure, so had time to paint and draw, to take photo- graphs and even to make sculpture. While high art remained the prerogative of the middle and upper classes, working-class artists were also finding ways of picturing the world.

The effects on people's art of compulsory free education, the opening of public art galleries and museums, and the reproduction of academic art in magazines were far-reaching. While working-class artists had previously called almost exclusively on their own experience, rooted in their own culture, they were now having to deal with imagery with which they rarely identified, with which they had little in common and whose complex language they often failed to appreciate. Illustrations and critical commentary proclaiming the values of, for example, abstract art encouraged working-class artists to copy style, but the results were poorly understood imitations. Such work looks, and often is, bad. More importantly, high art was put forward as superior to that by untrained artists, having the effect of suggesting that people's art was inferior and unimportant.

In the twentieth century further technical development affected the way art was perceived, presented and appreciated. The widespread use of photography and the appearance of high-quality reproductions of paintings in magazines and journals influenced artistic perception. The ability of the camera to produce an 'instant' image by the manipulation of basic equipment became for many artists a touchstone for what was considered 'good'. Many fine artists felt their role as individual creators was challenged by photography; art photographers claimed equal status with fine artists; and the representation of reality in photography seemed to

Plate 221 *Hammersmith Bridge on Boat-Race Day* by Walter Greaves, oil on canvas, 55 inches wide, painted around 1862 when the artist was about 16 years old

be the most accurate and desirable image. More sophisticated printing processes made reproductions of 'masterpieces' widely available at low cost, thus enabling virtually anyone to have a facsimile. This increased awareness of high art often resulted in a reproduction replacing home-made work, and in untrained artists modelling their work on that of the professional. At the same time many were encouraged and stimulated to produce their own work by emulating the aesthetics of high art.

The influence of the sophistication of the academic approach on a non-academic painter can be seen in the work of Walter Greaves (1846–1930). The son of a Thames waterman and boatman, Greaves trained in the technical aspects of painting while helping his father at Chelsea. At the age of 16 he painted 'Hammersmith Bridge on Boat Race Day', a crowded, jostling scene, primitive in feeling but highly evocative of mood and spirit (see Plate 221). A few years later he and his brother Henry met the American-born painter James McNeill Whistler and abandoned their own accomplished but naïve style in favour of aping, rather badly,

Whistler's Nocturnes. Walter Greaves's comment that 'Mr Whistler always used to say that to him a boat was a tone but to us it was always a boat', is an indication of the difference between them.

Partly in response to the use of photography and partly as a reaction to the changing attitudes of society in the early decades of the twentieth century, artists, dealers and critics started to evolve new theories of art which emphasised and confirmed its special role. The development of modernism, the general name given to the succession of avant-garde styles which have dominated art since the turn of the century, ensured that art remained within galleries to be appreciated by a relatively small group of well-educated and informed people. Ironically, the complex theories on which it relied made it, for some, even more inaccessible and remote, and artists and public turned to the direct and 'unsophisticated' qualities of 'naïvety' in art. Picasso and the cubists found great inspiration in the directness of African art while others were inspired by children's work or art by untaught artists. Painters such as Paul Klee, Henri Rousseau and L. S. Lowry quite consciously incorporated 'simple', 'primitive' and 'naïve' qualities in their work. As a result, their paintings communicated directly to people who failed to respond to the conventions of high art. L. S. Lowry's paintings of industrial cityscapes, for example, evoke the toil and weariness of factory work with which many identify. Yet Lowry was a professionally trained artist who deliberately chose to work in this particular style. His paintings of cities in which people seem to behave more like robots than human beings have a direct relevance and feeling conveyed by the apparent simplicity of the style, even though the painting was knowingly carried out and is actually highly sophisticated.

Many practising artists dubious of the ideas of modernism often responded quickly and positively to the work of untrained artists. In 1928 when Ben Nicholson and Christopher Wood came across the paintings of the retired fisherman Alfred Wallis in St Ives, Cornwall (whose work is discussed later in the chapter), their response was enthusiastic. Wood in particular was deeply influenced by Wallis's attitude and style and incorporated elements of it in his own work. Wallis, perhaps the best-known 'primitive' artist in this country, referred to Nicholson and Wood as 'real artists' without considering himself to be one.

Other discoveries came at much the same time. The poet and writer Valentine Ackland came across the work of John Craske in East Dereham, Norfolk. An ex-fisherman of Winterton, Craske had been paralysed as a result of being blown up in his ship whilst at sea during the First World War. He worked on almost any material to hand including cardboard, paper and pieces of wood. Other pictures were skilfully embroidered with bright wools on canvas or on one of his wife's pudding cloths. Dorothy Warren organised a successful exhibition for Craske in her London gallery.

In the 1930s a group of socially concerned artists, writers and photographers took a more systematic interest in the culture of the working class, setting up Mass Observa-

tion to study and record it. The artist Julian Trevelyan, a member of Mass Observation, in his autobiographical memoir *Indigo Days*, records meeting and admiring many self-taught 'Sunday painters' who had forged for themselves their own language. George, a Cockney market-trader, 'painted his own life, his wife ironing his shirt with the iron lying heavy on the place where the heart should have been, and himself selling stockings in the Caledonian Market'. A great admirer of abstract art, George was particularly impressed by the work of the Russian painter Vassily Kandinsky.

Trevelyan also mentions David Burton, a pavement artist, Stockley, a bus driver, and Madge Gill (1884–1933) who lived in East Ham, London. Each year in the East End Academy Gill showed paper rolls, sometimes as long as 100 feet, drawn with a pen. The line drawings, such as in 'Woman With Hat' moved tirelessly in and out creating 'strange flowers and sometimes strange faces that seemed to peer at one from another world'

Plate 222 *Woman with Hat* (detail) by Madge Gill, black ink on cardboard, about 39 inches tall, *c.*1950

(see Plate 222). She claimed to record messages from a spirit world that only she could tune in to; the scrolls were so long that she only saw them complete when displayed at the Whitechapel Gallery. As well as the scrolls carried out in coloured inks, she drew dark organic abstract designs, 'reminiscent sometimes of the hump-backed monsters of Miró or the prodigal nightmares of Ernst'.[3]

The creative exchange between high art and people's art, which has continued since the early years of the period, goes on. Such exchange includes subject matter, materials chosen and methods used, as well as in artistic interpretation (that is, what is accepted as constituting an aesthetic). Professional painters and sculptors draw on the energy and direction of art produced by working-class people: some adopt a clear, *faux-naïf* style such as in David Hockney's early paintings; others, like sculptor David Mach, utilise waste or scrap materials all want to devise an art form which has the ability to communicate as directly as possible with the audience. David Kemp (b.1945) draws ideas both from the discarded objects he finds, from the attitudes of society towards waste, and from religions of 'primitive' people. His sculptures assembled from scrap and discarded materials are shown in exhibitions with titles such as 'Immaculate Contraption', 'White Man's Magic', 'The Tailight Society' and 'The Refuse Collection'.

The naïve quality of people's art, however, is different from professional art; qualities often ascribed to people's art (such as 'simple', 'natural', 'spontaneous', 'unaffected' and 'unpretentious') signify immediate communication between the work, its maker and the viewer – terms rarely applied to academic art. Such terms also acknowledge the presence of a vital source, a creative urge, which flows from a knowledge of the material and gives it a sense of purpose and direction, positively identifying naïve qualities in the work. In contrast, professional naïve art is characterised by a particular use of colour, conscious stylisation in the representation of form and a deliberate avoidance of three-dimensional illusionistic painting. The artist who *knowingly* employs such a style is well aware of it and the effect fully intended. People's art arises through no conscious awareness about style but from a desire to express visually a feeling or impression, and the most effective way to communicate this is through painting or some other art form.

The description of the naïve qualities of people's art may imply that within each person there is an 'instinctive' or 'folk' memory, an inner sense of the visual, a common language which can be shared and understood which, given the right circumstances, will produce a free flow of imagery. The visual evidence of people's art – diverse, complex and variable – would refute such an idea. Communication occurs at many levels and is visually expressed in many styles, materials and forms. Some draws directly on tradition and some is modelled on the conventions of high art, but always extending and enriching it, its diverse manifestations within working-class communities still largely unstudied and unrecorded. This chapter sets out to discuss painting, sculpture and photography within its own contexts and institutions and to acknowledge the aesthetic intention of the maker.

PAINTING AND DRAWING

Painting and drawing are the most popular forms of people's art. Broadly, the diverse range of work produced can be discussed in two main though often overlapping areas. One is the work produced by artisan painters professionally concerned in some way with the painting trade – such as house, coach and sign painters – who also did portraits of people and animals, buildings, towns, ships, inn signs, police truncheons, even scenes on glass rolling-pins and the like. With no training in high art, their work is often described as 'naïve', 'primitive' or 'unsophisticated'. This category also includes itinerant artists who moved round the country seeking commissions. The other group is made up of artists, sometimes described as Sunday painters, who painted for their own satisfaction driven by an inner need, a desire to communicate through the visual image. Few had training as artists and most would claim to be 'self-taught' – truly artists who subscribed, quite unknowingly, to the notion of 'art for art's sake', picturing the world as a way of dealing with it.

Artisan Painters

As industry developed in the early years of the Industrial Revolution and the power of the industrialists grew, so the role of the church and the court in providing patronage for painters and sculptors diminished; the atelier system of training, of spending several years in the studio of an established artist, was largely replaced by study at an art academy. Although some had been set up in the seventeenth century it was not until the middle of the eighteenth century that a great expansion occurred and by 1790 well over a hundred art academies flourished throughout Europe including the Royal Academy in London which was founded in 1768. Industry and commerce encouraged a formal education in art and official support for academies increased. Inseparably linked to this was official enthusiasm for neo-classicism and the antique in general, which involved study of the great art of the past. At the same time a romantic notion developed around the artist, who was perceived as a genius who produced 'masterpieces' by dint of 'inspiration', who had a 'gift' to be nurtured. Thus the artist was seen as someone special and unique in society.

Traditionally, painters worked alongside other artisans in the decoration and ornamentation of buildings, often filling in the spaces between various architectural details according to what was required. The painters' guild ensured that all members received a proper training in the preparation and selection of pigments, the media in which they were mixed and the methods by which they should be applied to the surface. From 1625 it was obligatory for all shops and businesses to display a sign indicating their business and the nature of their trade, so giving employment to a large body of sign painters. William Hogarth (1697–1764), a great admirer of sign-painters' art, was greatly impressed by their ability to work to a strict set of requirements. In 1762 he organised what must have been the first exhibition of their work, partly as a spoof and partly as a means of drawing attention to them. The 'Grand Exhibition of the Society of Sign-Painters' was put on at Bonnell Thornton's Chambers

Plate 223 Painter's advertising sign by Andrew Doxsey, a 'Carriage and Likeness Painter Landscape and Herald Painter', which would be displayed in his workshop; oil on board, about 15½ × 13½ inches, c.1840. The portraits and vignettes show that the artist offered portrait and landscape, heraldry, sign and coach painting

Plate 224 *Tobacconist Shop* by Robert Allen, a 'writer and sign painter' who operated a tobacco and snuff shop, 1841

in London's Bow Street as a protest against the Italian 'grand manner' and as a demonstration of artists working outside establishment circles. An advertisement described it as 'a most magnificent collection of portraits, landscapes, seascapes, etc . . .'[4]

A law, passed in 1763, limiting the number of signs in the streets of London, had a profound effect on sign-painters who suddenly had no regular work and had to accept any painting jobs or else be forced to travel in search of work. These painters carried out portraits of prize animals often bred for their sheer size and splendour, as well as portraits of owners, coaches, houses and so on. In addition to painting houses, coaches and signs, artisan painters also depicted landscapes and portraits as well as their own compositions. Local trade directories listed names, addresses and professions: 'fine artists' were listed as 'Artists, Portrait, Landscape, Miniature', while artisan painters were found under 'Painters, House, Signs, etc'. Some were placed under 'Plumbers and

Glaziers'. A clear separation existed between the two groups both in social status and the professional way they approached their work.

With no academic training in anatomy, the theory of perspective or classical subject matter, artisan painters mainly took their subjects from the world in which they lived. Style was interpretative rather than realistic with its chief function to represent the subject and capture some essence of it. Andrew Doxsey's advertising sign (c.1840) indicates the artist's own ability at painting portraits, landscapes, notices and the like (see Plate 223). Sign-painters often decorated the outside of their shop to illustrate their skills with the brush and then painted a portrait of the building such as 'Tobacconist Shop' (1841), by Robert Allen, a 'writer and sign-painter'. The detailed and meticulous study illustrates the skills of the artist as well as serving as a useful advertisement for his services (see Plate 224). An unusual exception is the religious painting 'Abraham Offering Up his Son Isaac' (c.1830) by an unknown artist, which clearly calls on classical conventional art yet has its own naïve, highly expressive style (see Plate 225). Religious paintings are rare in Protestant Britain, but this picture vividly suggests the exotic location while conveying the narrative.

Reflecting the revolution taking place in agriculture, artisan painters carried out portraits of prize animals often bred for their sheer size and splendour. Painted portraits of such animals were virtually a pedigree, testimonies to the wonder of the animal and the skills of the farmer. A typical portrait, 'Oxford Down Ram' (c.1830), in Luton Museum, is by William Nicholls, a sign-painter who lived in Dunstable in the first half of the nineteenth century (see Plate 226).

The popularity of photography towards the end of the nineteenth century led to a reduction in painted portraits of people since these could more cheaply and quickly be supplied by photographers. Animal portraits, however, continued to be painted: the depiction of a favourite or prize animal in oil or watercolour was thought to be a more significant record than a photograph. Subjects included hens, dogs, horses, fighting cocks and sheep. A favourite subject in some areas was pigeons, some of the finest of which are by E. W. Windred who was working in the 1920s and 1930s. Windred, a barber with a shop in South London, painted in Kent and the south-east of England, invariably setting the finely painted pigeon in a loosely sketched-in landscape. A typical example of his work is 'Hawthorn Johnson' (see Plate 227), at the bottom of which, in copperplate script, are written details of the bird's racing success.

J. K. Browne, who worked at much the same time as Windred, travelled round the Midlands and in Northumberland and Cumberland; for small sums or even just a meal and a bed he would paint a portrait, but his paintings, though set out of doors, make little attempt to show the landscape. Another contemporary, Andrew Beer, painted many pigeon portraits between the wars. He lived in the Rhondda and like the others wrote the details of the bird's racing career at the bottom of the canvas. Inspired by this tradition painters who themselves were fanciers continue to paint pigeon portraits. Louis Nanton of Ruislip decorated several plates in the late 1970s, one – 'Old 86' – painted inside an ornately painted border, is a celebration of the bird and, of course, its owner (see Plate 228).

Artisan painters, borrowing little from the academic approach of trained artists, concentrated almost entirely on representational painting of specific subject matter; there was little attempt to suggest depth though a surprising amount of detail was often included to create an impression of accuracy as well as to record the chosen scenes or subject. John Bradley (1787–1844), a house and sign painter of Keighley in Yorkshire, was influenced by academic work. Like other artisan painters, he decorated the staffs of the parish constable and drew prize animals including the Airedale Heffer at Riddlesden ('She weighed 41 stones, 12 lb . . .') and, as late as 1837, was still taking work painting houses. Bradley's painting straddled both 'naïve' and academic work. Along with a tailor, a joiner and a reedmaker, Bradley

helped found the town's Mechanics Institute, becoming its first secretary, and he is thought to have given lessons in drawing to the Brontë family in Haworth who travelled to see him. Elizabeth Gaskill, a contemporary observer, thought little of Branwell's work or of sign-painting in general. Her biography of Charlotte Brontë describes Branwell's portrait of his three sisters, now in the National Portrait Gallery, London, as 'not much better than sign-painting'.

The sea and ships were attractive subjects for many artisan painters as well as other artists. As discussed in Chapter Five, sailors often painted a portrait of their ships on the inside of their sea-chests, stitched them in wool or scratched them on bone. Painters who did portraits of particular vessels, often known as pier-head painters, not only provided a record of appearance, but included relevant information about the ship, thus giving the work a functional as well as an artistic purpose. The ship was invariably shown in profile so that it looked as grand and impressive as possible. Pier-head painters such

Plate 225 *Abraham Offering Up His son Isaac* by an unknown painter, about 18 inches tall, early nineteenth century; the naïve style vividly depicts the graphic events of the story

Plate 226 *Oxford Down Ram*, a prize-winning ram by William Nicholls, a sign
painter; about 30 inches wide, early nineteenth century

Plate 227 *Hawthorn Johnson and Hawthorn Girsy* by E. W. Windred with details of the birds' successes written
along the bottom of the painting, about 29 inches wide, 1920s

as Michael Scurr (1800–1864) and William
Clark (c.1804–1883) followed the traditional
trade of sign and house-painter before concentrating on the sea, while Reuben Chappell
(1870–1940) worked for a photographer tint-
ing images.

John Ward (1798–1849) of Hull was a
leading painter of whaling and marine subjects. His earliest influences came from his
father, Abraham, a master mariner who is
credited with a whaling painting in the Hull
Trinity House. John Ward was apprenticed
to Thomas Meggitt, a Hull house and ship-
painter who encouraged artistic work among
his apprentices. As well as painting fine
depictions of the whaling trade, Ward also
carried out engravings and lithographs. Keen
to acquire first-hand knowledge of whaling,
Ward was the only Hull artist to definitely
visit the Arctic. In 'Whalers in the Arctic'
(c.1835) the detail describing the activities of
the whaling fleet is remarkable. The Arctic
landscape includes in the foreground a polar
bear about to eat a seal. Behind, a whale has
been successfully harpooned and is being
finally killed with a lance. Flensing (cutting
off the blubber) is in progress alongside the

Plate 228 Commemorative plate recording the success
of 'Old 86' by Louis Nanton, about 10 inches, 1970s

ship and a 'slip' of blubber is being hoisted
ashore (see Plate 229).

Pier-head painting was brought to an
end by the Second World War, the work
replaced by colour photography and social
change within the trade – seamen no longer
identified so closely with their vessel. Artisan
painters virtually ceased to exist. Fairgrounds,
circuses and seaside amusements became
major sources of employment for itinerant
painters as the traditional demands disappeared. Today the renewed interest in painted
inn signs has revived the art of artisan
painting, often adding a welcome addition to
anonymous buildings with lively, witty and
inventive work.

Plate 229 *Whalers in the Arctic* by John Ward, oil on canvas, 19 × 28½ inches, c.1835

The Painted World

There is no satisfactory name for art produced by artists who, without previous training, find painting and drawing a vital and satisfying means of creativity. At its most successful, their work is insightful, artistically confident, and visually strong with coherent if often idiosyncratic composition. Though painting primarily for their own pleasure and enjoyment, their art conveys their sense of the world to others. Many paint in their spare time, particularly at weekends, and have been dubbed 'Sunday painters'. 'Naïve', 'primitive', 'folk', 'intuitive', 'non-professional', 'outsider', 'visionary', and 'the innocent eye' are other descriptions applied to their art. One of the most notable Sunday painters was the Cornishman Alfred Wallis (1855–1942), whose telling phrase – 'what i do mosley is what use To Bee out of my memory' – conveys the spirit and intention of his and many other artists' vision.

Wallis often gave conflicting biographical information, claiming to have been a sailor before working in a marine shop in Penzance, though he later settled in St Ives. On his retirement and after the death of his wife, when he was 68, he started to paint 'for company', taking as his subject the sea and woodland, all painted in his own highly individual style. Using odd-shaped pieces of

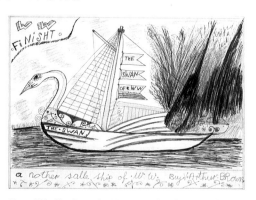

Plate 231 *The Swan* by Vernon Arthur Brown, coloured inks on paper, about 7 × 9½ inches; inscribed 'W W Finisht' and 'another salle ship of W W', this half-boat, half-swan is a magical fantasy which is both colourful and strongly conceived

cardboard scrounged from shops, he worked on his kitchen table, moving round it when he wanted to depict a different perspective. To represent a ship sailing down the picture as opposed to across he would sometimes simply turn the paper round to paint it. Paintings may combine several views: some objects are shown at eye-level, others are seen from above. The eye is made to swoop and soar, conjuring up the experience of seeing, selecting the view which can most clearly be recognised. His painting 'The Blue Ship' (see Plate 230) makes inventive use of perspective to depict the harbour, lighthouses and stormy sea. He either had little interest in, or knowledge of, the conventions of perspective, yet was vividly able to suggest space, direction and volume. Despite, or perhaps because of, the many viewpoints, his work has a powerful and convincing sense of space despite its unconventional perspective; the balance and weight of vessels, the shimmering water and cloudless skies are entirely convincing. It is as if we can see and experience for ourselves the many facets of his chosen view: the seas seem to swell and roar, the boats bob and rock; we can enjoy the work for its direct, visual qualities, its nautical subject matter and its highly individual style.

Sea and ships are the subject of Scottish-born artist Vernon Arthur Brown's pen and ink drawing, 'The Swan' (see Plate 231). This combines a powerful element of fantasy with

Plate 230 *The Blue Ship* by Alfred Wallis, oil on board, 17¼ × 22 inches, *c*.1934

Plate 232 *St Peter's Denial* by Joseph Browne, oil on board, about 30 × 120 inches, *c*.1795; the painter was a self-taught artist who was originally a coal porter

a realistic depiction of a sailing-ship, blending aspects of the observed world with an appealing element of fantasy to create an intriguing, almost diary-like narrative.

Not all painters followed such an independent path, and some modelled their work closely on academic art. Joseph Browne (1720–1800), originally a coal porter, taught himself to paint in his 30s, adopting the style and subject matter of contemporary academic painting. Subjects include a romantic landscape of 1767 and 'St Peter's Denial' (*c*.1795), a composition incorporating many classical elements (see Plate 232).

Elizabeth Ratcliffe, a lady's maid at Erddig, in Wales, the daughter of a Chester clockmaker, started work with the Yorke family and soon learned to make faithful copies of mezzotints and topographical studies in the conventional style of academic art. These included Newnham in Hertfordshire and Conway Castle (1782). She also made models of famous buildings, among them 'The Chinese Pagoda' (1767) in vellum, mica and fragments of coloured glass, based on an engraving in William Chamber's *Gardens & Buildings at Kew* (see Plate 233). Her most ambitious model, 'The Ruins of Palmyra' (1773), was based on a drawing in Robert Woods's book of the same name. A gifted artist as well as an excellent lady's maid, the family were keen she should stay, Dorothy Yorke writing in 1768 to a friend about her

misgivings at losing Elizabeth Ratcliffe's services because of her success as an artist, talent she did not want encouraged.

In contrast to the sophistication of

Plate 233 Model 'pagoda' by Elizabeth Ratcliffe, Mother of Pearl

Plate 234 *High Street, Richmond, Yorkshire* by J. S. Newton, 1847

Browne and Ratcliffe, who had clearly been influenced by academic painting, others used academic styles as starting points for their own work. Topographical views recorded and documented familiar streets and typical views. In 1883 in Perth a local chemist named J. D. Stewart painted a complex view of the town now in Perth Museum which includes portraits of contemporary personalities. There is a similar sort of close observation in 'High Street, Richmond' (Plate 234) where the daily scene is accurately suggested by the anonymous artist, and in 'View of the Thames at Putney Bridge' (Plate 235) where the semi-urban setting captures the activity of the city.

Many artists took as their subject the town in which they lived, concerned to record memories of their childhood as well as the reality of contemporary experience. There is some of this feeling in the work of Salford-born painter Ted Finlay (1908–1979). Finlay, who worked as a farmer, a street-sweeper and a museum attendant, painted in a conventional representational style to show scenes

from his daily life such as 'Neighbours' (Plate 236) which catches the relaxed times when work is over. In contrast, 'Eastwood Crown Brewery' (Plate 237) by F. L. Carter uses an aerial view he was unlikely to have ever seen yet he managed to evoke the feel of the building. It is probably based on the style of a contemporary advertisement.

More immediate experiences were depicted by other artists. W. G. Woods, serving as an air-raid warden in North London in the last war, painted 'The ARP Post' (c.1940), catching the atmosphere of this job. His painting evokes the ennui and isolation of the slowly passing hours that nevertheless had to be observed (see Plate 238). J. Ashford's portrait 'The Railway Worker and Child' (1953) is probably a self-portrait with his daughter. The affectionate way the child clings to the man's leg and the fact they both hold bunches of roses implies a close and loving relationship. The style of social realism catches the relaxed pose and the ordinary semi-rural setting. The smiles are those we usually see in a photograph, suggesting that this may have been the basis of the composition (see Plate 239).

Not all artists worked alone but gained from membership of art clubs and societies. One of these, the Triumph Art Circle, which started in 1934 in Coventry, was a major focus for Sunday painters bringing together self-taught artists within the factory. The circle regularly discussed 'modern art', and the work of 'controversial' artists including Rouault, Cezanne and Modigliani. The Post and Telecom's Art Club of Great Britain holds one of the largest annual shows in the country, including photography as well as painting and drawing, which is both popular and well supported.

One of the most successful art groups was that formed at Ashington, Northumberland in the 1930s, initially as a branch of the Workers' Educational Association. A class in Art Appreciation perplexed the tutor who did not at first know how to set about introducing art and its history to workers with little previous knowledge or awareness of it. He suggested they paint pictures themselves and, reluctantly at first, they agreed.

What had begun as art appreciation was taken over by an obsessive creativity as they painted familiar scenes from their daily lives such as down the coalmine and the fish and chip shop. Each painter developed his own style, unself-consciously enjoying the pleasure of making images. George Blessed's 'Whippets' (c.1939, Plate 240) has an attractive, pattern-like quality which catches the intensity of the training, while James Floyd's 'Pigeon Crees' (c.1938, Plate 241) uses a more realistic style to depict an equally popular leisure-time activity of coal-miners.

Julian Trevelyan in *Indigo Days* gives a contemporary account of meeting the miners:

> One of the unavowed leaders of the group was Harry Young, a pit blacksmith, whose work showed most clearly the poetic influence of David Jones. 'The Cock', a magnificent heraldic bird crowing in the twilight, and the 'The Knocker Up', the man who goes down the street waking up the sleeping miners for the early morning shift – these are two pictures that I remember best. Harry Wilson, another member of the group, had painted a strange picture called 'The Leek-stamper'. Leeks are grown for

Plate 235 *View of the Thames at Putney Bridge*, anon, oil on canvas, 25½ × 37½ inches, nineteenth century

Plate 236 *Neighbours* by Ted Finlay, a painting suggesting the intimacy of life in Salford, 1940s

prizes at Ashington, and a good leek is much coveted; so towards the time of the horticultural exhibition, in order to prevent theft, the owner stamps his name with a rubber stamp on the leaves of his plants. This strange ceremony, the importance of which would be missed by a non-Ashingtonian, was the subject of Harry Wilson's picture.

Trevelyan, together with Robert Lyon, organised an exhibition of 'Unprofessional Painting' which included work by the Ashington Group and other Sunday painters. It went to the Wertheim Gallery, the Peckham Health Centre, Fulham Town Hall, Mansfield Art Gallery and was then toured by the Workers' Education Association.

Oliver Kilbourn, a founder member of the Ashington Group, developed an independent reputation for his own work. Born in Ashington in 1904 he started at Ashington Colliery at the age of 13 and worked there until retirement. His interest in painting was stimulated by the formation of WEA classes, since when, he said, 'art has been my main

interest in life'. Many of his paintings are based on his everyday life such as in 'Proggin the Mat' (see Plate 141), and his life as a coalminer. These aimed to describe the work as it appeared to him, producing as many images as were required to depict the various activities or processes taking place. One series of three paintings shows the processes involved in filling a tub, all the paintings capturing the drama and excitement of work below ground in compositions which make effective use of powerful beams of light, of working bodies and cramped restricted space. There is little heroic in his work: the realism comes from the intensely-felt experiences convincingly portrayed.

For many miners-turned-painters the work of the collier with its drama, physical toil and ever-present danger has been, and continues to be, a popular subject, the autobiographical material inspiring vivid work. Notable among these painters are Ernest Walker and C. W. Brown. Walker was born into a coal-mining family in the Nottinghamshire coalfields in 1895 and, like Kilbourn,

Plate 237 *Eastwood Crown Brewery* by F. L. Carter, oil on canvas, 18 × 24 inches, 1898

Plate 238 *The ARP Post* by W. G. Woods, watercolour, c.1940

Plate 239 *Railway Worker and Child* by J. Ashford, oil on canvas, about 30 inches long, 1953. Ashford was a railway worker on BR Southern Region who lived in Brighton; the portrait may represent a father with his daughter

entered the pit when he was 13. He started to paint in 1960 when he retired, taking as his subjects aspects of the life and times of the coal-miner, including accidents, strikes, and stand-outs as well as various jobs carried out below ground. 'Summit Pit Gates' (c.1960) uses distorted perspective to depict the accident on the railway line (see Plate 242).

Unlike Walker, C. W. Brown (1882–1961) worked both on the land and down the coal-mine. As a lad of 13 he made sketches of farm life but the greatest part of his work was based on his time in the potteries, on the industrial landscape of the area and the life of a miner. Brown developed an unselfconscious style and directness of expression which gave his work warmth and conviction. 'Below Ground' (1938, Plate 243) is an expressionistic image of life in the coal-mine in which the individual figures are made tiny and unimportant. The warning expressed in 'Don't Ride on Conveyors' (c.1938, Plate 244) makes use of a cartoon-like approach and fairground lettering to make its point. While not seeking to recapture the innocence of the untrained eye nor continuing the unsophistication of the Sunday painters, Brown achieves a convincing strength and power; art painted very much as a reaction to the world in which he lived.

Nicholas Evans's (b.1907) response to the job of coal-mining in Wales is concerned with capturing the feeling of the work rather than merely seeking to describe appearance. His swirling and dramatic compositions with their repetitive, pattern-like quality evoke the experience of life below ground and the emotions conjured up by the job. His compositions are dominated by vivid impressions of dark, enclosed caverns deep in the bowels of the earth, the prevailing gloom and strong contrasts adding a particular mystery to the paintings. In 'Miners in the Cage' (c.1975, Plate 245) the individual identity of the workers is lost as they become part of a crowd which seems to loom out of the enveloping darkness to form a wall of half-seen faces, powerfully evoking the oppressive and claustrophobic atmosphere. His stark

Plate 240 *Whippets* by George Blessed, house paint or oil on cotton/muslin stuck to hardboard, about 25 inches wide, c.1939; the strong, pattern-like quality of the composition catches the mood of concentration

black and white paintings have a grim, convincing reality and are as much a metaphor for inner, deeper thoughts and feelings below the surface as they are of life underground.

The need to paint can become almost an obsession for some artists who often work in a style which conveys this feeling. James Lloyd (1905–1974) used tiny dots of paint to build up his compositions in which the engaging, slightly larger-than-life imagery is

Plate 241 *Pigeon Crees* by Jimmy Floyd, oil on wallboard, about 30 inches wide, c.1938. Each pigeon fancier kept the loft clean and freshly painted to their own design. A reminder of the industrial area is provided by the steam train pulling coal waggons from the colliery in the background

Plate 242 'Summit Pit Gates' by Ernest Walker, about 36 inches tall.
The railway crossing gates were closed when miners went to and from
work to prevent them taking short-cuts. In their haste, they often
crossed the tracks frequently causing serious accidents, even fatalities,
with men being knocked down by trains as in the incident shown in this
painting. Though an overhead bridge was required, one was never
built causing friction between railway workers and miners. The Lowry-
like composition describes a gruesome aspect of working life

almost obsessively shown. Lloyd's subject matter, based on his own life as a farm and factory worker, includes women, horses, children, dogs and the family living-room: all have a heightened, slightly exaggerated quality making them appear to invade, advance and threaten. Despite the intense, dotted style, Lloyd's figures and landscapes have great strength and solidity. In 'Woman With Horses' (c.1970) the intense impression is made more acute by the frozen action, as if some shutter mechanism has been involved enabling the artist to record a split second of a memory rather than real life (see Plate 246).

While Lloyd made effective use of dots

placed close together, Scottie Wilson (1888–1972) used numerous short pen strokes to create the patterns and motifs of his work. An ex-soldier and a dealer in 'junk', Wilson started to draw when he was attracted by the qualities of a large 'Bulldog' fountain pen. Images flowed from him in dense personal compositions, such as in 'Faces' (c.1940), involving threatening, evil faces, encroaching and ferocious; other compositions included symmetrically balanced trees on which carefully placed birds suggested an ordered, measured and controlled representation of life (see Plate 247). Wilson's painting was essentially for his own satisfaction, compulsively

Plate 243 *Below Ground* by C. W. Brown, 1938. The vast, yawning tunnels with their dramatic lighting make the miners seem tiny and insignificant as they direct the coal trucks along the railway lines

Plate 244 *Don't Ride on Conveyors* by C. W. Brown, ink and watercolour, 10½ × 14½ inches. Taking risks down coal-mines can lead to accidents, a point graphically made in the salutary incident depicted here, emphasised with the message 'That man did and is no more. Poor Fellow. He's Gone'. The use of fairground lettering effectively hammers home the point

Plate 245 *Miners in the Cage* by Nicholas Evans, about 22 inches tall, *c.* 1975. Despite the pattern-like quality
of the composition, the miners packed in a cage on their descent to the coalface create a haunting image of life
down a pit

Plate 246 *Woman With Horses* by James Lloyd, *c.*1970. The closely
worked dotted technique to build up the surface of the painting
creates a mood of intensity, despite the apparent ordinary everyday
activity portrayed

carried out and reluctantly parted with. When asked to sell his work he would either demand high prices or, occasionally, give it away to selected admirers. Showing people his work was like exposing a part of himself: he organised exhibitions in such unconventional spaces as bombed-out buildings, and viewers were left in no doubt about the honour it was to see his work; sales were of little importance and visitors were not allowed to take photographs. Despite being familiar with the work of contemporary artists and a regular visitor to galleries in London's West End, Scottie Wilson's work showed little or no influence of the art he saw, though surrealist artists have identified with the obsessive quality of his work.

Other artists too, despite being surrounded by academic art, pursue their own style without inhibition. Alexander Georgiou, born near Nicosia, Cyprus, in 1916, and usually known as Parafimou ('the famous one'), worked for some years as a warder at the Tate Gallery, London. But his imaginary, narrative dream-like paintings of half-human, half-animal figures, as well as people and animals, cannot be attributed to any identifiable influence. His 'Dream Sequence' (*c.*1980, Plate 248) depicts an event which has no literal explanation. Many other artists have called on dreams and their imagination to depict the complexity of their emotions. Pearl Alcock makes use of an almost instinctive sense of strong colour and flowing composition to conjure up intriguing images. In 'Waterfall' (Plate 249) the mystery and secrecy of the scene in the garden has an exotic quality. Equally convincing is the work of

Plate 247 *Faces* by Scottie Wilson, coloured inks on paper, about 12 inches tall, *c.*1940

London-born window-cleaner and odd-job man, Bob Williams. His chosen subjects include such religious themes as Madonna and Child as well as portraits and landscapes. The luscious use of colour and the visionary intensity in the miniature 'Green Landscape' (*c.*1980, Plate 250) were also used to great effect to paint the tops of tin tobacco-boxes.

Cleveland Brown (b.1943), a trained carpenter who arrived in Britain from Jamaica in 1961, became fascinated by the works of art while working at Sotheby's and wanted to become a painter himself. Scenes of London parks, such as in 'St James's Park' (1978), combine direct observation with sexual innuendo and a cheeky, witty sense of humour

Plate 248 *Dream Sequence* by Parafimou (Alexander Georgiou), acrylic on paper, about 12 inches long, 1980s. The 'incident' combines elements of fantasy and mythology with a powerful sense of drama to describe an event which cannot be simply explained

(see Plate 251). Brown paints slowly and produces at most only three pieces a year, which he will not sell until he feels he has fully enjoyed them himself. His paintings are highly personal responses to sexual desire and the constraints of modern life.

Characteristic to much people's art is a powerful inner drive which inspires artists without them feeling the need for any formal training. While much of the art is autobiographical and draws directly on the artist's own experience and perception, some is inspired by other events. Andrew Hay, a Scottish lorry driver and a member of the Transport and General Workers Union, was horrified by drivers who broke picket lines during the 1984–85 Miners' Strike. To express his anger he started to paint during the strike,

feeling that this was one way he could register his protest and give support to the National Union of Mineworkers. The influence of newspaper photographs is clear in his paintings, which include angry scenes on the picket line and in 'Coal Miner', portraits of figures directly involved in the strike (see Plate 252). Geoff Gibbons's painting 'Solidarity' (*c*.1985), which commemorates the same dispute, inventively makes use of the traditional format and emblems depicted on banners arranged in neat symmetry. It makes reference to local groups in Leicestershire and Warwickshire to suggest the need for unity and co-operation, asserting support for and solidarity with the beleaguered strikers (see Plate 253).

Plate 250 *Green Landscape* by Bob Williams, oil on board, about 13 inches wide, c.1970. A window-cleaner and odd-job man in North London, Williams painted his landscapes with an almost visionary assurance

Plate 251 *St James's Park* by Cleveland Brown, oil on canvas, about 50 inches wide, 1978. The sexual imagery and urban setting combines aspects of an idyllic setting with sexual abandon.
Opposite: Plate 249 *Waterfall* by Pearl Alcock, oil, about 13 inches tall, 1989. The bold, confident use of colour creates a vivid and mysterious incident in this exotic landscape

Plate 252 *Coal Miner* by Andrew Hay, oil on board, about 12 inches
tall. Painted during the Miners' Strike in the mid-1980s, the portrait
avoids any idealisation in favour of well-considered realism

Plate 253 *Solidarity* by Geoff Gibbons, oil on board, about 24 inches
tall. A miner at Coventry, Gibbons used the devices seen on banners
to commemorate the struggle of the Miners' Strike. In other paintings
Gibbons depicts pit life 'to try to show people what other jobs go
into keeping a coal mine open. I have been told that there is no
colour down the pit, but I find plenty. I paint what I see. I try to make
it as dark and dusty for you as it is for the miner'

SCULPTURE

The use of a term like 'sculpture' to describe works of art carried out in three dimensions by working-class artists raises more complex issues than painting and drawing. With its origins in classical Greek and Roman statues, sculpture has come to signify the highest and most prestigious art form in our society. The main materials of academic sculpture are bronze, marble and stone, with terracotta a less expensive alternative. Not only have most of these materials been denied working-class artists unless, like stone-carvers, they were professionally involved with handling them, but few working-class artists have sufficient working space to handle large pieces and messy processes.

In addition to the practical problems of space and the availability of materials, the concept of sculpture as a three-dimensional work of art produced solely for its expressive qualities, lies far outside the experience of most working-class men and women. Artisan carvers and modellers invariably worked to some practical requirement which served as a context for their work. In medieval times painters had their own guild but sculptors did not; they were instead identified with working particular materials such as stone or wood. Before the academic definition of a sculpture as a three-dimensional object for contemplation became common usage in the nineteenth century, sculptors were known by a particular activity rather than the abstract description, hence wood, stone and slate-carvers. Gargoyles on medieval churches and cathedrals and wooden carved seats were produced by artisans who would have been seen simply as carvers.

Throughout this book many sorts of three-dimensional objects have been referred to, such as models of engines and aeroplanes, miniatures of houses, furniture, churches and the like, but few makers of these pieces would think of themselves as artists or sculptors. The question of the status of carvers or modellers has also been touched on and once again the different materials and intention of the work separate it from the academic consensus given to sculpture. Nevertheless, three-dimensional sculptural forms expressive of makers' ideas are produced by working-class artists.

Carving, particularly of a hard and durable material such as rock or stone, or the working of concrete, are methods of making permanent and enduring objects. Stonemasons who carved heads and faces which were placed on the lintels of doorways and in the centre of the rounded arches of bridges were doing so both as a personal mark — evidence of their own skill and imagination — and as recognition of long and possibly pagan traditions. Gargoyles, too, exercised the wit and imagination of the carver as well as demonstrating skill. It was often the case that workers familiar with a material should want to handle it for creative uses; thus miners carved coal, slate-workers made decorative and functional objects out of slate and masons carved stone.

Carving and working on a large scale not only poses technical problems but practical issues also arise — such as where to display work. Carvings of stone frogs by Philip Pape, Barton-on-Humber, are many times life size and are worked and displayed outdoors (see Plate 254). Stephen Wilcock in Oakenclough, Lancaster, works on a similarly large scale with his vast carved statue of Jesus Christ.

Plate 254 Philip Pape carving a stone frog and other animals in his garden, Barton-on-Humber, 1950s

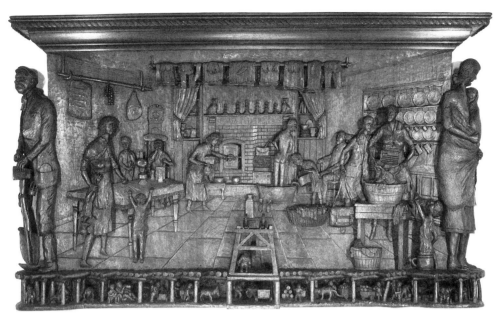

Plate 256 *The Miner's Kitchen*, carved in mahogany by Handel Edwards, about 36 inches long: 'It portrays life in the early 1930s when I was a boy. This was a typical scene in the home of a Welsh miner at that time'

Huge in size and controversial in the subject it depicts, Wilcock erected his 16-foot high sculpture in his garden without planning permission and local people objected to the presence of such a dominating feature. The ambitious, confrontational quality of the work is clearly conveyed (see Plate 255).

A contemporary wood-carver, Handel Edwards of Skewen near Neath, clearly fascinated by his chosen material, works on a smaller, more intense scale. He improvises methods and techniques to carve in wood scenes of his childhood, as well as modelling in clay, as a means of expressing his ideas and feelings. Born in a Welsh coal-mining family, Edwards was brought up in the 1930s and left school at 14. Though keen to study at art school, he became a plasterer in the building trade, and it was not until 1970 that he started to carve wood, learning the techniques from borrowed books, including how to sharpen his tools. An early piece 'The Miner's Kitchen' is set in the 1930s and is carved in mahogany (see Plate 256). The busy, detailed scene includes the whole family and depicts such activities as washing clothes, taking a bath in front of the fire and the preparation of food. Along the bottom, below ground, is a typical tunnel in a coal-mine

showing donkeys pulling wagons and miners heaving coal. The crowded, cramped conditions under ground echo the business of the domestic scene. The piece is now in the Ulster Museum, Belfast.

Following this came 'The Explosion', which was less to do with narrative and more concerned with conveying personal feeling. Carved in mahogany, measuring some 6 × 5 feet and weighing half a ton, it took over five years to complete. The composition consists of events from the life of Christ as described in The New Testament, (the initials of which TNT inspired Edwards' interpretation), and takes the form of an explosion harnessed by

Plate 257 *Cat* by Anthony Jadunath, wood and paint, 28 × 5½ × 10½ inches, late 1980s; carved from an old railway sleeper

Opposite: Plate 255 Stephen Wilcock working on a huge statue of Christ, Oakenclough, Lancaster

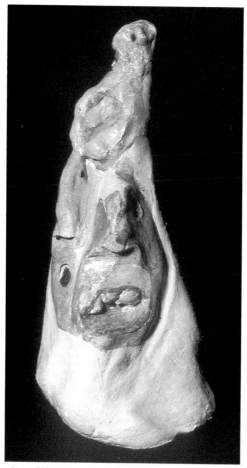

Plate 258 Figure modelled in self-hardening clay with paint and varnish by Albert Loudon, about 10 inches tall, 1980s

inventive use of found or waste materials, the odd and irregular forms suggesting subject matter, especially for domestic animals. Anthony Jadunath's 'Cat' combines two and three-dimensional aspects of the much-loved domestic animal to good effect, though whether the mouth is smiling or grimacing is an intriguing ambiguity (see Plate 257).

One of the most responsive and easily worked materials which has been widely used in the last 20 years is clay. It is cheap and lends itself to a variety of techniques. Whereas learning to throw on the potter's wheel or building up coil pots or making pots out of slabs of clay presents a technical challenge and may require good teaching, modelling forms out of clay can be direct and the necessary skills learned as the work is made. Albert Loudon (b.1945) models figures which combine the appearance of the body with powerful evocative elements, often suggesting inner hurt and pain (see Plate 258). Loudon's paintings have a similar sense of representing feeling and emotions, implying alienation rather than involvement. The models, carried out in self-hardening clay and painted with ordinary colour, call for no highly technical equipment and open up the medium to any artist.

Unlike such activities as embroidery or patchwork, clay requires a certain amount of equipment and a suitable space in which to work. In the past 25 years the popularity of pottery or modelling classes at evening

the wings of the messenger. In each of the 29 clouds given off by the explosion a scene depicts the life of Christ. When no permanent home could be found for 'The Explosion', in frustration Edwards carved 'Trapped', a small-scale piece in which he depicts himself held in by the tools of his trade unable to move into the world of art. Other pieces include 'Horizons Limited' (6 × 2 feet), a carving dealing with the rape of the green belt and the destruction of wildlife resulting in the trial of man by animals.

Frederick Richard Davies, a coal-miner of Stoke-on-Trent, took to whittling wood using his pocket knife while waiting for railway wagons to fill: 'The only training I received was as a little boy watching my father do fretwork. I carve for pleasure but have sold some of them to pay for the material that I used.'[1] Many artists make

Plate 259 *Christine's Frog* by Gary Cahalane, modelled, glazed and fired clay, about 6 inches tall, c.1985

institutes, community centres and the like have demonstrated the extent of the fascination of the material. The models of Gary Cahalane, who attends part-time classes in London, combine fantasy and narrative in an intriguing and highly personal way. Each piece, some six to eight inches tall, is modelled directly and painted with coloured glazes

to give the desired effect. Titles such as 'Christine's Frog' (see Plate 259), 'Creeping Paranoia' and 'Frankie Goes to Mothercare' suggest the autobiographical nature of the work. Most of Cahalane's modelling is done in his bedroom at home with the college providing technical advice, materials and firing facilities.

PHOTOGRAPHY

When Pip, the young hero of Charles Dickens's novel *Great Expectations* (published 1860–61), commented: 'I never saw my father, or my mother, and never saw any likeness of either of them (for their days were long before the days of photography) . . .', he was identifying a major difference between rich and poor and the vital role of photography in providing likenesses which could so significantly shape experiences and memory. As commercial photographers started to offer relatively low-priced images in the second half of the nineteenth century, so the less well-off could record their appearance, enabling them for the first time to acquire a visual history. While the better-off had long been able to commission portraits and surround themselves with paintings or sculptures of kith and kin, the poor had had no access to such images until the invention of photography. Now anyone could have their portrait taken, enabling an unprecedented group of people to have images of friends and relatives whom either time or circumstance had taken from them. Furthermore, events of working-class life such as daily activities, special outings, or festivities and so on, could be recorded and the images discussed.

Like academic art, photography has generally been seen as an activity for the middle classes, and little attention has been given to it as a means by which working-class men and women could document their own lives or use the medium as a form of artistic expression. Studies of photography usually concentrate on the work of famous

photographers, on technical processes, on photographic movements or subject matter, with little or no attention given to the social context or background of the photographer.

A fundamental question, therefore, is what are the likely differences between photographs taken by working-class photographers and those by the middle and upper classes? Photography is a notoriously difficult medium for critics and art historians to analyse or comment on without information about who the photographer was, the date of the work, some knowledge of the subject of the picture, the circumstances under which the photograph was taken and so on. Photographs are open to many sorts of 'readings' and few if any have a single intrinsic 'meaning' built in to them. Captions can fundamentally affect this by making place, time and possible intention of the photographer clear. Without such factual information, analysis remains speculative and any discussion of images by working-class photographers has first to establish the status of the photographer.

Such discussion has also to take account of the technical and practical aspects, as these are often restricted for working-class photographers. Until the end of the nineteenth century cameras and developing equipment were large, bulky and expensive. Photography tended to be the prerogative of the well-to-do who had financial resources and time to devote to it. Equally relevant are the aesthetic considerations for evaluating the images. These are particularly important as the characteristics of a 'good' photograph are likely to be based on the aesthetics of high art.

The aesthetics of photography have tended towards adopting the classical and academic criteria of fine art, discussing images in terms of such concerns as light and shade, composition, photographic technique and so on; a 'good' photograph was considered to be one which came closest to these values. Within this process, the content of the photograph, which is the major concern of working-class photographers, is seen as secondary and of less importance. Recording and documenting what is seen without being deterred by aesthetic considerations are intrinsic aspects of working-class images.

Equipment and Subject

The invention of a relatively simple and small camera in the late 1880s and the introduction of celluloid roll film by the American George Eastman brought about an aesthetic and practical revolution in the medium. By simplifying the technical aspects of photography Eastman not only made the medium more portable and reduced the costs of taking photographs, but over time brought this fascinating and remarkable medium within the reach of workers on modest incomes. What had been a skill which only the wealthy and leisured could enjoy was dramatically changed by Eastman's camera. 'You press the button, we do the rest' was his proud advertising boast. His first 'Kodak' – a word intended to represent the click of the shutter – was introduced in 1888. By offering specialist developing and printing services Eastman was able to claim that photographs could be taken by 'anybody, man, woman or child who has sufficient intelligence to point a box straight and press a button'.

Eastman's advertisements were aimed at the middle classes – 'Travellers and Tourists, Artists, Sportsmen and Camping Parties, Surgeons, Bicyclists and Boating Parties' – and it was some time before the price was sufficiently low to come within the range of the skilled worker. In 1910 the cost of a No.2 Brownie camera was about 35 per cent of the average wage of a Kodak factory worker; by 1920 the proportion had fallen to 20 per cent. In 1920 five times as many cameras were sold as in 1914. By 1930 the cost of a No.2 Brownie camera represented some 15 per cent of the average weekly wage of the Kodak factory worker. In 1939 the real cost of a five-shilling camera, allowing for inflation, was about one-hundredth that of the first Kodak camera in 1888.

The reduction in cost and the greater simplicity of operation had by the early years of the century brought hundreds of thousands of new photographers. The *Daily Mail* reported 'the demand for snapshot cameras has this year beaten all records . . . it would appear as if the photographic "craze" . . . is likely to continue!' Women as well as men took to photography: over a third of the participants for a day's competitive photography at London's Wembley Park in 1903 were women. Two years later the *Photographic News* in September 1905 reported from a Birmingham newspaper: 'Thousands of Birmingham girls are spattered about the holiday resorts of Britain this month, and a very large percentage of them are armed with cameras.'

The working class themselves were popular subjects for nineteenth-century (and twentieth-century) photographers, and distinctions have to be made between photographs taken *of* the working class and those taken *by* them. Documentary evidence is needed to identify the photographer, essential information if any analysis is to be made on how aspects of class influenced and determined the sort of images taken. What can be said, however, is that the more sophisticated and flexible the equipment, the more expensive it was. A simple camera could only produce a limited range of images. Technical sophistication, finely ground lenses, the processing involved in taking photographs (until Eastman came along, everything had to be done by the photographer who was in charge of the production of the image from exposure to final print) and the equipment needed, meant that it was only the middle and upper classes who could afford to take photographs.

From the 1850s until the 1870s some of the most creative work was done by wealthy, gifted, amateur photographers trying out different techniques and experimenting with various processes. Many belonged to the Photographic Exchange Club, one of the most notable of the amateur societies whose members included a wool merchant, a timber merchant, medical doctors, solicitors and artists. However, when the availability of photographic services and equipment put photography within the reach of thousands of new enthusiasts, most of the distinguished early amateurs withdrew, saying that photography had become an inert craft rather

than an art. Though commercial photographers grew greatly in number, they concentrated on methods which produced reliable results rather than experimenting with new processes.

In large industrial cities such as Leeds, Liverpool and Glasgow, local councils appointed official photographers to record the living conditions of the poorest in society. Such photographs, often taken by professional 'objective' photographers, served several purposes: they documented how people lived, often showing the poverty and the crowded life of too many people in too small a space. While such images were ideal propaganda material in the fight for better housing, proper sanitation and so on, they could also serve as evidence of the 'base' nature of human beings who were prepared

Plate 260 Workers in a stall, clog and legging level, Pontypool, by William Edmund Jones, c.1914

Plate 261 *Children by the Pond*, a page from a family album, by Frank Pitcher, c.1914

to do little to improve their lot. Many of these photographs, while technically excellent, were unlikely to reflect the way working people saw themselves. These photographers, acting in official capacities, were outsiders giving an observer's rather than a participant's point of view. Unfortunately, cameras and photographic equipment were not available to the people who lived in such tenements or slums – they were only the subjects of the work and we can only speculate on the sort of images they would have taken.

While the middle classes could, and did, photograph working-class people in their homes, the reverse could rarely occur. Not only were there virtually insurmountable practical problems but the middle classes were inaccessible to outside observation. In comparison to working-class life, much of which was public and could be readily investi-

gated (or at least in part), the middle classes lived lives of seclusion or privacy in walled or hedged gardens, their homes protected from photographic intruders.

An important aspect of working-class photography was the urge to photograph themselves at work, at leisure and so on. Remarkable early photographs of coal-miners and family life are held in the Welsh Industrial and Maritime Museum in Cardiff, taken by a Welsh miner William Edmund Jones (1890–1985). Some, such as 'Workers in a Stall, Clog and Legging Level, Pontypool' (c.1910), were taken down the pit (see Plate 260). Jones went to work down the mine aged 13 and seven years later had acquired sufficiently sophisticated equipment to take photographs below ground. A Thornton Packard half-plate camera with a tripod was used in conjunction with either a flashpan filled with magnesium powder or a magnesium strip, in 'safe', gas-free areas. Jones photographed other miners as well as typical working conditions below ground with no attempt to romanticise the work or gloss over the oppressiveness of the cramped spaces, the dirt and the sheer physical hard labour of coal-mining. Other images depict home life, a travelling fair at Pontypool Park (c.1920) and a gipsy encampment (c.1914). Jones has not tried to construct or arrange artistic settings, and the outdoor photographs made use of the strong contrasts of sunlight. All have an unself-conscious directness in which the artifice of the image – the careful static pose, the arrangement and so on – are those imposed by the medium itself.

Edward Ward, a printer and bookbinder active from the 1880s, took some two thousand photographs tracing the line of the Manchester Ship Canal before work began. His unfussy documentary approach was imaginatively conceived and carried out, and his photographs are now held in the local history collection of Bolton Museum. In the Grange Museum, Neasden, two collections of photographs taken at the turn of the century reflect similar concerns. One is a set of quarter-plate glass negatives taken by a Metropolitan Railway worker which include local views as well as family portraits. The other group, by Frank Pitcher, is technically more ambitious and autobiographical. These include images of indoor life, kitchens and portraits as well as 'Children by the Pond' (c.1910), a scene of children fishing and enjoying a picnic (see Plate 261). Some local photographers, whose income derived from studio portraits or weddings, used their spare time to photograph subjects of their own choosing. William Thomas Whiffin (1882–1957) took his quarter-plate reflex all over London, photographing topical events and buildings, including Barnet Horse Fair, St Paul's Cathedral and the 'Coronation Celebration' of King George VI (see Plate 262). Whiffin, a cockney, was born in Poplar and recorded events in West India Dock Road where he lived, street-life and the effects of

the 1926 National Strike.

The advent of war in 1914 brought a boom in photographic businesses which reached a peak in 1917. Joining the armed forces was considered an heroic deed which should be recorded. Cameras were bought to photograph loved ones going to war – many never to return. A few soldiers acquired cameras to carry with them despite the fact that possession of such equipment while on active service in the front line was a court-martial offence which, in some circumstances, could result in the death penalty. Though the same ban applied to officers, a few were able to get round these regulations and many important photographs were taken on the battlefields. This proved to be much more difficult for non-commissioned soldiers and only a few images have come to light which can be accurately attributed.

The problem of identifying such photographers without documentary evidence is almost insurmountable. Of the many thousands of photographs stored in archives and albums, only a relatively small number can be properly credited to particular photographers. Few photographs were signed (a signed print by a professional is still comparatively rare) and little study has been devoted to working-class photographers nor much attempt made to identify them. The excellent Manchester Studies Archives of Family Life (Manchester Metropolitan University) and Beamish Open Air Museum have thousands

Plate 262 Street celebration between the wars by William Thomas Whiffin

Plate 263 *The Tally Men, Gloucester Street* by Jimmy Forsyth ('The tally men came Thursday night collecting for the credit shops'), 1957

of photographs of working-class life; their classification is based on the subject of the photograph with little if any information recording the name or status of the photographer, and while it is tempting to identify images taken by working-class photographers, this may be misleading. A few valuable collections are fully documented.

In post-Second World War Britain, equipment and processing has become even cheaper, bringing the medium within the reach of many. Local art exhibitions regularly include photographic entries. Images often borrow heavily from established genres of professional photography such as pictorialism and portraiture, the technical achievement all but eliminating individual expression. There are, however, notable exceptions. Photographs by Jimmy Forsyth, a docker in Newcastle, record the geographical and social change of the area in which he lives. Forsyth moved to Tyneside from his home in Barry to do war work, but after an industrial accident he lost the use of an eye and found jobs difficult to get. Conscious of the radical social changes that were imminent in 1954 he

started documenting his immediate surroundings, learning his skills as a photographer through trial and error. Unable to afford a light meter he had to guess exposure times. To fund the purchase of film Forsyth made portraits of people on the street, in shops and in their homes, selling prints processed at the chemist for two shillings.

'Scotswood Road', an exhibition of his photographs (Side Gallery, Newcastle-upon-Tyne), took the name of the street where he lived. The photographs picture the process of the decline of the area from a thriving community in the mid-1950s to an urban wasteland some ten years later. 'The Tally Men, Gloucester Street' (1957) pictures two local characters (see Plate 263). The value of Jimmy Forsyth's work lies as much in its unassuming documentary approach as in its beguiling honesty, and is a rare example of a working-class community documented by a photographer who is part of it.

Community life in a small mining village in all its material poverty and diversity has been recorded by Jack Hulme (b.1906) in Fryston, Yorkshire. Once a thriving colliery village, Fryston has changed immensely; with the mine closed and the old back-to-back homes pulled down, the population has dramatically altered. Jack Hulme started taking photographs when he was 14 with a camera acquired for 2/6d (25p), and has taken pictures ever since with a variety of cameras. His chosen subject matter has been life in the small, close-knit community, recording family and friends at work and leisure. Daily tasks such as donkey-stoning the front doorstep (see page 140), black-leading the grate, bathing in the kitchen sink, or public festivities, capture at first hand life in the village. 'George Wagstaff and His Dog' (see Plate 264) records the eccentric behaviour of a local figure in a street free of motor cars. Despite the air of nostalgia, of images of time gone by, there is a convincing sense of reality in Hulme's photography which neither sentimentalises nor romanticises the life he portrays.

Post-war photography is dominated by the 'family album', the central focus for working-class imagery. Albums are both fascinating accounts of family life, recording not only the epic celebrations of birth, marriage, outings and holidays as well as everyday experiences, but often have an aesthetic appeal quite different from that of the professional

Plate 264 *George Wagstaff and His Dog* by Jack Hulme, 1950s

Plate 265 Page from the family album of Cathy Peters, 1940s

variety of family images (see Plate 265). Photographs taken between 1935 and 1950 by Graham Smith, now in the Victoria and Albert Museum, picture his family on holiday and evoke comradeship and family feeling of shared experience without artifice or sophistication.

The availability of a wide range of advanced technical processes at relatively reasonable cost has brought highly skilled techniques within the range of many. Colour photography has virtually replaced black and white for most photographers, as the developing and printing costs are often the same or even lower. Within the visually more sophisticated colour process, working-class photographers have produced individual works. Images by Cole Joseph, a taxi-driver living in London's East End, have a surreal element particularly noticeable in his photograph 'The Pig's Head' (1975), which was taken in an abattoir (see Plate 266). His work was considered to be of sufficient merit to be included in the Arts Council book *About 70 Photographs* (1981). Retired coal-miner Cliff Grist has photographed his village and coalmine in South Wales creating visually accomplished images. 'The Last Day of Steam' is both a clear documentary image and one evocative of time and place (see Plate 267).

Photography has also become a means by which the working class can record,

image. While some occasions are accepted as suitable for recording on film, there is as yet no tradition of photographing sadder, more reflective, events such as death or funerals. Much of the excitement and delight in family history as recorded in photographs was well captured in the exhibition 'Exploring Living Memory' at the Royal Festival Hall in London in 1984. Louise Savage showed photographs which included street parties and the first Zeppelin; there were photographs by Londoners who annually spent holidays picking hops on Kent farms, and a notable family album by Cathy Peters which includes a

Plate 266 *The Pig's Head* by Cole Joseph, 1975

Plate 267 *The Last Day of Steam, Cefn Coed Pits, Crynant* by Cliff Grist, 1980s

Plate 268 *Women's March, August 1984* by Teresa Dronfield

document and report on the world as they see and experience it. During the Miners' Strike of 1984–85, the workers, with time, if little money, on their hands, recorded the strike. Dave Dronfield, a striking miner at North Markham Colliery, North Derbyshire, and his wife Teresa Dronfield, produced impressive work, some of which has been exhibited while others have appeared in the press. 'Women's March, August 1984' is a relaxed, informal and involved view of the supporters (see Plate 268).

Today, interests are extending into video recording. Again the existence of low-priced advanced technology has made available a highly sophisticated filming method, although so far, the results by working-class videoists have yet to be seen.

Chapter Seven

PEOPLE'S ART EXAMINED

Chapter One raised some of the issues involved in appreciating people's art which have been taken up throughout the book. The complex and closely argued aesthetic which evolved in academies and art institutions for analysing the fine arts, particularly in painting, drawing and sculpture, though useful when discussing people's art, is of limited value because it evolved within a different context and these differences need to be clearly established. Little of the work described in this book has been produced either within the aesthetic of high art or with an understanding or knowledge of it. Aestheticism developed as part of the mystique around art of a particular class and as an aspect of commodity production. Even though artists have a special 'bohemian' status within the capitalist economy, they are still seen as producers, heavily influenced by and responsive to a thriving expanding art market.

People's art is very different: it is rarely produced for sale and may have little or no monetary value; individual artists or makers may be reluctant to sell their work at any price but may give it to friends or family. Value lies in the power of the work to serve as a means of communication, a way of making a statement about life and work. Within the society in which it is produced, people's art uses visual means to respond in an individual manner to the world in which it is created. For some it is a way of dealing with the experiences of everyday existence, for others it is a way of responding to the wider and often traumatic forces of life. Much of the work is simple in form and direct in its statement: to a sophisticated eye familiar with the complexities of the fine arts of painting and sculpture, some may even appear crude. Such work can only be classified and assessed by its own rules or conventions, for it is a powerful and personal form of expression.

Appreciating the diverse qualities of people's art involves recognising the context within which it was produced, the audience to whom it was addressed and the purpose for which it was made. Like academic art, people's art has a history both in the form it has taken and in its use of various subjects, though it is largely unrecorded and unstudied. The use of particular imagery is related both to the familiar, which may come from the past or the present, and to the need for new statements as a response to changing times. While it is only possible here to touch on the history of patterns and designs used in people's art, the technology which influenced it, and the territory it covers, it is sufficient to suggest the complexities and richness of working-class culture.

AESTHETICS AND SOCIAL USAGE

As pointed out earlier there are limitations in making use of the high art divisions of painting, sculpture and drawing to discuss people's art. Aesthetic analysis of people's art forms an objective point of view, which, though a useful part of the process of evaluation, must be related to the intention of the artist or maker and the time and place in which it was created. While a wooden Aunt Sally is carved and painted, a clay candelabra modelled, an inn sign painted and an inscribed decoration on a plate drawn – and so may appear to conform to the fine art divisions of painting, sculpture and drawing – such definitions fail to recognise the intention or value of the work. Neither can people's art usefully be considered alongside works by such fine artists as Rembrandt, Picasso, Michelangelo, Van Gogh or Henry Moore for they are part of a different type of art. Within any art form there are hierarchies of genre with minor and major artists; the lives and work of 'great artists', for example, have been recorded, annotated and discussed to fully substantiate these judgments. Other artists are accepted as not being so talented and are thus thought to produce work of lesser value. Similar difficulties occur in making judgments about people's art, for not all is equally effective in its handling of material or so powerful in conveying its visual 'message'.

Comparisons of different art forms which rely entirely on outward appearance or formalist values result in limited appreciation. Virtually any organised mass can be classified as sculpture, any applied colour described as painting or incised lines as drawing following, literally, fine art categories, but such a system omits the functional qualities of the piece, removes it from the cultural context in which it was conceived and made and ignores the purpose for which it was intended. While some people's art can be considered within fine art categories, most will defy such classification. Items such as carved seashells, ships in bottles, grottoes made of shells, or whalebone incised with carefully drawn scenes or patterns, are made to preserve a memory, signify an event or give physical substance to the free play of the imagination, and fall totally outside any fine art category both in their use of materials and their aesthetic quality. This does not prevent them being seen as art objects, but evaluation must recognise social as well as artistic intent. People's art requires a broader spectrum of

categories to reflect the breadth of the work.

There is a need to look beyond outward appearances and apparent similarities for other qualities in the work. One such aspect is the use of inscription, signature or marks of identity which not only serve as decorative motifs but as part of the individual response linking maker and user. For some items these may be one and the same person. It is a form of expression in which makers, or users, extend themselves into objects thus turning these into an extension of themselves.

The importance of the individual sign indicating intent and direction is central to the appreciation and expectation of high art: the signature of the artist (or patron) legitimises price and status. Such signs and markings have a different and more complex role in people's art. Markings on tools by makers or owners may be highly elaborate and involve a personal mark, initials or a name. The signature is not only a sign of its maker but is also a proclamation of involvement and achievement. Stonemasons traditionally fashion a stone face or head on a bridge they have built, devising their own method of adding evidence of the maker's artistic and physical involvement.

Sewers of bedspreads and makers of patchwork quilts often say about their work that their lives are there – not only have they spent many hours over the piece, but the fabrics are often recycled cast-offs which relate to particular occasions, people and events. Knitters, too, convey their own identity in their work, whether in the form of particular patterns they and others will recognise, or in adaptations of traditional designs which are still clearly part of the past but which are creative interpretations.

The greatest and perhaps most effective signature is personal adornment, whether in the form of specially made costumes, hairstyles or tattoos. Identity is created by and is an intimate part of a personal statement about the relationship between individuals and society. The genre includes objects entirely detachable from the body – such as jewellery and clothes, to styles and markings which are an integral part of the body and contribute to physical and social appearance. Clothes, hairstyles and ornament convey a particular social image according to whether they are worn by fisherfolk, by Pearly Kings and Queens or by teds and punks. Costumes such as smocks worn by farm workers served as protective covering and hence had a utilitarian purpose. Form, material, colour, pattern and decoration, though informed by tradition and social convention, can also be influenced by fashion and social class as much as by practical considerations of weather. Outfits worn by punks and teds are a response to a wide range of social concerns which owe little or nothing to such considerations (see Plate 269).

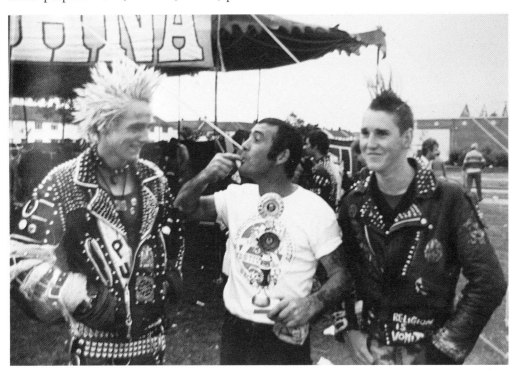

Plate 269 Two punks and friend, photographer unknown, c.1985

TASTE

Art historians are familiar with attempting to make sense of objects which are relics from another age and, deprived of their original function, can only be appreciated through their material and their form. This is often sufficient for these pieces to be seen as genuine works of art. Objects from so-called 'primitive' societies such as bronzes, masks, carved stone and totem poles, though now devoid of their original mystical content or ritualistic power, can take on new meanings in a different society. Within the culture in which such objects were made, no explanation of form, decoration or sign was required for they were an integral part of the society which produced them. Viewing these products away from their original context means either attempting to assign their cultural significance or objectifying them as art pieces. People's art poses many of the same problems.

In theory, the philosophy of the beautiful in art, such as that put forward by Kant, ought to apply to all art, but it is not readily applied to people's art. In order to judge whether an object merits the label 'art', an evaluation may take into account not only academic knowledge about the object, but also taste, considerations which are over and above any physical characteristics. Taste is a combination of a wide range of responses associated with materials and fashion, and involves the emotions as well as a sophisticated visual language. A rational assessment which makes use of a generally agreed canon of taste is required if these judgments are to be more than personal prejudice. These need to identify and analyse the underlying concepts of a taste evaluation, for the verdict of taste is a claim to make universally valued that which is individually appreciated. Objective proof, substantiating taste, can only be put forward through an agreed series of arguments. Clearly, they cannot be measured and proved in the way that scientists understand such concepts, but they can follow an agreed system of analysis. One method is to identify various categories of evaluation which not only take into account the characteristics of the object and its functional forms (if any), but also attempt to assess how well the object succeeds as a communicator of ideas and ideals set up by the maker and the user.

While in high art there are recognised types of painting or sculpture judged by the content or subject-matter (that is, still-life, landscape, portraiture, history painting, etc), the categories or genres for people's art are not so clearly established. There has been virtually no discussion of what constitutes a genre nor, fortunately, is there any academy, accepted authority or educational body to decide what compositional consideration a piece must conform to if it is to qualify as artwork. Any useful attempt to classify people's art according to various genres requires investigation of the entire range of items produced bearing in mind the way culture identifies them; attention also has to be given to the principles of evaluation followed by the makers and the users. Such classification needs to take account of the material used, the pictorial effect achieved, whether the object is faithful to the purpose for which it was intended according to accepted social usage, its artistic plastic quality and the extent of its aesthetic expression.

Three major areas can be identified as a part of the process, although they are closely interlocked. The first, *form*, includes the organisation and arrangement of the mass, the handling of materials, decoration, and the quality of making. The second, *function*, relates to the relationship between form and purpose and involves assessing how well the object will work and how successfully it has been adapted to the purpose for which it was intended. The third and most complex area is that which involves *idea* and *intention*; this not only includes the creative and aesthetic content but must also take into account the intention of the maker of the piece and, to some extent, the perception of the recipient of the object.

These three aspects can be further divided into a more detailed spectrum which extends from a primary consideration of function to one of appearance and meaning.

1.   Function

Objects which have a clear purpose are likely to be closest to traditional work. The form and inventive use of material are directed by the need for the object to carry out its allotted task. Such objects often have a strong visual harmony arising partly from the constraints of the practical form and partly from the skill of the making. Items such as those produced by basket-makers, traditional potters and straw-plait weavers are examples of material and function influencing form.

Perception of the aesthetic intention of the maker is integral to the way the object operates and is enmeshed with considerations of 'fitness for purpose'. Such items are produced to be used rather than to be admired as decorative forms. The requirements of function set the limits within which shape and materials vary though the creative element, expressed in the working of the material and the use of particular designs or decorations, is present.

2. Form and Function

Although informed by aesthetic intention, it is both the functional purpose and a feeling for shape as well as an inventive use of materials which determine the form and appearance of these objects. This may echo traditional styles but allow a considerable creative input from the maker. Overall, the effect achieved is a dynamic balance between the demands of use and the imaginative handling and treatment of materials and techniques. Many of these items are ingenious and skilful, intended for use within the household; examples are items of furniture such as those made in parts of Scotland from found wood, either collected on beaches or recovered from peat bogs, pegged rugs made from discarded fabrics and sewn quilts. The purpose of the piece is clear, the use of material and form shaped by tradition and the wit of invention and improvisation. There is also the intention to make such objects do more than function well; as major items in the home they fulfil a decorative as well as a functional role in conveying pride and status.

3. Form, Function and Decoration

A clear indication of the aesthetic intention of the maker is suggested by the nature and amount of decoration on the object when material and shape are determined by function. Embellishment beyond that required by function or form may include carving, the use of colour and the making of inscriptions. Decoration may celebrate the qualities of the material or it may express a desire to embellish simply for the visual effect it achieves. Such objects usually have special significance with much time and care taken in their production, even though they still retain a functional purpose. The maker and the user are likely to fully appreciate this ambivalence. Seen out of context, this work is likely to be discussed almost exclusively on the handling of the material, the quality of making and, especially, on the success of the decoration. Typical examples are modelled watch-stands in clay, fancy dress and lacemakers' bobbins.

4. Form, Function, Decoration and Ritual

Form, function and aesthetics determined by cultural rituals, celebrations, festivals and processions result in objects which reflect the occasion in a multitude of ways. Into this extensive group fall objects made for religious use (relatively few in Britain), for celebratory parades, for trade processions and for festivals in general. Items include wassailing-bowls, harvest-jugs, trade-related objects such as apprentice pieces, and objects made to be carried or worn in processions. Makers are well aware of the significance of these pieces which have an important role in educating the audience as well as celebrating shared concerns. While many of these objects continue to relate to their original function, they take on the additional role of demonstrating how skilled the work can be and hence the objects are at their most inventive.

For objects which are part of an accepted ritual or shared concept, users expect the highest level of making. Enjoyment is heightened because it is recognised that the maker is responding to such knowledge with a demonstration of skill and inventiveness. When taken out of their original context these objects lose much of their significance, though they are still effective as 'art' objects. Today we are often denied the excitement of appreciating the work as it functioned in such settings as workers' parades, wassailing parties, harvest celebrations and carnival processions. Such cultural occasions re-created today as entertainment have little of their original power of significance.

5. The Aesthetic Object

Objects which are primarily decorative and ornamental with no use in the practical sense come closest to the category of fine art. These objects do have a function in the way they serve as vehicles for communication, presenting ideas and commenting on events or experiences. But the intention of the makers of these pieces is likely to be very different to those of fine artists who consciously seek to produce works of art. In addition, the style will usually belong to an artistic tradition which is part of popular culture rather than that of the ruling élite. Much of this work is used to decorate the environment or the body, the objects displaying status and identity; aesthetic intention and pleasure are intimately bound up together. This work may not have the sophistication of high art in its use of the visual language, but may fit well into the concepts of painting, drawing and sculpture though this is unlikely to be the intention.

COLLECTIONS AND MUSEUMS

A significant aspect of people's art, given the large quantity produced, is that so little of it has found its way into museums and galleries. Traditionally, people's art has had little or no value either in monetary or aesthetic terms beyond the community in which it was produced. Hence it had no market value and was of little interest to collectors. Museums directed their attention to the fine and classical arts, anthropology and natural history, with curators and keepers reflecting their own taste. Educated to degree level and coming from a well-organised and influential class, they collected objects with which they were familiar. The People's Palace on Glasgow Green is the single exception. Since the turn of the century it has sought out, collected and displayed the visual art of the working class of Glasgow, placing it as far as possible in its relevant context, revealing some of the richness of working-class culture.

More recently, other museums have set up departments of social history which include such work, but often objects are likely to be scattered in various departments and no coherent listings are available. Despite the restrictions and limitations of museum funding and lack of staff, some museums have become aware of this area of work and of the need to represent it. Generally, however, there is a lack of commitment to collecting, analysing and presenting people's art, and without this no serious in-roads can be made.

The growing awareness of people's history has resulted in new museums. The Museum of Naïve Art in Bath collects objects and paintings up to 1900, many of which constitute people's art. The Black Cultural Archive collects material relating to the history of black people in Britain, while the Museum of Labour History in Manchester concentrates on organised labour, as do the recently opened Labour History Museums in Liverpool (1986) and The People's Story in Edinburgh (1989). However, concentrating on labour, with the emphasis on trades, professions and union organisation rather than wider cultural concerns, prevents them from truly being museums of working-class life. The Manchester Studies Collection has an extensive photographic archive of images of working-class life, but little or no information on the photographers. This is the basis for an extensive network of participating history projects in the community. Other museums catalogue aspects of particular industries, of a trade union, or groups of industries. An important body of work has been built up by London's Outsider archive of paintings, drawings and sculpture by men and women whose work comes from a powerful inner drive. Few have had professional training, many are working class, and include carpenters and museum attendants. Their work is visually powerful, often having a compulsive quality which speaks directly to others.

Such collections are all fragmented; a rich but dispersed representation of a culture which has produced visual art as skilled and inventive as any other. Major centres are needed for the presentation, study and documentation of historical and contemporary working-class life. These should take in all aspects of workers' lives and culture as well as visual art, bringing together oral and visual memories and include objects associated with work, politics and the home. Exhibition space and display areas could show work being done today to ensure that they are living museums, places of educational activity, drawing on the living memory of the community. As well as forming an historical resource, such a centre would give working-class culture an equal status alongside that of the middle and upper classes, able to be studied and enjoyed, an affirmation of values and ideals. Contemporary work would recognise achievement and a continuing, if changing, tradition. Funding for such a centre should be made from central government as well as from the labour movement itself; the wider involvement of trades unions in the visual arts and a genuine regard for their inheritance is long overdue.

PEOPLE'S ART TODAY

Tradition and innovation, so vital a part of people's art, remains a central concern for the discussion and appreciation of contemporary work. Influences are drawn from a wide variety of sources, and as people become better informed and educated so creative work changes. Television, with its diversity of news, cultural information and comment, serves as a vital source of visual material and ideological standards. Leisure time and unemployment have rarely been so great. Generally, there is a renewed awareness of 'cultural heritage' demonstrated by the growth in attendance at festivals, country houses, leisure parks, castles, churches and the like. Many of these occasions and establishments are associated with nostalgia and an invented past which reflects little of the realities of working-class life, nor do they give any meaningful recognition of history. In addition, the 'heritage' that is presented is that of the ruling élite from which the values of the working class are omitted and hence given little or no value.

Tourist centres at these places invariably include a shop selling a range of craftwork in clay, iron or wood, much of which is made in imitation of country and traditional crafts. These objects relate to a real but now dead tradition and use it as a curiosity and as a selling point, making no attempt to suggest the skills involved or the way that such objects formed a meaningful part of life. Dolls in regional costumes are often on display, again evoking a long tradition which may, in reality, have only a short history. All are lifeless reproductions in terms of the vitality and purpose of the originals; the justification for such work arises out of commercial concerns and hence any original intention or significance is lost. These items serve as mementoes, souvenirs of a visit or an occasion – they are romantic and unreal in their use of the people's art tradition, concerned only with superficial appearance. This is not people's art.

Equally problematic in terms of its effect on people's art is the growth of interest in painting and drawing. Do-it-yourself books and programmes on television have rarely resulted in a more revealing search for personal creativity, but have instead – by suggesting what techniques to use and what subject-matter to attempt – followed the aesthetics of high art. The result is art which apes that seen in art galleries rather than expressions of more individual experiences.

Today there is a pluralism in the production and evaluation of people's art and in artistic expression. As well as objects made by individuals there is a considerable body of work produced outside the walls of art galleries and institutions which goes largely unnoticed. Art forms of many sorts flourish, much of them without identifiable artists, sometimes without an object to exhibit, without academies or schools, without commission from patrons, with no prestigious galleries in which to display the work and with no awards or prizes.

There is, for example, public art, seen on houses and buildings or worn in the street. It is embroidered on clothes, expressed in elaborate hairstyles, in tattoos, decorated ghetto-blasters, painted on cars, motorbikes and pushbikes, it is sprayed on walls – mark-making of the most direct kind. It is also enshrined in festivals and parades, some of which date back into history while others reflect the more affluent times in which we live. Some thrive on a vibrant community involvement. Many of these occasions may make use of mass American pop culture, of the science fiction fantasy *ET* or any other popular expression, and it is problematic to reconcile the use of this mass-produced commercial culture with ancient pagan or religious processions; such diversity indicates how people can respond imaginatively to contemporary influences and use them for their own forms of expressions.

There is also house art in which the whole of the decoration and care of the home becomes not only a focus for individual and artistic expression but also an important statement of identity. This may involve painting and decorating the building as well as adding patterns or designs to the outside. It is also expressed in garden art, whether in the caring and cultivation of window-boxes, in the designing of gardens and lawns, in the care and presentation of vegetable plots, or in the construction of such items as elaborate bird-baths or wind indicators.

Do-it-yourself kits, efficient mechanical tools, home embroidery sets and knitting-machines, while offering opportunities for creative work, are often accompanied by suggested designs rather than explanations of

technique which would enable the operator to do more experimental work. Magazines, periodicals, books, dictionaries, encyclopaedias and practical guides stimulate interest in craftwork and provide much information. The number of clubs and associations increases, giving direction and bestowing legitimacy, serving as arbiters of quality and influencing taste. Working side by side with all these activities are painters, sculptors, photographers, metalworkers, potters and so on, most of whom have trained full-time in art schools learning traditional skills but interpreting them in a contemporary form.

Today, as for many years, people's art and high art exist alongside each other, with limited exchange of ideas and information. The artist-potter borrows heavily from the techniques of the country-potter; textile artists, studio glass-blowers, silk-screen printers have all adopted for their own craft traditions which formed a part of people's art in the past. The professional naïve artist has codified a style of art while sculptors using scraps and waste material have taken up concepts central to people's art. While many artists and craftspeople borrow freely from artisan skills, this does little to enrich working-class culture which becomes even more threatened by middle-class values.

Although complex and diverse, people's art has recognisable forms and recurring patterns – established genres which give the territory shape. Some pieces can be described as 'works of genius', just as some fine art objects can. But these pieces are far less common; the process of creating hierarchies of the finest and best is not important, for this attempts to emulate high art too closely. People's art represents no vested interests, commercial or aesthetic; it does not claim to be intrinsically or aesthetically superior because it is made by the artistically untrained or unsophisticated, but it does merit consideration alongside it.

As this book shows, working-class creativity is as powerful, as moving and as relevant to society as that of any other, displaying a visual imagination which nourishes and enriches, and the cultural signifi-cance of people's art is slowly being recog-nised. Conventional art history has largely ignored such work or else relegated it to a tiny and insignificant part of its concerns. This will no longer suffice. Ironically, work-ing-class art can only be acknowledged: it cannot be formally taught, ordered or directed. It is a visual expression which comes out of a deep-felt need for communication and identity. It has to be recognised and cherished for what it is, and if this presents a radical challenge to the usual view of art, it is one which has to be met.

NOTES

Chapter One

1. Woodward, Sir Llewellyn, *The Age of Reform 1815–1870* (Oxford: Clarendon Press, 1962)
2. Ibid.
3. Ibid.
4. Ibid.
5. Ibid.
6. Ibid.
7. The *Daily Telegraph*, 2 January 1987
8. Woodward, *The Age of Reform*
9. Ibid.
10. Ibid.
11. Ibid.
12. Dhondy, Farrukh, *Race Today*, May–June 1978

Chapter Two

1. Hajdamach, Charles, 'A Finer Substance than Anything', *The Antique Dealer and Collector's Guide*, November 1986
2. Nichols, Marian, *The Popular Arts in Luton Museum* (Luton: Luton Museum and Art Gallery, 1982)

Chapter Four

1. Gryspeerdt, Mary, *Rag Rugs in Somerset Rural Life Museum* (Glastonbury: Somerset Rural Life Museum, c.1980)
2. Quoted in Young, G. M. (ed.), *Early Victorian England, 1830–1865*, Vol. I, by Mrs C. P. Peel, 'Homes and Habits' (London: Oxford University Press, 1934)
3. Quoted by Marghanita Laski in Nowell-Smith, Simon (ed.), *Edwardian England, 1901–1914* (London: Oxford University Press, 1964)
4. Merthyr Tydfil Engine House Museum
5. Ibid.

Chapter Five

1. The *Guardian*, 31 August 1983
2. Hollingstead, John, 'On the Canal', *Household Words*, 18 September 1858

3. Trevelyan, Julian, *Indigo Days* (London: MacGibbon and Kee, 1957)
4. See Ayres, James, *English Naive Painting* (London: Thames & Hudson, 1980)

Chapter Six

1. Letter to author, 1983

OBJECT CREDITS

Abingdon Museum 219, 220; Abbot Hall Museum of Lakeland Life and Industry 75, 142, 145; Arbroath Museum 65, 66; Arts Council Collection 251, 266; Baysgarth Museum 254; Beamish Open Air Museum 5, 30, 42, 135, 136, 137, 138, 143, 144, 146, 147, 170, 178; Blaise Castle House Museum 85; Bristol Museum and Art Gallery 14, 39, 90; Bristol Industrial and Maritime Museum 96, 190, 193; Broadfield House Glass Museum, Dudley 49; Bruce Castle Museum, London 238; Castle Museum, Norwich 232; Castle Museum, York 7; Chatterley Whitfield Mining Museum 181; Cheltenham Museum and Art Gallery 9; Crane Gallery, London 223; Cumnock and Doon Council 127; Exeter Museum and Art Gallery 38; Devon Folk Life Register 118; Glasgow Museum and Art Gallery 78, 79, 80; Horniman Museum 9; Huntly House, Edinburgh 89, 97; Imperial War Museum 200, 201, 202, 203, 204, 207, 209; Ipswich Museum and Art Gallery 8, 17, 18, 157, 173, 211; John Gorman Collection 98, 100, 101, 102, 103; John Sturrock, Network 271; Kelham Island Industrial Museum, Sheffield 44; Kings Lynn Museum 123, 192; Kingussie Folk Museum 41, 48, 162; Kirkcaldy Museum and Art Gallery 72; Luton Museum and Art Gallery 54, 55, 56, 82, 128, 150, 152, 154, 155, 157, 197, 218, 226; Lyth Arts Centre 13; Manchester Museum and Art Gallery 36; Manchester Studies Archives of Family Photographs 107, 109, 110, 112; Museum of English Rural Life, Reading 4, 11, 33, 53, 130, 131, 133, 149, 153, 159, 174, 214; Museum of Labour History 99, 239, 253; Museum of London 224; Museum of Naïve Art, Bath 10, 21, 22, 23, 55, 58, 84, 151, 156, 158, 161, 167, 168, 195, 206, 225, 234, 235, 237; National Library, Wales 245; National Trust, Dinas, Betws-y-Coed 233; Neasden Museum 261; Newarke Houses Museum, Leicester 15, 169, 170, 171; Northampton Leather Museum 81; Oldham Museum and Art Gallery 28; Outsider Archive, London 222, 231, 247, 248, 249; People's Palace, Glasgow 19, 47, 87, 88, 93, 212, 252, 257, 258; Perth Museum and Art Gallery 92; Portland Museum 215; Queensferry Museum 43, 63; Royal Air Force Museum 208; Ruddington Lace Museum 76; Science Museum 40; Salford Museum and Art Gallery 225; Salt Museum, Northwich 94, 165; Sotheby's 24, 32, 35, 160; South Wales Miners' Library, Swansea 99; Southwold Museum 26; St Helens Museum and Art Gallery 50, 51; Stoke-on-Trent Museum and Art Gallery 243, 244; Swansea Industrial and Maritime Museum 12, 196; Tate Gallery 221, 230; Town Docks Museum, Hull 191, 198, 229; Townley Hall Art Gallery, Burnley 17, 31; Tyne and Wear Museum 45; Valence House Museum, Dagenham 114; Welholme Galleries, Grimsby 25; Welsh Folk Museum 29, 34, 60, 61, 62, 77, 132, 166, 260; Whitehaven Museum 72; Wisbech and Fenland Museum 20.

BIBLIOGRAPHY

While there are many books which touch on people's art, none deals with it in detail. The following books look at different aspects of the subject.

GENERAL

Art for Society – Contemporary British Art with a Social or Political Purpose (London: Whitechapel Art Gallery, 1978)

Ayres, James, *British Folk Art* (London: Barrie & Jenkins, 1977)

Ayres, James, *The Art of the People in America and Britain* (Manchester: Cornerhouse, 1985)

Baynes, Ken and Alan Robinson, 'Work', *Art & Society Times* (Lund Humphries/Welsh Arts Council, 1970)

Baynes, Ken, *Art in Society* (London: Lund Humphries, 1975)

Bennett, Tony, Richard Middleton and John Muncie, *Popular Culture and Hegemony in Post-War Britain* (Milton Keynes: Open University Press, 1981)

Boshier, Derek, *Lives* (catalogue of an exhibition of artists whose work is based on other people's lives), Arts Council of Great Britain

Brears, Peter, *North Country Folk Art* (Edinburgh: John Donald, 1989)

Burnett, John, *Useful Toil: Autobiographies of Working People from the 1820s to the 1920s* (London: Allen Lane, 1974)

Carrington, N., *Popular Art in Britain* (London: Penguin, 1945)

Christopher, Thomas, *Autobiography of an Artisan* (London: 1847)

Cork, Richard, *Art for Whom?*, exhibition catalogue, Arts Council of Great Britain, 1978

Cork, Richard, Batraj Khanna and Shirley Read, *Art on the South Bank: an Independent Report*, commissioned by the GLC, 1986

Durr, Andy and Helen Martin (eds.), *A Common Tradition – Popular Art of Britain and America*, Brighton Festival catalogue (Brighton: Brighton Polytechnic, 1991)

English Naïve and Provincial Art, Sotheby's Sale Catalogue, London: 17 July 1985

Exploring Living Memory, Life History Projects in London 1985, Exhibition at the Royal Festival Hall, London 1985

Finnegan, Ruth and Kenneth Thompson, *Popular Culture and Everyday Life* (Milton Keynes: Open University Press, 1981)

Fletcher, G. S., *Popular Art in England* (London: George G. Harrap, 1962)

Ford, Colin and Brian Harrison, *A Hundred Years Ago: Britain in the 1880s in Words and Photographs* (London: Allen Lane/Penguin Books, 1983)

Galbraith, John Kenneth, *Economics and the Arts* (W. E. Williams Memorial Lecture, 18 January 1983), Arts Council of Great Britain

Gorman, John, *Images of Labour: Selected Memorabilia from the National Museum of Labour History, London* (London: Scorpion Publishing Ltd, 1985)

Graham, Llewellyn F., *Arts & Crafts in the Age of Unemployment*, the Crypt Association Wolverhampton (unpublished BA degree thesis, Middlesex Polytechnic)

Grant, I. F., *Highland Folk Ways* (London: Routledge and Kegan Paul, 1961)

Harrison, Tom and Charles Madge, *Britain by Mass Observation* – see Introduction by Angus Calder (London: Cresset Library, 1986)

Hartley, Dorothy, *Made In England* 4th edn (London: Eyre Methuen, 1974)

Hobsbawn, E. J., *The Age of Revolution, Europe 1789–1848* (London: Weidenfeld & Nicholson, 1962)

Husa, V., *Traditional Crafts and Skills: Life and Work in Medieval and Renaissance Times* (London: Hamlyn, 1967)

Jones, B., *The Unsophisticated Arts* (London: The Architectural Press, 1951)

King, Elspeth, *The People's Palace and Glasgow Green* (Glasgow: Richard Drew Publishing, 1985)

Lambert, M. and E. Marx, *English Popular Art* (London: Batsford, 1951)

Lewery, A. J., *Popular Art, Past and Present* (Newton Abbot: David & Charles, 1992)

Klingender, F. L., *Art and the Industrial Revolution* (London: Paladin, 1972)

Mayhew, Henry, *Mayhew's Character*, edited by Peter Quennell (London: Spring Books)

Nichols, Marian, *The Popular Arts in Luton Museum* (Luton: the Borough of Luton Museum and Art Gallery, 1982)

Official Catalogue of the Wisbech Industrial Fine Art Exhibition (Wisbech: 1866)

Oral History (Journal of the Oral History Society, edited by June Freeman and Moira Vincentelli), vol. 18, no. 2, Autumn 1990 – a special issue which covers aspects of people's art

Pacey, Philip, 'Family Art: Domestic and Eternal Bliss', *Journal of Popular Culture*, Summer 1984 (Bowling Green State University, Ohio)

Painter, Colin and Anne Painter (eds.), 'Art, Leisure, Education and Purpose in the '80s', *Aspects*, no. 18, Spring 1982

Pittaway, A. and B. Scofield, *Traditional English Country Crafts* (New York: Pantheon Books, 1975)

Rattenbury, Arnold, *Ardudwy*, exhibition catalogue, Coleg Harlech Arts Centre, 1975

Roberts, Robert, *The Classic Slum: Salford Life in the First Quarter of the Century* (Manchester: Manchester University Press)

Spriggs, Gareth M., 'Maidens' Garlands', *Folk Life*, vol. 21 (1982–83), 12–32

Telford Community Arts, Report May 1981–April 1982 (Telford: 1982)

Thompson, F., *Larkrise to Candleford* (OUP, 1939; repr. Penguin, 1973)

Wiener, Martin J., *English Culture and the Decline of the Industrial Spirit 1850–1980* (Harmondsworth: Penguin, 1981)

'A People's Autobiography of Hackney', *Working Lives, 1905–45* vol. 1 (London, *c.* 1985)

CHAPTER 1
WORKING CLASS ART: WORKING CLASS ARTIST

Hole, J., *Light, More Light*, On the present state of education amongst the working classes of Leeds and how it can be improved, 1860

Laski, Marghanita, *Domestic Life in Edwardian England 1901–1914* (London: Oxford University Press, 1938)

Smith, M. A., *Leisure and Society in Britain* – see chapter by J Mott (*Miners, Weavers and Pigeon Racing*), pp. 86–96 (London: Allen Lane, 1973)

Young, G. M. (ed.), *Early Victorian England* vols. I and II (Oxford University Press, 1934)

CHAPTER 2
'PURE GENIUS'

Gray, Richard (ed.), *Working Lives, Volume One, 1905–45* (London: Hackney WEA, c. 1983)

Wood

Gardiner, F. J., *A History of Wisbech and Neighbourhood 1848–1898* (Wisbech: 1898)
Gardiner, F. J., *The Fiftieth Birthday of a Model Institute 1864–1914* (Wisbech 1914)
Stammers, M. K., *Ships' Figureheads* (Princes Risborough: Shire Publications Ltd, 1983)
Staniforth, Arthur, *Straw & Straw Craftsmen*, (Princes Risborough: Shire Publications Ltd, 1981)

Clay

Brears, Peter C. D., *English Country Pottery, its History and Techniques* (Newton Abbot: David & Charles, 1971)
Cooper, Emmanuel, *A History of World Pottery* (London: Batsford, 1988)
Cruickshank, Graeme and Godfrey Evans (ed), *Aberdeen Ceramics* (Aberdeen Art Gallery and Museums, 1981)
Draper, Jo, *Dated Post-Medieval Pottery in Northampton Museum*, Museums & Art Gallery, Northampton Borough Council's Leisure and Recreation Department
Holland, Fishley, 'Fifty Years a Potter', *Pottery Quarterly*, Tring
Hunt, C. J., *The Lead Miners of the Northern Pennines in the Eighteenth and Nineteenth Centuries* (Manchester: Manchester University Press, 1970; repd. Newcastle-upon-Tyne: Davis Books, 1974)
Jugs, Jars and Jolly-Boys: Tradition in English Pottery (Manchester: Whitworth Art Gallery, 1983)
Leary, Emmeline, 'By Potters Art Skill: Pottery by the Fishleys of Fremington', *Ceramic Review* 91, January/February 1985, pp. 10–12
Lewis, J. M., *The Ewenny Potteries* (Cardiff: National Museum of Wales, 1982)
Lloyd-Thomas, E. and E., *The Old Torquay Potteries* (London: Stockwell, 1978)
Phillips, Phoebe, *The Encyclopaedia of Glass* (London: Heineman, 1981)
Rigg, Hubert R., *Museum of Local Crafts and Industries* – see especially Cliviger Pottery, pp. 14–15 (Towneley Hall Art Gallery & Museum, Burnley Borough Council, 1974)
Tyler, Sheila, *Buckley Pottery: the Craft and History of the Buckley Potters from the 1300s to the 1940s* (Llandudno: Mostyn Art Gallery, 1983)
Willett, Henry, *Catalogue of a Collection of Pottery and Porcelain Illustrating Popular British History*, The Bethnal Green Branch, Victoria & Albert Museum, London (HMSO, 1899)

Metal

Addy, John, *A Coal and Iron Community in the Industrial Revolution, 1760–1860* (Harlow: Longman, 1969)

Glass

Dodsworth, Roger, *Glass and Glassmaking* (Princes Risborough: Shire Publications Ltd, 1982)

Glassmaking on Wearside (Tyne and Wear County Council, 1979)

Hajdamach, Charles, 'A Finer Substance than Anything: Friggers and Novelties in English Glass', *The Antique Dealer and Collector's Guide*, November 1986, pp. 52–54

Levitt, Sarah, *Pountneys, The Bristol Pottery at Fishponds 1905–1969* (Bristol: Redcliffe Press, 1990)

Polak, Ada, *Glass – its Makers and its Public* (Weidenfeld and Nicolson, 1975)

Seago, T. Taylor, 'From the Glassworker's Idle Moment', *Country Life*, 24 October 1963, pp. 1058–1059

Seago, T. Taylor, 'Glasshouse Friggers and Nursery Friggers', *Pottery Gazette*, 1946, p. 524

Witt, Cleo, *Bristol Glass* (Bristol: Redcliffe Press Ltd, 1984)

Woodward, H. W., *The Story of Edinburgh Crystal* (Edinburgh: DEMA Glass Ltd, 1984)

Straw

Davis, Jean, *Straw Plait* (Princes Risborough: Shire Publications Ltd, 1981)

Fearn, Jacqueline, *Thatch and Thatching* (Princes Risborough: Shire Publications Ltd, 1976)

Lambeth, M., *A Golden Dolly – the Art, Mystery and History of Corn Dollies* (London: John Barker, 1969)

Lambeth, M., *Discovering Corn Dollies* (Princes Risborough: Shire Publications Ltd, 1974)

Staniforth, Arthur, *Straw and Straw Craftsmen* (Princes Risborough: Shire Publications Ltd, 1981)

Slate

Caffell, Gwenno, *The Carved Slates of Dyffryn Ogwen* (Cardiff: National Museum of Wales, 1983)

Fairweather, Barbara, *A Short History of Ballachulish Slate Quarry* (The Glencoe & North Lorn Folk Museum, c.1970)

Harrod, Tanya, 'Carved in Slate', *Crafts* magazine, no. 72, January/February 1985, pp. 36–39, London

Coal

Gray, Douglas, *Coal: British Mining in Art 1680–1980* (London: Arts Council of Great Britain, 1982)

Waste

Beeby, K. J., *The Wonderful Story of Leather* (London: The Leather Institute, nd)

Thomson, Roy, *Leather Manufacture in the Post-Medieval Period with Special Reference to Northamptonshire* (Museum of Leathercraft, Northampton; reprinted from *Post-Medieval Archaeology* 15, 1981, pp. 161–175

Waterer, John W., *Leather* (Northampton: The Museum of Leathercraft; reprinted from Singer and Holmyard, *History of Technology* vol. II, Oxford: Clarendon Press)

CHAPTER 3
ART FOR ALL

Braithwaite, D., *Fairground Architecture* (London: 1968)

Campbell, Thalia, *100 Years of Women's Banners* (Wales: Women for Life on Earth, Art and Publicity, and Arts for Labour, *c*.1985)

Deshpand, Chris, *Diwali Celebrations* (London: A. & C. Black, 1985)

Dexter, T., *The Pagan Origin of Fairs* (London: 1930)

Disher, M., *Fairs, Circuses and Music Halls* (London: 1941)

Gorman, John, *Banner Bright: an Illustrated History of the Banners of the British Trade Union Movement* (London: Allen Lane, 1973)

Malbert, Roger (ed.), *Masquerading: The Art Of Notting Hill Carnival* (London: Arts Council, 1986)

Rattenbury, Arnold, *About Goose Fair*, Poster/Catalogue, Nottingham Castle Museum, Nottingham 1979

Rawe, Donald R., *Padstow's Obby Oss and May Day Festivities: A Study in Folklore and Tradition* (Padstow: Lodenek Press, 1982)

Rites and Riots: Folk Customs of Britain and Europe (Poole: Blandford Press, 1981)

Rooke, Patrick, *The Trade Union Movement* (London: Wayland Publishers, 1972)

Starsmore, Ian, *The Fairground*, exhibition catalogue (London: Whitechapel Art Gallery, 1977)

Walford, C., *Fairs Past and Present* (London: 1883)

Weedon, Geoff and Richard Ward, *Fairground Art: The Art Forms of Travelling Fairs, Carousels and Carnival Midways* (New York: Abbeville Press; London: White Mouse Editions, 1981)

CHAPTER 4
PRIVATE WORLDS: HOME, HEARTH AND HAVEN

Lace

Freeman, Charles, *Pillow Lace in the East Midlands* (Luton: Luton Art Gallery and Museum, 1958)

Hopewell, Jeffrey, *Pillow Lace and Bobbins* (Princes Risborough: Shire Publications Ltd, 1975)

Knitting

Harvey, Michael and Rae Compton, *Fisherman Knitting* (Princes Risborough: Shire Publications Ltd, 1978)

Freeman, June (ed.), *Knitting: A Common Art* (Minories/Aberystwyth Arts Centre, 1986)

Lansdell, Avril, *Occupational Costume and Working Clothes, 1776–1976* (Princes Risborough: Shire Publications Ltd, 1977)

Palmer, Marilyn, *Framework Knitting* (Princes Risborough: Shire Publications Ltd, 1984)

Wright, Mary, *Cornish Guernseys and Knit Frocks* (Penzance: Alison Hodge, 1979)

Quilting and Patchwork

Allan, Rosemary E., *North Country Quilts and Coverlets from Beamish Museum, County Durham* (Beamish North of England Open Air Museum, 1987)

Anthony, I. E., *Quilting and Patchwork in Wales* (reprinted from *Amgueddfa, Bulletin of the National Museum of Wales* 12, Winter 1972)

Clabburn, Pamela, *Patchwork* (Princes Risborough: Shire Publications Ltd, 1983)

Colby, A., *Quilting* (London: Batsford, 1964)

Freeman, June, *Quilting, Patchwork and Appliqué, 1700–1982: Sewing as a Woman's Art* (Colchester: Minories, 1983)

Garrad, Larch S., 'Quilting and Patchwork in the Isle of Man', *Folk Life* vol. 17, 1979, pp. 39–48

Hake, E., *English Quilting Old and New* (London: Batsford, 1937)

North Country Quilting, catalogue (Barnard Castle, 1963)

'Notes on Quilting in the Isle of Man', from *Manx Folk Life Survey* (Douglas: Manx Museum)

'Patchwork', *Embroidery Magazine* vol. 29, No. 2, Summer 1978, p. 38

Swain, Margaret, *Figures on Fabric* (London: Adam & Charles Black, 1980)

Rae, Janet, *The Quilts of the British Isles* (London: Constable, 1987)

Osler, Dorothy, *Traditional British Quilts* (London: Batsford, 1987)

Ward, A., *Quilting in the North of England* (Bradford: Bolling Hall, 1966)

Rugs

Felcher, C., *The Complete Book of Rug Making – Folk Methods and Ethnic Designs* (London: Robert Hale, 1982)

Finch-Dawson, F., *Notes on Rag Rugs* (leaflet, Abbot Hall Museum, 1982)

Gryspeerdt, Mary, *Rag Rugs in Somerset Rural Life Museum* (Glastonbury: Somerset Rural Life Museum, c.1980)

Clothes

Brooks, Peter F., *Pearly Kings and Queens in Britain* (Chichester: Barry Rose Publishers, 1974)

Hall, Maggie, *Smocks* (Princes Risborough: Shire Publications Ltd, 1983)

Jarvis, Anthea and Patricia Raine, *Fancy Dress* (Princes Risborough: Shire Publications Ltd, 1984)

Lansell, Avril, Occupational Costume (Princes Risborough, Shire Publications Ltd, 1977)

Nichols, Marian, *Smocks in Luton Museum* (Luton: Luton Museum and Art Gallery, 1980)

Treen

Harrison, M., *People and Furniture: a Social Background to the English Home* (London: 1971)

Pinto, Edward H., 'Love Spoons', *Apollo*, January 1951, pp. 24–27

Pinto, Edward H., *Treen* (London: G. Bell and Sons, 1970)

New Communities

Hebdige, Dick, *Subculture – The Meaning of Style* (London: Methuen, 1979)

Knight, Nick, *Skinhead* (London: Omnibus Press, 1982)

Barnes, Richard (compiler) *Mods!* (London: Eel Pie Publishing, 1979)

Polhemus, Ted, *Body Style* (Luton: Lennard Publishing, 1988)

Steele-Perkins, Chris and Richard Smith, *The Teds* (London: Travelling Light/Exit, 1979)

Wylie, Gus, *Flags of Recognition: The Iconography of Rock 'n' Roll* (London: MA degree thesis, Royal College of Art, 1991)

CHAPTER 5
HOME FROM HOME

Sailors

Adamson, Peter, *The Great Whale to Snare: The Whaling Trade of Hull* (City of Kingston-upon-Hull Museums and Art Galleries, Kingston-upon-Hull, nd)

Banks, Steven, *The Handicrafts of the Sailor* (Newton Abbot: David & Charles, 1974)

Boswell, D., *Catalogue of Ship Models in the Doughty Museum* (Libraries and Museum Committee, County Borough of Grimsby, 1964)

Cook, Olive and Edwin Smith, 'Ship Shape', in *The Saturday Book*, edited by Leonard Russell (London: Hutchinson, 1950) pp. 57–80

Credland, Arthur G., *The Diana of Hull* (Kingston-upon-Hull: Museums & Art Galleries, 1977)

Credland, Arthur G., *Wales and Whaling* (Princes Risborough: Shire Publications Ltd, 1982)

Hansen, H. (ed.), *Art of the Seafarer* (London: Faber & Faber, 1978)

Marcombe, David, *The Victorian Sailor* (Princes Risborough: Shire Album, 1985)

Ritchie, C., *Scrimshaw* (London: 1972)

Trench

Liddle, Peter H., *Voices of War 1914–1918* (London: Heinemann, 1988)

Royle, Trevor, *The Best Years of Their Lives* (London: Michael Joseph, 1986)

Prisoners

Carrell, Christopher and Joyce Laing (eds.), *The Special Unit Barlinnie Prison* (Glasgow: Third Eye Centre, 1982)

Levin, Angela, 'The Rebirth of Jimmy Boyle', in *You* (The *Mail on Sunday* magazine), 26 May 1985

Riches, Colin, *There is Still Life – a Study of Visual Art in a Prison*, (London: MA degree thesis, Royal College of Art, 1991)

Canal

Chaplin, T., *A Short History of the Narrow Boat* (London: Geoffrey Dibb, 1967)

Gladwin, D. and J. White, *English Canals: Part Three, Boats and Boatmen* (Oakwood Press: 1971)

Lewery, A., *Narrow Boat Painting* (Newton Abbot: David and Charles, 1974)

Regan, Michael, *Canal Boat Art* (London: Victoria & Albert Museum, nd)

Rolt, L., *Narrow Boat* (London: Eyre and Spottiswood, 1971)

Smith, Peter L., *Canal Barges and Narrow Boats*, Shire Album 8 (Princes Risborough: Shire Publications Ltd, 1983)

CHAPTER 6
PICTURING THE WORLD

Painting

Ayres, James, *English Naive Painting, 1750–1900* (London: Thames & Hudson, 1980)

Bloore, Carolyn and Grace Seiberling, *A Vision Exchanged – Amateurs and Photography in Mid-Victorian England* (London: Victoria & Albert Museum, 1985)

British Naive Painters (London: Register of Naive Artists (RONA), 1985)

Creation for Liberation, catalogue for the Third Open Exhibition of Contemporary Art by Black Artists (London: Brixton Recreation Centre, 1985)

Delderfield, E., *British Inn Signs and their Stories* (London: Dawlish, 1965)

Delderfield, E., *British Inn Signs and their Stories* (Newton Abbot: David & Charles, 1969)

'Don't ask me, I can't draw': Community Arts in Yorkshire 1983–84 (Yorkshire and Humberside Association for Community Arts, 1983)

Feaver, William, *Pitman Painters, The Ashington Group 1934–1984* (London: Chatto & Windus, 1988)

Finch, C., *The Ship Painters* (Dalton: 1975)

Finch, Roger, *The Pierhead Painters* (London: Barrie & Jenkins, 1983)

Finch, Roger, *The Ship Painters* (Lavenham: Terence Dalton Ltd, 1975)

Keen, Richard, *Coalface* (Cardiff: National Museum of Wales, 1982)

Kilbourn, Oliver, *My Life as a Pitman* (Nottingham: Midland Group, 1977)

Klingender, F. L., 'The Portraits in the Servants' Hall', *Picture Post*, 24 December 1943, pp. 22–24

Larwood, Jacob and Camden, John, *English Inn Signs* (London: Chatto & Windus, 1951)

Levy, Mervyn, *Scottie Wilson* (London: Brook Street Gallery)

Lister, E. and S. Williams, *Twentieth-Century British Naive and Primitive Artists* (London: Astragal Books, 1977)

Melly, George, *A Tribe of One: Great Naive Painters of the British Isles* (RONA and the Oxford Illustrated Press Ltd, 1981)

Melly, George, *Its all writ out for you – The Life and Work of Scottie Wilson* (London: Thames & Hudson, 1986)

Mullins, E., *Alfred Wallis, Cornish Primitive Painter* (London: Macdonald, 1967)

Musgrove, Victor, *Outsiders: an Art Without Precedent or Tradition* (London: Arts Council of Great Britain, 1979)

New Frontiers of Naive Art in Europe, Royal Festival Hall catalogue (RONA and Muller, Blond & White Ltd, 1984)

Osman, Colin, *Pigeon Painting* (Nottingham: Midland Group, 1979)

Trevelyan, Julian, *Indigo Days* (London: MacGibbon and Kee, 1957)

Vigurs, Peter, *C. W. Brown – the Potteries' Primitive* (Stoke-on-Trent, Stoke-on-Trent City Museum and Art Gallery, c.1980)

Ward-Jackson, C. H., *Ship Portrait Painters – Maritime Monographs and Reports* (National Maritime Museum, 1978)

Waterson, Merlin, 'Elisabeth Ratcliffe, an Artistic Lady's Maid', *Apollo*, vol. CVIII, No. 197, July 1978

Photography

Daniels, Jeffery, *Lousey but Loyal: Royal Jubilees in the Geffrye Museum* (London: 1977)

Hirsh, Julia, *Family Photographs: Content, Meaning and Effect* (New York and Oxford: Oxford University Press, 1981)

Hulme, Jack, A Photographic Memory (Pontefract: Yorkshire Arts Circus, 1986)

Smith, Derek (ed.), *Scotswood Road: Photographs by James Forsyth* (Newcastle-upon-Tyne: Bloodaxe Books, 1986)

CHAPTER 7
PEOPLE'S ART EXAMINED

Brett, Guy, *Through Our Own Eyes: Popular Art and Modern History* (London: Heretic/GMP, 1986)

Henry, Stew, *Skinheads Photobook* (Barrow-in-Furness, Henry, 1977)

Williams, Raymond, *Culture* (London: Fontana, 1981)

INDEX